THE

KOREAN

WAR

THE ESSENTIAL BIBLIOGRAPHY SERIES

Essential Bibliographies
Series Editor
Michael F. Pavković, Ph.D.
U.S. Naval War College

For general and expert readers alike, volumes in the Essential Bibliographies series combine an authoritative historiographical essay and current bibliography on significant subjects drawn from world military history, ancient times through the present.

THE

KOREAN

WAR

THE ESSENTIAL
BIBLIOGRAPHY SERIES

ALLAN R. MILLETT

Potomac Books, Inc.
Washington D.C.

Library of Congress Cataloging-in-Publication Data

Millett, Allan Reed.
  The Korean War : the essential bibliography / Allan R. Millett. — 1st ed.
      p. cm.
  Includes bibliographical references.
  ISBN 978-1-57488-976-5 (alk. paper)
  1. Korean War, 1950-1953. 2. Korean War, 1950-1953—Bibliography. I. Title.
  DS918.M514 2007
  951.904'2—dc22

                              2006039674

ISBN 978-1-57488-976-5

(alk. paper)

Printed in the United States of America on acid-free paper that meets the American National Standards Institute Z39-48 Standard.

Potomac Books, Inc.
22841 Quicksilver Drive
Dulles, Virginia 20166

First Edition

10 9 8 7 6 5 4 3 2 1

CONTENTS

ACKNOWLEDGMENTS

In fifteen years of producing books written and edited, writing essays in books edited by others, and publishing scholarly and popular articles on the Korean War, I am sure I have exhausted the patience of the Korean studies and military history scholars of three continents from whom I've asked help. No homage to all of them is possible here. I hope I have duly recognized them in the acknowledgments in two of my books: *Their War for Korea: American, Asian and European Combatants and Civilians, 1945–1953* and *The War for Korea, Volume I: A House Burning, 1945–1950.* Nevertheless, I have at various times dragooned my colleagues into specific bibliographical tasks, important but thankless, and therefore I want to acknowledge their help here. First, I thank Ms. Frances Russell of the Mershon Center, The Ohio State University, whose assistance has been irreplaceable. During their tours of duty as history doctoral students, a series of my graduate students served as Korean War bibliographical explorers: Ms. Katherine Becker, Dr. Leo J. Daugherty III, Dr. William B. Feis, Dr. Mark Jacobson, Dr. Maj. Park Il-song, Dr. Cmdr. Cho Duk-hyun, Dr. Kim Taeho,

Maj. Son Kyeung-ho, and Dr. Kim Young-ho. I also had the pleasure of working with two Chinese American scholars, Dr. Yu Bin (Wittenberg University) and Dr. Li Xiaobing (Central Oklahoma University), who guided me through Chinese language sources on the war, assisted by Ms. Bao Ying, another Ohio State graduate student. Maj. Jon Anderson, a U.S. Air National Guard officer and a north Asia intelligence specialist, performed essential searches for Korean and Chinese sources. Majors Park and Son did equal duty in the same linguistic domain. Dr. Maj. Bryan Gibby (USA) shared sources on the Korean Military Advisory Group, as did Dr. Maj. Thomas Hanson on the Eighth U.S. Army and Dr. Lt. Col. Kelly Jordan on the same force. I often consulted Dr. Col. Jiyul Kim (USA) on Korean and Japanese sources. My experts on Russian sources are Dr. Kathryn Weathersby; Col. Viktor Gavrilov (Institute of Military History, Russian Federation Ministry of Defense); and Dr. George M. Hudson (Wittenberg University).

I want to thank—again—Dr. Timothy K. Nenninger for his expert guidance on the records of the United States armed forces, especially in the twentieth century, now catalogued and stored in Archives II, National Archives and Records Administration, College Park, Maryland. Whatever Tim's actual job title and real work may be, many of us call him for prompt, hands-on, and accurate archival guidance. He is the ultimate archivist, an educated, published history doctorate from a distinguished department, the University of Wisconsin–Madison, who thinks and writes as a scholar and understands that finding documents is an imaginative and continuing process. During the summers of 2005 and 2006 I consulted the extensive

Asia Collection, Hamilton Library, the University of Hawaii–
Manoa with the invaluable assistance of Dr. Chun Kyungmi,
the library's specialist on Korean language sources.

At various times I have relied upon the bibliographical
services of four key research centers in the United States and
one in Korea: the U.S. Army Military History Institute, now
part of the Army Heritage and Education Center, Carlisle Barracks, Pennsylvania; the U.S. Air Force Historical Research
Agency, Air University, Maxwell Air Force Base, Alabama; the
Naval Historical Center, Washington Navy Yard, D.C.; and
the History and Museums Division, Headquarters U.S. Marine Corps, now part of the Marine Corps University, Quantico,
Virginia. Of the many librarians and archivists who have ad-
vised me, Mrs. Louise Arnold-Friend has been a stalwart con-
tributor to all my research for almost thirty years. Mr. David
Keough, also a MHI research specialist, and Mr. James Zobel,
archivist, the MacArthur Library, are Korean War experts without peer. The library of the Institute for Military History Compilation (formerly the Korean Military History Institute), the
Korean War Memorial, Yongsan, Seoul, Republic of Korea,
can provide reference services for its multilingual collections,
but not that of the more limited files and library of the joint
and combined history office, Combined Forces Command and
U.S. Forces Korea, housed in the General William F. Dean
Heritage Center, South Post, Yongsan U.S. Army Base. Drs.
Cho Sung-hun and Suh Yong-sun have been generous with
their time and expertise. The center for Korean War studies in
the People's Republic of China is the People's Liberation Army's
Academy of Military Science, and we have all benefited from
the AMS staff's Korean War research.

I also acknowledge the permissions I have received to use portions of my earlier work to shape this guide. The first chapter, a short history of the Korean War, is drawn from two entries I wrote on the war for *Encyclopedia Britannica*, one in English and the other in Korean (translated by Dr. Lee Choonkun and Dr. Maj. Park Il-song) and published in the most recent editions of the *Encyclopedia Britannica* in English and Korean. I want to thank Encyclopedia Britannica Inc. of Chicago, Illinois, for permission to use a version both expanded and revised. Ms. Sylvia Wallace represented the EB. Much of the rest of this book began as a historiographical essay I wrote for *The Journal of Strategic Studies*. The journal is edited by Dr. John Gooch, The University of Leeds, and Ms. Jan Dennyschene, who represents the publisher, Frank Cass Ltd., London, England. Frank Cass's journals may be reviewed at www.tandf.co.uk. The appendixes come from *Their War for Korea*, published by Potomac Books under its earlier identity as Brassey's, Inc.

As it had for thirty-eight years, the Mershon Center for International Security Education has supported my work. For the last thirteen years, a generous alumnus, Maj. Gen. Raymond E. Mason Jr. USAR (Ret.) has shared the financial burden of supporting my research. General Mason's encouragement and appreciation is priceless. My new sponsor, the University of New Orleans, especially Dean Robert Dupont, has encouraged my continued work on the Korean War.

Mr. Don Bishop, a former student and career foreign service officer, reviewed the Korean and Chinese titles for accuracy.

My wife Martha and daughter Eve continue to share our journey of understanding about Korea.

A work like this book inevitably leads to personal judgments about and omissions of someone else's work. I have tried to be comprehensive and fair in deciding what to include and what to omit. I have applied twin criteria: lasting significance and general utility. I am solely responsible for this evaluation, although I'm sure I have been influenced by other historiographical studies. There are already some very good introductions to Korean War studies, and I will identify them and explain why I think they are useful. At the same time, I hope this book will "raise the bar" and that someone else will take on the task in the future and do even better.

ALLAN R. MILLETT
NEW ORLEANS, LOUISIANA ·
MARCH 2007

This book is a guide to the study of the Korean War, whether the reader is only interested in a particular engagement or an entire campaign or the reader is interested in the common soldier or General of the Army Douglas MacArthur.

The individual chapters require some explanation. The book begins with a long narrative chapter about the war. Chapter 1 provides the historical context for the following chapters, which introduce major areas of study. I have placed the chapters that deal with the Asian belligerents first because their story is the least known, and yet in terms of the stakes and the losses, it was the Koreans' war and became the Chinese war. Although I am a latecomer to Asian studies—and set new records for linguistic ineptness at Yonsei University's Korean Language Institute—I have visited much of Asia, including China and Japan, multiple times. Since 1986 I have been a regular visitor to the Republic of Korea, most recently in 2004. I have been along almost all the Demilitarized Zone (DMZ), down into two infiltration tunnels, and to many of the Republic of Korea's battlefields. Despite South Korea's urbanization and reforestation, one can still find the signs of war at "the Punchbowl," Chipyong-ni, Tabu-dong, "Heartbreak Ridge," Wonju, Obong-ni Ridge, Yonhui Ridge and Hill 296 (Ansan) in western Seoul, and Munsan-ni. I have been into the mountains of Kangwon province and the Chiri-sans of southern Korea, where a guerrilla war continued from 1948 into the mid-1950s.

I have talked to many Koreans from Gen. Paik Sun-yup to Republic of Korea (ROK) private soldiers about their wartime experiences. I have had similar conversations with American and other United Nations Command (UNC) veterans. The difference between these two groups of veterans is dramatic. No doubt the Americans' wartime experiences shaped their lives, but they lived in the United States, untouched by that war in a direct way. Even those veterans who continued to serve, who finally retired as generals, colonels, and master sergeants, would admit they put the war behind them to defend Europe and to fight in Vietnam. For the Koreans, the war is still an everyday influence. It explains the existence of the draconian National Security Act of 1948 and the tragedy of separated families; why primary education in both Koreas includes a large dose of political indoctrination and counterespionage advice, the longevity of the Kim family dynasty in Pyongyang, the continued presence of 25,000 American military personnel on Korean soil, and the 1.1 million North Koreans under arms from a population of only 23 million with a per capita income of $969 a year. (The per capita income of South Koreans is $14,000.) It also explains why Koreans hate replays of the TV series *M*A*S*H* and its contemptuous silliness.

Barriers of language, culture, and social experience will perpetuate Koreans' and Americans' different perceptions of the war, but these differences are no excuse for ignoring the literature about the war that clearly sees it as a "total," not limited, conflict. The war is certainly not "forgotten" but remembered with pain and grief. It is a mistake, however, to assume the Asian participants were simply victimized by the Soviet Union and the United States. The Koreans and Chinese made the Korean War possible; indeed, the Soviets and Americans did not fight each other by proxy for Austria or Yugoslavia. Koreans killed Koreans, making the war a self-perpetuating feud, not the German form of peaceful unification.

The experience of Korea, the end of the Cold War not withstanding, is still important as a way to understand the possibilities and problems of nation-building as well as the perils of postcolonial politics. Only the dead, to paraphrase Plato, have seen the end of violent regime change by whatever name.

1 THE KOREAN WAR

The Korean War (1948–54) began with the Japanese Empire's surrender at the end of the Second World War in September 1945. The leaders of the Allied coalition had decided the Japanese Empire's fate at the Cairo Conference, held in December 1943, when they declared Japan could not keep any territories it had conquered with military force after 1895. These territories included the former Kingdom of Chosun (Korea), a protectorate of Japan after the Russo-Japanese War (1904–1905) and then annexed in 1910. Unlike China, Manchuria, and the former European colonies seized in 1941–42, Korea and Formosa did not have acceptable native governments or a European colonial regime ready to return or both. Instead, Korean nationalism had been brutally suppressed within Korea since 1919; most claimants to power were harried, isolated exiles in China, Manchuria, Japan, Russia, and the United States.

Although badly divided by internal rivalries, the Korean nationalists fell into two broad groups. The first rebels were committed Marxist revolutionaries who had embraced the anticolonial struggle in the 1920s and fought the Japanese in the Chinese-dominated guerrilla armies in Manchuria. Some Communist partisans, driven out of Korea and southeastern Manchuria, took refuge in the Asian provinces of the Soviet Union. One of these exiled partisans was a minor but successful guerrilla leader named Kim Sung-ju, age thirty-two in 1945, who had taken the nom de guerre of Kim Il-sung. The Communist partisans advocated redistributing land, nationalizing manufacturing and extractive industries, abolishing the traditional Korean class and Confucian social conventions, and confiscating all Japanese property.

A rival revolutionary movement had borne much of the struggle against Japanese domination since the 1890s, but it had lost much of its force by the 1940s. Similar to the Communists, it exhibited strong hostility to the Japanese and Confucian past and had an authoritarian leadership. It was also just as revolutionary in its own way as the Marxist-Leninist coalition it faced. Largely influenced by Western political and economic values, infused with evangelical Christianity, and filtered through an Asian culture that was 4,000 years old, Korean ultranationalism drew its modernism from the best of science, education, and industrialism in Great Britain, France, Germany, Japan, and the United States. The Nationalists' Christianity, however, seemed more like that of the Roman era and the English Revolution, not that of the twentieth century. The Nationalists remained Korean at the core, bedeviled by uncompromising rivalries and enduring hatreds.

Although the American government had never supported the Korean ultranationalists, private citizens and missionaries (primarily from the Methodist and Presbyterian churches) provided Korean dissidents with diplomatic protection, sponsorship, employment, and educational opportunities in the United

States and Korea. After the failure of the March First Movement of 1919, a massive public protest against Japanese rule, the Korean leaders split into two rival factions. The first was the Provisional Government in Exile, formed in Shanghai and then fled to Chungking, and led by a veteran anti-Japanese terrorist and popular hero, Kim Ku.[1] The second faction centered on Syngman Rhee (Yi Sung-man), a venerated nationalist educated in the United States. Rhee had formed the Korean Commission, a group of American and Korean lobbyists who worked with the media and political elite in New York and Washington. While Kim Ku slipped in and out of temporary alliances with the Communists in China, Rhee faced no such necessity in the United States and formed alliances with American sympathizers. Kim and Rhee each viewed himself as the savior of his country.

In the hurried effort to disarm the Imperial Japanese Army and repatriate the Japanese population in Korea, estimated at 700,000, the United States and the Soviet Union agreed on August 12, 1945, to divide the country at the 38th Parallel for administrative purposes. At least from the American perspective, the geographical division was an expedient and not the first step in dividing Korea into two rival political systems. The Russian reign of economic and physical terror in northern Korea, however, almost immediately politicized the division as hundreds of thousands of refugees fled the hardships of Russian occupation. The returning expatriate leaders of every political persuasion also regarded the two occupation administrations as potential patrons.

1. With some exceptions, Chinese names are in pinyin, but Korean names are given in the Romanized form used in 1945–53 rather than in the new system adopted in 2000.

The Japanese surrender in 1945 set off a complicated internal struggle among all the Korean factions that eventually brought on a vicious partisan war in southern Korea in March and April 1948, a border war the following year, and a full-scale, internationalized conventional war in June 1950. The internationalized phase is the war known outside Korea. The partisan war, in fact, cost the lives of almost 8,000 members of the South Korean security forces and at least 30,000 lives of other Koreans of all political persuasions and degrees of belligerency. The potential for an internal uprising—with popular ire focused on the American military government—first appeared in the Autumn Harvest Uprising (October and November 1946), which disrupted half of southern Korea and inflicted an estimated 5,000 casualties (more than a thousand dead) and produced 10,000 arrests. The American troops' involvement in crushing the uprising persuaded U.S. officials to speed up the process of independence.

After the United States and the Soviet Union failed to agree on a trusteeship formula to produce a unified Korea—a commitment both sides made in Moscow in December 1945—Harry Truman's administration in 1948 went to the United Nations (UN) and persuaded it to assume responsibility for Korea. Although the U.S. military government remained nominally in control, more and more Koreans entered official positions. Both the Korean National Police and the Korean Constabulary doubled in size, providing a security force of about 80,000 by 1947. In the meantime, the Communist regime in Pyongyang—dominated but not yet controlled by Kim Il-sung and his partisan comrades—strengthened its party apparatus, administrative structure, and military forces. In 1948 the North Korean military forces and police numbered about

100,000 and were reinforced by a group of southern Korean guerrillas who had established their headquarters at Haeju, a small city in central-western Korea on the Ongjin Peninsula. Other Communists created underground guerrilla bands and infiltrated the Korean Constabulary—as did some ultra-rightist groups associated with Kim Ku, who resented Syngman Rhee's growing power.

Partisan War, 1948–50

Determined to block the creation of an independent South Korea, southern dissidents, primarily members of the South Korean Labor (Communist) Party (SKLP), attempted to throw southern Korea into chaos with a general strike in March 1948. With much greater effectiveness than they had shown in 1946, the National Police and Constabulary broke the strike. American troops, reduced to about 10,000 officers and men, did not have to face the mobs. On the island of Cheju-do, effectively South Korea's ninth province and located eighty-five miles off Korea's southern coast, the partisans struck government offices and police stations on April 1 and 2, 1948, and were aided by a mutiny in the Constabulary regiment stationed on the island. The Cheju-do uprising, led by the charismatic Kim Talsam, was not easily defeated. The SKLP infrastructure was too deeply embedded in the island's population of 300,000, the grievances against the government were real, and the mountainous terrain provided ample sanctuaries for the guerrillas. Moreover, the Korean security forces were poorly led, trained, and manned and riddled with spies and informers. The strongest officers of the Constabulary (many with counterguerrilla experience in Manchuria as officers of the Manchukuo Army) and the U.S. Korean Military Advisory Group (KMAG) came to Cheju-do to run the campaign, and they called for more Constabulary units to sweep the villages and mountainsides. The revolt did not prevent the creation of the Republic of Korea in August 1948 with Syngman Rhee as president.

The Cheju-do rebellion proved to be only the tip of the insurrectionary iceberg. In the autumn of 1948 the partisan war engulfed parts of every mainland Korean province below the 38th Parallel. In its larger purpose—to destroy the Republic of Korea (ROK) at birth—the uprising failed. Nevertheless, its damage to political unity, economic development, governmental legitimacy, and military effectiveness was severe enough to set the stage for the invasion of June 1950. In addition, the partisan war expanded into a border war between the South Korean Army (ROK Army, as the Constabulary became known in December 1948) and the North Korean border constabulary, which became the North Korean Army (known as the Korean People's Army). Although the incursions became a test of political will, the border war had a direct military purpose: to assist guerrilla columns in penetrating the ROK Army's defenses and drawing its units away from the guerrilla-suppression campaign in the southern provinces. The ten border-crossing expeditions were organized by the exiled leader of the southern Communists and vice premier of the Democratic People's Republic of Korea (DPRK), Pak Hon-yong, and his guerrilla lieutenant, Kim Tal-sam, who had escaped from Cheju-do. In 1949, however, Kim Il-sung put his own comrades in charge of the operation, fearing too much independence and popularity for Pak.

The partisans in South Korea enjoyed a dangerous level of popular support. An estimated 50,000 Communist cadres and workers joined the revolt. The leaders had a high level of military competence drawn from the disaffected ranks of the Constabulary (the number of mutineers, deserters, and purged soldiers may have exceeded 8,000) and from Communists who had served in the Japanese armed forces. The spark for the mainland uprising was the October mutiny in the Constabulary's 14th Regiment in Yosu, a southern seaport. At least four other regiments lost soldiers to the guerrillas. Defectors even seized two ROK Navy gunboats and sailed them north. Although the government forces crushed the Yosu revolt, which had spread to the neighboring city of Sunchon, they could not prevent more than 1,000 armed rebels from finding sanctuary in the Chiri-san mountains, which became a guerrilla stronghold along with the Odae-san and Taebaek-san ranges to the northeast. Moreover, many victims of this war were neither security forces nor armed guerrillas but people whom the belligerents identified as either "rightists" or "reds." The guerrillas targeted the Korean National Police and paramilitary youth associations, and they reciprocated the violence. Small-scale atrocities became a way of life, and terrorists stalked notable supporters of the ROK government, especially Christian leaders and landowners. The Communists portrayed the enemy as dupes of the hated Japanese, while the government painted the guerrillas as tools of Soviet communism.

The partisan war divided even those Korean politicians who opposed the Communists. President Syngman Rhee and his supporters sponsored the National Security Law, which gave the government broad powers to crush political dissent, but members of the National Assembly also approved another law in 1948 that made anyone who had the slightest association with the Japanese colonial regime subject to prosecution as a "collaborator." The target group included most of the senior officers of the Korean National Police and the ROK Army. Communist intelligence operatives, numerous and active in South Korea, had reason to report that dissension in the police and army made more defections very likely in a crisis. They did not report to Pak Hon-yong, however, that the South Korean security forces had whittled the active guerrilla combatants down from a force of 5,000 to about 1,000 by early 1950.

Nevertheless, the partisan war delayed the training of the South Korean Army. In early 1950, the KMAG advisers judged fewer than half of the army's infantry battalions were ready for war. Staff work and logistics support for divisional operations were nonexistent. The army had only six battalions of artillery, armed with a lightweight version of the American 105mm howitzer with half the range and bursting effect of the North Korean Army's Russian guns. The South Koreans had no tanks, only a squadron of American scout cars with 37mm guns. American disengagement from the military crisis on the Korean Peninsula stemmed principally from the Department of Defense, while the Department of State wanted to keep a regimental combat team (2,000 officers and men) near the 38th Parallel.

The American military position on Korea, shaped by Gen. Omar N. Bradley (chairman of the Joint Chiefs of Staff [JCS]), Gen. J. Lawton Collins (Army chief of staff), and Gen. Douglas MacArthur (commander in chief, Far East Command [CINCFECOM]), was essentially a U.S. Army position. With reduced ground forces and slumping budgets for operations and weapons maintenance, the generals wanted no American units in Korea and proposed only limited military assistance to the Koreans. Facing the creation of a North Atlantic Treaty

Organization (NATO) armed forces and upset with the Chinese Nationalists' equipment losses in 1948–50, the generals wanted few weapons sent to Asian armies. General MacArthur also argued his four weak divisions in Japan (the U.S. Eighth Army), not the Koreans, required more support. The U.S. Navy and Air Force backed the U.S. Army's position since the joint service plans for a war with the Soviet Union included using Japanese bases for air and naval operations. The Joint Chiefs and President Truman made this conclusion public well before Secretary of State Dean Acheson discussed Korea's lack of importance in America's strategic planning in January 1950, but his accompanying remarks about the American commitment to protect Korea through the United Nations escaped notice.

American military leaders used incautious statements by Rhee and some of his generals about "marching north" to justify the low level of U.S. military assistance. They also encouraged Brig. Gen. William L. Roberts, USA, the commander of KMAG, to make misleading statements about the South Korean Army's battle readiness. The justification for portraying the South Korean Army as more than equal to its North Korean counterpart was that such glowing statements increased the pressure from "Asia First" Republicans to send more military aid to Korea and the Nationalist forces on Formosa. The Defense Department would thus retain control of its military assistance program, but it would not have to send scarce first-line aircraft, artillery, and tanks to Asia. From South Korea's independence in August 1948 until June 1950, American military assistance to Korea amounted to $141 million, largely drawn from American surplus equipment and supplies. Funds provided through the Economic Cooperation Administration for the same period totaled $53.7 million. Although Congress eventually passed a new military assistance bill for Korea in March 1950, allotting $10.2 million in new funds and credits, little of this money had gone to military equipment, and none of it would have created a force that equaled the North Korean Army's heavy firepower.

Emboldened by their control of the Communist factions in their own regime and convinced the rebellion against Syngman Rhee had brought the Republic of Korea to the brink of collapse, Kim Il-sung and Pak Hon-yong pressed their case with Josef Stalin that they could destroy the South Koreans with a conventional invasion. After considering all their arguments in early 1949, Stalin gave the Koreans a firm *nyet* (no). Stalin's refusal was conditional, however; it was really a "not yet," not a *nyet*. The critical obstacles to a 1949 invasion were the remaining U.S. combat troops in Korea, the incomplete Chinese Revolution, the uncertain state of the partisan war in South Korea, and the relative unpreparedness of the North Korean armed forces. At the political level Stalin also wanted to ensure that Chairman Mao Zedong would share the risks of a general war in Asia.

In the course of the next year (1949–50), the Communist leadership built the Korean People's Army (KPA) into a formidable offensive force modeled after the Soviet Army. The Chinese provided two Korean divisions for redesignation as the KPA 5th and 6th Divisions. By the end of 1949, the KPA deployed five divisions and two brigades (one of two tank regiments) to the border areas. The military preparation's pace increased in early 1950, including the formation of Soviet-trained aviation squadrons, naval forces, and commandos. In April 1950, the Chinese released more Korean veterans from the People's Liberation Army (PLA) to form the KPA 7th

Division. The Russians and North Koreans organized several youth training centers that could be converted to additional divisions or various types of internal security forces. The Soviet Army provided the essential armaments and field equipment for an invasion army of three tank regiments (identified as the 105th Tank Brigade and then converted into a division) and seven infantry divisions. Since the South Korean Army could deploy only about half its under-armed divisions to the 38th Parallel, the Communists would probably have at least a 2:1 manpower advantage, enhanced by superior air support and firepower. Each KPA division would have the support of four artillery battalions, one with self-propelled SU-76 guns. The North Koreans would deploy 150 T-34 tanks while the South Koreans had no tanks at all. The North Koreans in 1950 enjoyed substantial advantages in every category of equipment and in rigorous training and staff work directed by a Soviet operational training mission headed by Maj. Gen. Ivan V. Vasilyev, an accomplished armor commander in the war against Germany.

After Kim and Pak visited Moscow again from March 30 through April 25, 1950, Stalin approved final preparations for an invasion of South Korea sometime in the summer of 1950, probably in August after the summer rains ended. Stalin had every reason to feel the forced unification of Korea could be accomplished at an acceptable risk. No one then (or now) knew exactly what factors convinced Stalin to change his *nyet* of 1949 to a *da* (yes) in 1950. However, the Soviets had exploded their first nuclear weapon in September 1949 and thus announced their willingness to match the American strategic nuclear deterrent force. Although the Allies had formed a European defense force as part of the North Atlantic Treaty (1949), in reality NATO depended on American forces and weapons, which could

not be sent to Asia. Important developments in Asia drama-
tized the Communists' militancy: the declaration of independence of the People's Republic of China (PRC) in October 1949,
opposition to the signing of an American-Japanese peace treaty,
the withdrawal of American troops from Korea, the potential
assistance of the surviving insurgents, the distrust and internal
plotting within the South Korean political and military elite,
and Mao Zedong's agreement to support the North Koreans.
The Soviet leverage that would ensure Chinese participation
was the Sino-Soviet Treaty of Friendship, Alliance, and Mutual
Assistance signed in February 1950. The Communist allies
pledged to oppose any return of Japanese imperialism, aided
by any other nation, meaning the United States and the Chinese Nationalists. In return for cash payments and economic
resources, the Soviets would provide for the air defense of China
proper and rearm the People's Liberation Army with standardized Red Army weapons.

The Soviet and North Korean war planners reached the
documentation stage in April 1950, and the written plans reflected their optimism about a speedy victory. After initial deep
penetrations to the Han River valley in a matter of days, the
North Koreans hoped the Rhee government and the ROK
Army (ROKA) would collapse. If they did not, the offensive
would continue for an estimated three or four months until
the KPA and its guerrilla allies controlled the whole country.
Seaborne special operations forces would attack and seize Korea's
southern harbors, including Pusan, thus sealing off Korea from
outside forces. The timing still had to be settled. Kim Il-sung
pressed for an invasion in June, not later, because more time
might bring more U.S. military assistance to the South Koreans and might compromise the invasion plans through inevitable leaks.

ROK intelligence operatives provided accurate predictions of the attack but without a specific date; line crossers also reported all sorts of preinvasion indicators but not a date. Assessing all the indicators—the movement of troops and supplies, the mobilization of additional manpower, increased internal security arrangements, communications patterns and message content, and other clues—the Korean and American intelligence officers in Korea predicted an imminent invasion. Unfortunately, they had already done so several times and had been wrong. The chief of staff of the South Korean Army, Lt. Gen. Chae Byong-duk, instead declared the last weekend of June a limited leave period, granting the troops a respite from the alerts and actual operations along the 38th Parallel. Two KPA officers (one was a pilot) defected in June and claimed an invasion was only days away. The local American military leaders (only Col. W. H. S. Wright in Korea and General MacArthur in Japan) did not feel sufficiently alarmed to raise the issue of war with Washington, knowing the Truman administration did not welcome pleas to defend Korea. In any event, preparations that would have reversed the situation—for example, transferring medium tanks, aircraft, and artillery from Japan to the South Korean Army—would have taken weeks to accomplish. Advanced basing for American fighter-bombers in Korea did not exist outside of Kimpo Airport, a prime Communist objective in the Han River valley. Time had run out for the Republic of Korea.

The Traditional War, 1950–51

Executing plans developed in April through June 1950 and issued as orders on June 18, the Korean People's Army struck across the 38th Parallel in the predawn hours of June 25 behind a thunderous Soviet-style artillery barrage. The KPA, divided into the I and II Corps, attacked along four axes of advance. The principal offensive by the I Corps (five divisions, one tank brigade, and one separate tank regiment of 53,000 men) drove toward Seoul along the Kaesong–Munsan-ni axis across the Imjin River and along the Uijongbu-Seoul axis, the most direct route from the border. The opposing South Korean 1st and 7th Divisions probably numbered no more than 10,000 men because half of the troops had taken short leaves. Many officers had gone to visit their families and attend a party in Seoul. The KPA II Corps (four divisions, one tank regiment, one motorcycle regiment, and two commando battalions of 54,000 soldiers) attacked along two widely separated axes. One advance was supposed to take the KPA 2d Division with the tanks and motorcycle infantry through the city of Chunchon to Hongchon and Suwon, thus cutting the ROK Army in half and cutting off the Seoul garrison. The KPA 5th Division attacked down the east coast road toward Kangnung, aided by amphibious landings behind the ROK Army's lines. The ROK 6th Division defended Chunchon, and the ROK 8th Division stood in front of Kangnung. Their combined strength should have been around 17,000 men since they had not granted leaves.

The Korean People's Army won the campaign north of the Han River valley and its adjoining corridors in four days, entering Seoul in the afternoon of June 28. Although the initial offensive ruined four ROKA divisions (1st, 7th, 2d, and Capital) and forced the ROK 6th and 8th Divisions to fall back to the south, the North Koreans did not accomplish their goal: causing the collapse of the Rhee government and the disintegration of the South Korean Army. The Communists' operational successes were predictable. The South Koreans did not have the tanks, artillery, antitank guns, and mines to stop a combined arms enemy, and their demolitions were not plentiful enough to block the critical passes. South Korean engineers blew up some bridges, and suicide squads attacked and destroyed T-34s and Su-76s with antitank guns and satchel charges. Long-range artillery, tank fire, and determined North Korean infantry, however, eventually swept the battlefield. The independent ROK 17th Regiment on the Ongjin Peninsula and the ROK 6th Division, however, not only held their positions but counterattacked successfully. Plagued by KPA commandos, the ROK 8th Division fought its way south in good order, but it opened the East Sea coastal road for the KPA.

The campaign was lost along the roads that led to Seoul. Gen. Chae Byong-duk contributed to the uneven battle by committing the reinforcing ROK 2d Division in piecemeal fashion and by ordering the destruction of the three bridges over the Han River the night of June 27–28 before his remaining troops, ammunition, supplies, and vehicles could evacuate Seoul. The remnants of the Seoul-area ROK forces and seven battalions from the ROK 3d and 5th Divisions formed a defensive line south of the Han River, organized by Maj. Gen. Kim Hong-il, a former division commander in the Chinese Nationalist Army. If the ROK Army was to hold, it would need help from the American armed forces.

Within hours of the attack, reports of the North Korean invasion reached Japan and Washington through war correspondents, the Korean Military Advisory Group, and the U.S. Embassy. Messages from the United Nations mission in Korea verified their reports. The Rhee government confused the reports by issuing radio messages of ROK Army counterattacks. These bits of wishful thinking were designed to deter a panic-stricken evacuation of Seoul and to boost morale, but they only provided grist for the Communist propagandists, who claimed the South Koreans attacked first. Without guidance from Washington, Ambassador John Muccio encouraged Syngman Rhee to stay in Seoul, but Muccio's mission and all the KMAG advisers were supposed to either move south to evade capture or leave Korea by ship or plane through Kimpo and Inchon. Orchestrated by Secretary of State Dean Acheson and with President Truman's approval, initially the JCS ordered General MacArthur to transfer munitions to the ROK Army and to use American air cover to protect the evacuation of American citizens. Washington issued this instruction on the evening of Sunday, June 25, but it was executed late on Monday, June 26 in Korea and Japan.[2]

When President Truman and his principal diplomatic and military advisers assembled for the first time in Washington on Sunday evening, June 25, they knew the Republic of Korea might be conquered. They did not spend much time debating the wisdom of the impending U.S. intervention. Correctly believing Stalin had encouraged and supported the attack—a conclusion shaped as much by communications intelligence as by historical analogies to Adolf Hitler—the American leaders saw

2. Time zones and the International Date Line make Korean time (KT) and Washington time (WT) confusing. In June 1950 there were twelve time zones between Seoul and Washington, and Washington was on daylight savings time, which added a thirteenth hour to the difference. For example, if Seoul was at 6:00 a.m. on June 26, 1950, Washington would be 5:00 p.m. on June 25, 1950. If Seoul was at 6:00 p.m. on June 26, 1950, Washington would be at 5:00 a.m. on the same day. In this essay, the days are given as they fell in Korea unless attached to actions taken by Washington or the United Nations headquarters in New York.

the invasion as a direct challenge to the American policy of "containing" Communism and Russian imperialism and the U.S. strategic corollary of forward, collective defense and nuclear deterrence. If the United States allowed Korea to be conquered, what chance did the NATO alliance have if the American willingness to risk war became doubtful? What chance did a peace treaty and possible military alliance with Japan have?

The Americans' debate focused on the political authority for intervention. Instead of pressing for a congressional declaration of war, which Truman regarded as too alarmist and potentially dilatory when time was of the essence, the administration went to the United Nations for sanction. Under American guidance, the United Nations first called for the invasion to halt (June 25) and then for the UN member nations to provide military assistance to the Republic of Korea (June 27). By charter the Security Council considered and passed the resolutions, which could have been vetoed by any permanent member of the council, including the Soviet Union. The Soviet Union, however, was boycotting the council over the issue of admitting Communist China to the United Nations. Even had the Soviets vetoed the Korean resolution, it would have received General Assembly approval, as did other Korean War measures of equal importance. The Soviets wanted no obvious association with the war, so their boycott would have been consistent with the same primitive dissembling as the order that no Russian advisers would accompany the North Korean Army across the 38th Parallel. Congressional and public opinion in the United States supported military intervention without significant dissent.

Having demonstrated its will, the Truman administration faced the unhappy truth it did not have enough effective military power to meet the invasion. The first obvious action was to send American aircraft and warships against the North Koreans, first only south of the 38th Parallel (June 26) and then extending into North Korea (June 29). The first American combat deaths of the war were six crewmen of the U.S. Air Force (USAF), killed June 27 in raids on targets in the Seoul area. Jets and propeller-driven light bombers (the B-26) flew initial air strikes in attempts to halt enemy columns and supply and troop trains sent from Pyongyang to Seoul.

In the meantime, General MacArthur ordered the KMAG advisers back into the war, sent an observer mission to join the Korean military and political headquarters at Sihung and Taejon, and then went to Korea himself. He took his staff and a group of correspondents up to the ROKA line south of the Han and watched Seoul burn. He then reported to Washington that the ROKA lacked the morale and training to halt the Communists and recommended committing American ground troops, perhaps as many as two of the four divisions of the U.S. Eighth Army in Japan. His request caused some anxiety in Washington, but on June 30 Truman authorized the commitment of at least a regimental combat team and later the same day extended it to cover all of MacArthur's initial request. Neither the press release from the White House nor the JCS internal deliberations suggested a larger and longer commitment.

Despite brave talk in Washington and Tokyo and even with the help of the Fifth Air Force's fighter-bombers and B-26s and the Far East Air Forces (FEAF) Bomber Command's B-29s, the U.S. Eighth Army had no more success than the ROKA in halting the North Korean advance. The American ground force commitment—three infantry divisions in July 1950—only expanded the scope of the defeat. In the same eight-week period, the prewar South Korean Army shrank to half its June 25 strength through deaths, surrenders, a few defections, and substantial desertions. No units, however, changed sides, and the South Korean Army's ranks began to climb back toward 100,000 with true volunteers (including college students) and impressed men as the South Koreans fell back. American units fought near Osan, along a defense line at the Kum River, in front of and into Taejon, and back along the highway and railroad that went south to Taegu. At these and other obscure locations, American soldiers fought and died. Some fled.

Frustrated by their strategic stalemate, the North Koreans rushed more supplies and reserve divisions south. The advance developed into three major thrusts, all aimed at the critical port of Pusan, where Kim Il-sung promised to hold a victory parade in mid-August. The KPA I Corps directed two divisions along the Taejon-Taegu axis. It also sent the crack 6th Division and a mechanized regiment into southwestern Korea to occupy the two Cholla provinces in conjunction with Communist partisan units, which had emerged from the hills and added new recruits. The KPA II Corps drove down the eastern coast road toward Yongdok and Pohang with the 5th Division and an attached separate regiment, while the 12th and 8th Divisions slid inland to menace Taegu from the east. The KPA high command committed the reserve 1st, 13th, and 15th Divisions to the central advance.

In the first weeks of August, the ground forces of United Nations Command (UNC, as MacArthur's theater forces had become known on July 8) started to slow, if not halt, the North Koreans and to do so at great cost to the Communists. The gradual reversal of fortune came from several sources. First, the U.S. Eighth Army, under Lt. Gen. Walton H. Walker, USA, and the ROK Army—now under the direction of Maj. Gen. Chung Il-kwon, a youthful American favorite—simply grew in numbers with less ground to defend. One of the best corps commanders in Europe in 1944–45 and a protégé of Gen. George Patton's, the irascible Walker proved an adequate army commander, especially after Washington sent proven officers for his staff. Walker's basic problem was he did not worship MacArthur or his chief of staff, Maj. Gen. Edward M. Almond. MacArthur and Almond gloried in second-guessing Walker and doing so in front of uncritical members of the press corps, often favored for their loyalty to MacArthur.

Walker's most pressing problems, however, were military and solvable if the U.S. Army in Japan and the United States helped. First, he needed a secure and efficient port at Pusan. The South Koreans made the first contribution to saving Pusan when a ROK Navy corvette, the *Paektusan*, sank a North Korean commando transport headed to destroy Pusan's docks on June 25–26. Also, Walker needed port logistics troops or civilians, supporting railroads, and trucks to supply his troops. Undermanned by Americans, the Eighth Army logistics system depended on Korean and Japanese technicians and common labor to work. The Eighth Army's shortages of logistics and engineering units did not improve for more than a year. Meanwhile, the numbers of combat troops increased more rapidly than the service troops to support them, which forced the army to recruit thousands of untrained Korean laborers, a long-term boon for Korea but a short-term burden for the U.S. Army. Another change saw the integration of Koreans into the Eighth Army itself. The least satisfactory expedient was the Korean Augmentation to the U.S. Army (KATUSA) program, which brought ill-trained and motivated Korean conscripts into the ravaged U.S. infantry regiments' ranks. Some KATUSAs proved loyal and solid fighters; most were not dependable in a serious fight. For nonfighting tasks they were welcome manual labor. The army had better luck with regular ROKA liaison officers, civilian interpreters, Korean National Police field battalions, and assorted hangers-on of many ages and both sexes. Some teenage boys became effective members and lifelong alumni of American units. In addition to housekeeping, the Koreans provided essential intelligence, cultural guidance, and an insider's skill in sorting out the loyalties of other Koreans. Christians, for example, were prima facie to be trusted since they were key Communist targets. Without the Koreans' assistance, American units could never have coped with the serious rear-area threat posed by Communist partisans.

Someone still had to stop the T-34s and their supporting artillery and infantry. The American armed forces provided the solutions: M4A3E8 Sherman and M26 Pershing medium tanks, new 3.5-inch rocket launchers, direct and indirect fire artillery pieces, mobile antiaircraft machine guns and cannons of devastating effect upon infantry and all light artillery and vehicles, and close air support aircraft. Most of the firepower went to American units, but Gen. Paik Sun-yup's ROK 1st Division received a tank and two American artillery battalions when it proved its fighting prowess in defending Taegu.

Adopting a system of airborne forward air controllers (codenamed "Mosquito"), the Fifth Air Force provided close air support to all units. Forming new squadrons of F-51 Mustangs, a piston-driven World War II fighter-bomber, the air force could use the primitive forward bases in Korea that were closed to its jet F-80s and F-84s. The B-26s and B-29s normally attacked the KPA's logistics systems, but they also attacked KPA units.

The ROK Air Force began its real life as a fighting force as an F-51 squadron of American and Korean pilots, commanded by the legendary Maj. Dean E. Hess, a minister turned World War II close air support hero. The tactical air capability took another jump with the arrival of two Marine Corps F4U Corsair squadrons embarked on U.S. Navy (USN) light carriers. These squadrons could fly missions anywhere along the front in quick response. On the east coast the ROK forces absorbed the student volunteers, who died by the hundreds in close combat. The ROK forces also benefited from the U.S. Navy's cruiser and destroyer forces and the ROK I Corps' seagoing heavy artillery as American KMAG advisers and U.S. Navy liaison teams ensured the shells and air attacks went to the correct targets.

The Eighth Army also needed more American infantry in addition to the three divisions sent to Korea: the 24th Infantry Division, the 25th Infantry Division, and the 1st Cavalry Division. The one division remaining in Japan, the 7th Infantry Division, had been stripped to supply men for the other divisions. The additional forces began to arrive in August: the 2d Infantry Division from Fort Lewis, Washington; the 29th Infantry Regiment from Okinawa; the 5th Regimental Combat Team (RCT) from Hawaii; and the 1st Provisional Marine Brigade from California. Except for the 29th Infantry, which was ambushed and nearly wiped out at Hadong on July 27, the new units brought not just numbers but a higher level of training and experience to the battlefield. All of them, however, had to endure the inevitable adjustment to a real war in a strange land where it rained one minute but then baked a man the next, the water was undrinkable, the language incomprehensible, the enemy undetectable, and the hills unclimbable.

Veterans all remember the rice paddies fertilized with human waste; most of them thought this smell symbolized all things Korean.

Concerned the shift of combat power toward the Eighth Army would continue in August and September 1950, the KPA field commander, Gen. Kim Chaek, ordered a three-axis advance against the U.S.-ROK forces defending the Masan-Naktong River-Taegu-Yongdok line, or the "Pusan Perimeter." Continuous and mounting UN Command air attacks had made the KPA's road and railroad resupply and reinforcement increasingly costly. Its tank force had been cut by more than half, and the KPA faced shortages of artillery ammunition and other munitions. Probably one-third of its original soldiers had become casualties and could be replaced only with North Korean conscripts, ROKA prisoners, and South Korean youths dragooned into its ranks. Pyongyang sent one new division and elements of two others south, but UNC manpower increased more rapidly. The North Koreans, however, reduced the allied firepower's effect by changing to night operations, emphasizing infiltration tactics, and establishing ambushes and raids on rear-area positions, especially with the Communist partisans' help. This tactical adaptation allowed the KPA to stay in the fight for another seven weeks despite its dwindling manpower. As allied troop strength mounted past 100,000 men, the North Korean forces fell to 70,000 effectives.

The first North Korean offensive began in the first week of August and continued for almost three weeks (August 4–19) until it collapsed. The major effort, made by seven divisions and most of the remaining T-34s, was a double envelopment of Taegu that was supplemented by drives at both the southwestern and northeastern coastal anchors of the Pusan

Perimeter. Although all of the KPA attacks scored local successes and caused General Walker some anxiety, none reached significant objectives. Allied infantry performance continued to be uneven. While the best Korean and American units fought with skill and élan, other units showed considerable reluctance to hold their positions.

As radio intercepts and agents warned of attacks, Walker met each crisis with select reserve forces such as the 5th RCT and the 1st Provisional Marine Brigade. Regiments of the 2d Infantry Division fought engagements along the perimeter's northern edge and as far south as "the Naktong bulge," well south of Taegu. One of the great successes of the defense was the Battle of Tabu-dong, or "the Bowling Alley," in which the ROK 1st Division and the U.S. 27th Regimental Combat Team defeated the North Koreans' main armored thrust toward Taegu (August 18–26). On the eastern coast the ROK I Corps fell back under a heavy KPA attack, losing Yongdok and Pohang in a battle that surged back and forth through the coastal cities in vicious, close urban warfare. In the southern sector, the 5th RCT and the Marines stopped the coastal thrust, then turned north, and joined part of the 2d Infantry Division in driving the KPA from its positions east of the Naktong River. General Walker's "Stand and Die" order of July 29, MacArthur's idea, produced more dying and some standing.

The Korean Peoples' Army made one more desperate attempt to win the war when it renewed the offensive on August 27. Within the next week the KPA had penetrated the UNC positions in five different locations, all sites of its earlier attacks. Again, the Eighth Army gave ground, sometimes without orders, but Walker now enjoyed some manpower superiority, even in "foxhole strength" or actual combat troops. The

North Korean losses reduced the two KPA corps to around 60,000 men while the U.S.-ROK divisions, now reinforced by a British brigade, numbered more than 150,000 soldiers. Neither opposing force showed much tactical skill; American losses in the first two weeks of September 1950 were the highest of the war to date. The three original American divisions and the five divisions of the ROKA had few veteran infantrymen left, and their fillers did not have any real precombat training, a guarantee of high and futile losses. Out of thirteen army infantry regiments in the Eighth Army, only three could be counted as fully reliable for staunch defense and determined attacks. By September 12, however, the North Korean Army had lost its capability for offensive action, and it had been driven back in most places to positions beyond the Naktong River and well away from Taegu and Pohang.

General MacArthur knew he could lose the war if Walker failed to hold the Pusan Perimeter, but he did not believe he could win the war without a deep amphibious turning movement that would change the entire strategic balance. He thought about a landing somewhere behind enemy lines in early July 1950, and he delayed the commitment of the 1st Cavalry Division because he saw it as his landing force. With the 7th Infantry Division reduced to cadre status, MacArthur needed a landing force from outside his theater, and he argued for the deployment of the 2d Infantry Division and 1st Provisional Marine Brigade for a landing in August or early September. These forces, too, went instead to the hard-pressed Eighth Army. Encouraged by two Marine Corps generals, MacArthur and the Joint Chiefs of Staff decided to form the 1st Marine Division and make it available for a landing in mid-September. They felt the 7th Infantry Division could be brought up to strength with Korean fillers and American soldiers shipped from the United States. As the force developed, it also included two South Korean marine battalions, an elite ROK infantry regiment, and an assortment of corps support troops from the U.S. Army and Marine Corps. The entire force was designated X Corps. Commanded by Maj. Gen. Edward M. Almond, still FECOM's chief of staff, MacArthur's landing force became part of an amphibious task force (Joint Task Force 7) directed by Vice Adm. Arthur D. Struble, USN.

As difficult as it was to form X Corps—the Marine Corps had to activate its reserves and strip the 2d Marine Division to form its division as well as plead for the return of the 1st Marine Brigade—selecting a landing site added special drama to the campaign. MacArthur himself fixed on Inchon in late July on the belief that landing there would lead X Corps to capture Seoul quickly and disrupt the KPA's major supply line and political base in South Korea. Always influenced by emotional factors, MacArthur wanted Seoul retaken and Syngman Rhee returned to his capital only ninety days after the original invasion. He also thought beyond the landing to a campaign into North Korea itself to destroy the Kim government and to unify all Korea under a non-Communist regime. MacArthur was not alone in wanting to use the United Nations Command to liberate and unify Korea. This change in war aims had already been supported by a powerful faction of Asianists in the State Department, had won over the U.S. delegation to the United Nations, and captured the hearts and minds of Truman's most influential advisers. The skeptics remained. Secretary of Defense Louis Johnson and the JCS, supported by military intelligence specialists and the Central Intelligence Agency (CIA), worried about Chinese and Russian intervention. Never one to draw attention to threats he chose to ignore, MacArthur argued his case based on the element of surprise against the North Koreans. He did not focus on the Soviet air and naval threat from the nearby Russian bases on China's Liaoning Peninsula.

Against this background of promise and risk, MacArthur had to win over his theater navy and Marine commanders and to convince the JCS that the Inchon option offered great strategic gains with little operational risk. Some problems applied to any landing on Korea's western coast: wide tidal variance, restricted channels, primitive beach exits, a crazy quilt of islands and shoal waters, and coastal hills of tactical advantage to the defender. Inchon had all these problems plus its proximity to the KPA garrison of Seoul, reinforcements from North Korea, a mining program just under way, and vulnerability to Russian naval and air forces. MacArthur brushed off these concerns as "mere technical details" and argued the navy and Marines had never failed him in World War II. Doubters thought a landing closer to the Eighth Army would allow a coordinated campaign in which X Corps and the Eighth Army could support each other and crush the KPA between them.

MacArthur would not be moved. By August 23 he had won over his fellow commanders and the JCS. Truman, however, reserved the right to keep the operation, code-named "Operation Chromite," under examination because he was about to fire Johnson and appoint retired General of the Army George C. Marshall to the post of secretary of defense. Truman hoped Marshall would provide the statesmanship conspicuously absent in his chairman of the Joint Chiefs of Staff, General Bradley. Against some uncertainty—complicated by the Pusan Perimeter battles and the approaching typhoon season—

planners continued to organize Operation Chromite because, as one admiral observed, "it was not impossible."

Not all the national leaders who watched Chromite develop—and it could hardly be kept a secret—worked in Washington. In Beijing, Mao Zedong, Zhou Enlai, and other key members of the Central Military Commission (CMC)—the Chinese equivalent of the National Security Council (NSC) and Joint Chiefs of Staff—watched the North Korean offensive slow with alarm. The Chinese mission in Pyongyang warned the Koreans to expect an amphibious landing, probably at Inchon. The Koreans ignored that advice, and a Korean-Russian engineering team proceeded to mine first the harbors of Wonsan and Chinnampo. Mao believed the United Nations would allow a Japanese-American coalition to attack the People's Republic of China and roll back its socialist revolution, but he could get the CMC to approve only a precautionary policy of transferring four elite Chinese armies (each of three or four small divisions or the equivalent of an American corps) from southern China to Manchuria, where they became the Northeast Border Defense Army. Mao continued to press the issue while facing both political and military resistance. In mid-August the consensus within the Central Military Commission began to shift toward military intervention, provided the Chinese armies could be reinforced and the Russians would honor their treaty promises of military assistance. In the meantime, Chinese observers at the UN and higher officials in Beijing started a series of public warnings, and the Chinese government initiated a "Hate America" campaign of public propaganda throughout China. By the end of August, MacArthur's intelligence service reported the presence of 260,000 frontline troops of the People's Liberation Army in Manchuria, which gave Mao an intervention capability. In the first week of September, Mao told an assembly of key party leaders that he saw no alternative to fighting the United States in Korea.

As the U.S. Navy and Marine planners tried to match fire support and the scheme of maneuver ashore with the available shipping, the strategic context in which Chromite would occur ripened. In the United States the Truman administration assumed great things of the Inchon landing. By September 11 the National Security Council (less the president) approved a final version of NSC 81/1, a policy memorandum that urged the unification of Korea by military action and a political settlement under the United Nations' auspices. It stipulated that MacArthur could cross the 38th Parallel with his ground forces in pursuit of the KPA, but if he faced Russian or Chinese military intervention, he had to restrict operations until Washington sorted out the crisis. Although the South Korean Army would be part of the "march north," MacArthur could not allow the current Rhee administration to govern the liberated people above the 38th Parallel. Although Truman withheld final approval of NSC 81/1 (he wanted Inchon in and Johnson out), the JCS sent MacArthur the gist of the guidance the very day X Corps made Chromite a reality.

After a naval gunfire and aerial bombardment on September 14, the Marine landing force the next day assaulted a key harbor defense site, Wolmi-do Island, and then in the late afternoon took Inchon itself. The North Korean resistance was not stubborn, and the armored counterattacks over the next two days did little to slow the 1st Marine Division's advance on Seoul. With Kimpo airfield secured on September 18, the 1st Marine Division put all three of its infantry regiments across the Han River (September 20–25) and captured Seoul with some last-minute and largely unnecessary help from the ROK 17th Infantry and an American infantry regiment. The rest of the 7th Infantry Division advanced to Suwon, where it contacted the lead elements of the Eighth Army on September 26. After Almond's premature declaration of victory on September 25, the Marines actually cleared the city two days later. MacArthur and Rhee marched into the damaged capitol building and declared South Korea liberated.

The Inchon-Seoul campaign did not have quite the outcome MacArthur anticipated. First, the Eighth Army had to fight for four days (September 16–22) before its I Corps (three divisions and the British brigade) could break out of the Taegu front and drive north toward Seoul. The ROK I Corps (two divisions) advanced up the east coast road. The ROK II Corps (three divisions) moved slowly up the central corridors toward Wonju while the U.S. IX Corps (two divisions) liberated the western provinces and tried to round up the remaining Communist partisan bands. As an organized field force, the Korean People's Army disintegrated south of the 38th Parallel. It had lost 13,000 prisoners and 50,000 casualties in August and September. Nevertheless, about 25,000 of its best troops abandoned their heavy weapons, took to the mountains, and marched home as cohesive units. Another 10,000 troops remained in South Korea as partisans. As the Communists headed north, they left thousands of South Koreans executed in their wake and took additional thousands with them north as hostages and slave labor. The ROK Army and national police showed little sympathy to any southern Communists they found or suspected, although they did on occasion actually set up military tribunals to screen suspects. With American aircraft attacking people and places with little restraint, the last two weeks of September repeated the excesses of the Thirty Years War. On September 27 the JCS gave MacArthur final authority to conduct operations north of the 38th Parallel with Truman's complete approval, although the cautions about Russian and Chinese intervention remained in force. No geographic limits to the UNC advance had yet been established, and MacArthur's OpPlan 9-50 covered only operations that would place UNC ground forces on a line that ran roughly from north of Pyongyang to north of Wonsan on the east coast or across the so-called waist of Korea.

In October 1950, the Korean War became a wider and longer conflict in four brief weeks. For the United Nations Command its mission was to occupy all North Korea and eliminate the Korean Peoples' Army as a threat to the political reconstruction of the two Koreas as one nation. Under Syngman Rhee's prodding, on October 1 the ROK 3d Division crossed the 38th Parallel on the east coast, but the real march north started on October 7, when the 1st Cavalry Division crossed the border above Kaesong. The U.S. I Corps took the main highway toward Pyongyang, fighting one major battle at Sariwon, but was otherwise slowed more by logistical restraints than by stubborn defense. The ROK II Corps advanced more slowly on its right (inland) flank, sliding to the northwest in echelon behind the lead divisions. The IX Corps and two ROK divisions remained in the south for counterguerrilla operations while the ROK I Corps marched rapidly up the east coast highway. The Koreans won the race for Wonsan because the X Corps, assigned another landing, took more than a week to re-embark at Inchon and Pusan and then arrived at Wonsan to find the harbor so heavily mined that it required another two weeks to clear a path to the docks. Wonsan fell on October 11 and

Pyongyang on October 19. The remnants of nine KPA divisions fell back to the mountain town of Kanggye with the Kim Il-sung government. Two other divisions—and the Russian advisory mission and air defense forces of Pyongyang—struggled northwest toward the Yalu River and the Chinese border. The United Nations Command assumed the KPA had lost its will to fight, not that it was awaiting rescue.

On October 15 President Truman and General MacArthur met at Wake Island to share the reflected glory of their victory for the media and to discuss the rest of the war. MacArthur assured Truman the Chinese had missed their opportunity to intervene when they let Pyongyang fall, and he told Truman American air power would "slaughter" any Chinese forces that appeared in Korea. Communications intelligence showed troop concentrations in Manchuria; it also reported Soviet passivity in the face of the advance north. The two men, in fact, spent much of their limited time discussing the progress of building a peace with Japan and the reconstruction of South Korea. They barely discussed Chinese threats of intervention made to third parties in Beijing and New York. MacArthur's only concern was overcoming his logistical problems.

As Truman and MacArthur basked in victory, the political temperatures in Beijing and Moscow turned chilly. On October 1 Mao Zedong finally received a plea for direct military aid from Kim Il-sung. The chairman immediately called a meeting of the Standing Committee of the Politburo, joined by the top PLA commanders, for the following afternoon. Mao probably drafted a telegram to Stalin, indicating his willingness to intervene and requesting Soviet assistance. After long discussions with his colleagues, Mao made his commitment more conditional, suggesting internal opposition to his intervention plan could only be met after receiving generous assurances of Soviet air support, enough munitions and ordnance to modernize the PLA, and Russian assistance in creating a Chinese air force and armaments industry. Doubters around Mao were powerful military and political figures, including his most accomplished general, Lin Biao, and a domestic policy czar, Liu Shaoqi. Mao brought Gen. Peng Dehuai to Beijing to brief him on his new command, the Northeast Border Defense Army, and sent Zhou Enlai and Gao Gang, the pro-Soviet Manchurian party boss, off to Moscow to arrange an aid package that would silence the dissenters in Beijing.

Mao Zedong could not save Pyongyang as he hoped on October 2. When he finally sent Chinese service units into Korea, he faced considerable uncertainty about the scope and type of Soviet support. The principal issue was the employment of Soviet air power. Russian aviation units and antiaircraft artillery had already assumed the air defense of major Chinese cities; furthermore, Stalin promised to extend these air defenses to a corridor above the Yalu, which would protect the air bases in Manchuria and the hydroelectric plants on the river. The Soviets agreed to hurry the training of Chinese pilots and the creation of PLA aviation squadrons. In return for money and raw materials, the Russians would transfer arms and limited factory facilities to the Chinese. But the Russians would not send an expeditionary air force into Korea to build bases and mount air attacks on UNC ground forces or even to protect the Chinese armies from air attack. After much debate and some recrimination, Mao sent definitive orders on October 18 for his expeditionary force—the Renmin Zhiyuanjun, or Chinese People's Volunteers Force (CPVF)—to cross into Korea on the night of October 19–20 and blunt the Eighth

Army's northward movement, which was now past Pyongyang and entering the watershed of the Chongchon River, the last major terrain feature short of the twin cities of Sinuiju-Antung on the Yalu River.

The Chinese First Offensive (October 25–November 6, 1950) had the limited objective of testing the U.S.-ROK fighting qualities and slowing the pace of the UNC's pursuit of the KPA north toward Kanggye. The Chinese main force—the Thirteenth Army Group (fifteen infantry divisions and three artillery divisions)—directed four armies against the Eighth Army and one against the X Corps. In the battle of Onjong-Unsan along the Chongchon River, the Chinese ruined seven Korean and American regiments, including the only Korean regiment to reach the Yalu, cut off in the vastness of the cold northern hills. Only hard fighting by the U.S. I Corps extracted its two endangered divisions and provided some safety for the wreckage of the ROK II Corps. To do so, the 24th Infantry Division and 27th British Commonwealth Brigade first had to extract themselves from fixing attacks by the CPVF Sixty-sixth Army while the Thirty-eighth, Thirty-ninth, and Fortieth Armies fell on the rest of the I Corps and the ROK II Corps. On the east coast the Forty-second Army ambushed elements of the ROK 3rd Division and the 1st Marine Division and lost most of a division in fighting around Sudong. Even though they suffered 10,000 casualties, the Chinese thought they had found a formula for fighting the United Nations Command: attack at night, cut off routes of supply and withdrawal, ambush counterattacking forces, infiltrate past infantry positions and assault artillery units, and exploit all forms of concealment and cover, including hiding in caves and setting forest fires to produce blankets of smoke to foil UNC aircraft. Stunned by the suddenness of the Chinese onslaught and by suffering almost 8,000 casualties (all but 2,000 of them Koreans), the Eighth Army fell back to the Chongchon's south bank and tightened its overextended lines. Logistical scarcities and the beginning of the harsh Korean winter made the pause a wise move. The real source of the new caution in Walker's headquarters was the growing awareness that the regular Chinese Army had entered the war and in numbers quadruple those published by MacArthur's chief intelligence officer (G-2), Maj. Gen. Charles A. Willoughby.

Another matter of concern was the dramatic appearance of the Soviet first-line air superiority fighter, the jet MiG-15, in combat above North Korea. Flown by Russian pilots masquerading as Chinese and Koreans, the MiGs of the 64th Fighter Air Corps challenged UNC air superiority. In one week's action (November 1–7), the Russians stopped most of the daytime raids on North Korean targets with worrisome losses, especially to the B-29s. MacArthur chose to meet the challenge by ordering bombing raids on all North Korean cities and on the Yalu River bridges, which, to be effective, meant violating Manchurian air space. The Far East Air Forces balked at MacArthur's plans, and the air strikes were canceled or changed upon JCS review. MacArthur did not take the decision well, but the U.S. Air Force immediately dispatched a crack wing of F-86 Sabre jet interceptors to Japan to tackle the MiG problem, thus beginning a two-and-a-half-year air battle over North Korea. The F-86s also ensured Ilyushin bombers based in Manchuria would not bombard the Eighth Army.

Convinced the Chinese force could be defeated, MacArthur prepared another offensive toward the Yalu River for mid-November, but Walker, pleading logistical problems that were real enough, obtained a week's postponement. Walker's immediate concern was bringing his IX Corps up from South Korea and committing it to the critical upper reaches of the Chongchon River valley and the Onjong-Unsan battlefield of October. The I Corps slipped left to a sector anchored on the West Sea with the battered 1st Cavalry Division in army reserve. The IX Corps did not fully appreciate its peril since it came to a quiet sector and spent much of its time issuing cold weather clothing and Thanksgiving dinners. The reformed ROK II Corps guarded the army's eastern flank with its three divisions in echelon. The Koreans knew thousands of Chinese hid in the hills to their front, but they could not communicate their anxiety to the Americans. Irritated by MacArthur's cavalier conduct of the exploitation campaign, Walton Walker did all he could to keep his army well in hand and adequately supplied for the ill-considered offensive he would have to mount before November ended.

The fate of the fighting forces rested on decisions in Washington and Beijing. The JCS reviewed the situation and recommended that the United Nations Command hold the Pyongyang-Wonsan line and see what the Russians and Chinese might do. Truman and Acheson, soothed by MacArthur's assurances, did not intervene to stop MacArthur's November offensive. In part they awaited results from the revived air campaign, but the reports suggested limited success in stopping the flow of men and material from Manchuria. The U.S. Air Force turned its fury on all the structures that might shield the Chinese from the cold; villages and towns all over North Korea went up in flames. The air assault did not halt Peng Dehuai's build-up for a second offensive, this time a counterstrike against an anticipated UNC offensive. Peng's plan assumed the doubling of his own army to 400,000 and the concentration of the Thirteenth Army Group around the Eighth Army. The new Ninth Army Group would encircle the forward elements of the X Corps. The 1st Marine Division, doubting Almond's optimistic operational assumptions, moved cautiously northward. It detached forces to maintain its route to the Hungnam-Hamhung area, which was occupied by the newly arrived 3rd Infantry Division. To the north the rest of the 7th Infantry Division and the two divisions of the ROK I Corps reached the Yalu and Korea's most northern coastal cities. The advance had some urgency since the Communists had started a pogrom against any suspected dissidents. In the Hungnam-Hamhung area the numbers of disinterred victims may have been as high as 10,000 people or twice the numbers of the worst atrocity in South Korea, the Taejon massacre of 5,000 people in September.

Having assessed the results of his first offensive, Peng Dehuai agreed with Mao Zedong that the CPVF should strike again before MacArthur abandoned his plan to drive on to the Yalu. Peng's instructions to his army commanders stressed the necessity to lure the Americans and "puppet troops" out of their defensive positions between the Chongchon River and Pyongyang and to give the impression of weakness and confusion while Peng Dehuai deployed his much-enlarged force of 420,000 Chinese and North Korean regulars. Thirty CPVF divisions and a KPA corps of two divisions deployed in a wide semicircle from the West Sea to the Taebaek mountain range. The new Ninth Army Group (twelve divisions in four armies) deployed along the eastern ridges of the Taebaeks to catch X Corps. The new offensive would focus on the 1st Marine Division and a regimental task force of the 7th Infantry Division crawling forward along either side of the Changjin Reservoir ("Chosin" in 1950) and separated from the sea by one narrow, vulnerable road through several mountain passes and one bridged chasm. Three armies would try to annihilate the Americans around the reservoir while the remaining divisions would try to pin the rest of the 7th Division and the ROK I Corps to enclaves between Hamhung and the Russian border. If the Chinese could push all the way to the coast, most of X Corps would be cut off and forced to evacuate by sea. Such results represented the most optimistic planning by the Chinese. Their more modest goal was to eliminate one or more American divisions, which would send the South Koreans into a panic and weaken the Americans' resolve to continue the war. Even a limited victory might drive the United Nations Command out of North Korea, Mao's immediate goal.

In probably his only real military mistake of the war, General MacArthur ordered the Eighth Army and X Corps northward into the Chinese trap on November 24, despite his earlier report that the Chinese force "threatens the ultimate destruction of my command." MacArthur later argued the offensive was really a reconnaissance in force, a brilliant plan to spring the Chinese trap before Peng's snare was fully set. Generals Walker and Almond and their division commanders did not see the plan that way. Almond hectored his commanders to attack north while Walker, who had no faith in MacArthur's genius, cautioned his generals to go slowly and watch their flanks. Neither commander was really aware of the disaster they faced as the snows fell and the temperature plunged to zero. Loose military lips, careless reporters, and barracks rumormongers all spread the tale that the Americans would be home by Christmas.

From late November 1950 until May 1951, the Chinese People's Volunteers Force did its best to drive all of the UNC forces from the Korean Peninsula. In four major offensives—November–December 1950, January 1951, February 1951, and April–May 1951—the Chinese expeditionary force battered the Eighth Army (of which X Corps became a part in December) back below Seoul and to the 37th Parallel. The Second Offensive of November 25–December 14, 1950, did, in fact, drive United Nations Command back to South Korea, but Mao did not quite win the moral victory he sought over the American army. Falling upon the IX Corps, new to the Chongchon River front, the Chinese almost destroyed the 2d Infantry Division, sweeping upon it through the ROK II Corps from the east and opening up a gap to the west through the 25th Infantry Division. Walker secured his right flank with a newly arrived Turkish brigade, the 1st Cavalry Division, an airborne regimental combat team, and a British brigade. In the meantime, the I Corps and the 25th Infantry Division disengaged from their advanced positions north of the Chongchon and fell back toward Pyongyang, fighting through Chinese forces that had infiltrated and established roadblocks along the major roads. Nevertheless, the Eighth Army had slipped the noose by December 1 and now enjoyed the advantage of shipborne resupply up the Taedong River to Pyongyang.

The situation for the X Corps, however, seemed fraught with potential disaster. The CPVF Ninth Army Group sent one army against the isolated regimental combat team of the 7th Infantry Division and virtually destroyed it, two armies attacked the 1st Marine Division at Yudam-ni and Hagaru-ri, and a fourth army moved against the main road to Hungnam deep in the rear, where it ran into more Marines and the 3rd

Infantry Division. Under the worst possible weather conditions, the 1st Marine Division fought its way south and destroyed seven Chinese divisions in the process before reaching the Hungnam enclave on December 11. Allied casualties reflect the Chinese main effort. The Marines had 4,418 battle casualties in the breakout, while the ROK 3rd Division disengaged to the north and reached Hungnam with less than 1,000 losses.

At the height of the crisis, MacArthur called Walker and Almond to Tokyo for a midnight conference on November 28–29. They agreed both the Eighth Army and X Corps should escape their respective traps and establish enclaves in North Korea that would preserve the option of holding the Pyongyang-Wonsan line. At least that is what MacArthur told the JCS—or what the JCS believed he told them—on November 30. MacArthur and the JCS seemed mesmerized by the peril to the X Corps, and they missed the real story: Walton Walker had already started the Eighth Army's move south, abandoning the possibility of a Pyongyang enclave. Walker's first movements were logistical: he canceled rail and shipping resupply to Pyongyang and sent major logistical units and whatever they could carry south as far as the Han River valley. Walker had finally gotten his revenge for all of MacArthur's meddling and posturing; the Eighth Army commander would save his army first and explain it later. MacArthur kept his eye and the JCS's eyes on X Corps, and on November 30 Truman approved a JCS directive to MacArthur that allowed him to withdraw from all of *northeast* Korea above Wonsan. By December 6, with confusion reigning in Washington and Tokyo, the Eighth Army had broken contact with the Chinese (much to Peng Dehuai's dismay), destroyed everything it could not carry, and had taken the road for Seoul. Walker's initiative may have saved his army, but it also meant that the United Nations Command had forfeited any chance to organize a strategic defense north of the Han River valley. Much of the rest of the war would be fought as a UNC effort to return to the ground Walker surrendered with so little effort. The general never had to answer for his decision, for on December 23 he died in a traffic accident just north of Seoul.

Heartened by the surprising ease with which the CPVF had driven the United Nations Command out of North Korea, Mao Zedong demanded that Peng Dehuai continue the offensive. Mao expanded the war aims: the Chinese Army must unify Korea and drive the Americans and "puppet troops" off the peninsula. He believed the CPVF could continue its offensive without air support and without any parity in artillery strength. He ignored the likely problems of supplying the CPVF as it marched farther south. Peng attempted to dampen the chairman's enthusiasm, but Mao had succumbed to "victory disease." Peng's concern did not abate even after the Chinese Third Offensive (December 31, 1950–January 5, 1951) retook Seoul and drove the Eighth Army out of the Han River valley. This time the Eighth Army retreat, under its new commander, Lt. Gen. Matthew B. Ridgway, USA, did not endanger any American divisions, but the ROK Army showed growing signs of defeatism even in its best divisions. The campaign of 1950 had cost the South Koreans too many of their trained troops and best officers. Ridgway, therefore, had to rely in the short-term on his American divisions, many of which had now gained infantry units from other United Nations participants. In addition to the British Commonwealth, which had two separate brigades in Korea, Turkey had sent an infantry brigade of good fighting qualities. France, Belgium, the Netherlands, and Greece sent battalions late in 1950, and other infantry battalions from Colombia, Thailand, Ethiopia, and the Philippines joined the allied army in 1951. The United Nations consistently rejected the option of introducing Chinese Nationalist divisions, but Quomindang and Japanese veterans participated in the war as individual intelligence agents, transportation experts, and technicians. Pulling his multinational force together, Ridgway challenged MacArthur's judgment that the UNC ground forces could not hold, and on January 15 he tested his army with a limited advance north. The initial probe showed the Chinese ready to give ground, so Ridgway kept up the offensive pressure for the next four weeks until the Eighth Army reached the approaches to the Han River valley.

Now reinforced with a reborn North Korean Army, the Chinese launched their Fourth Offensive on February 11, 1951. Again the initial attacks struck ill-prepared South Korean divisions and opened a large salient between the Seoul area and the central corridor to Hoengsong and Wonju. The U.S. I Corps and IX Corps gave ground but retained their cohesion in the western sector, but the X Corps suffered serious losses in the ROK 3rd and 8th Divisions and the U.S. 2d Infantry Division in a week's fighting. Two UNC actions blunted the Chinese offensive: the stand by the 23rd Regimental Combat Team at Chipyong-ni and the defense of Wonju by American and Korean units, an action in which American heavy artillery caught the Chinese Thirty-eighth and Fortieth Armies in the open and stopped them without major infantry combat.

For the next two months, the Eighth Army fought its way methodically back to the Han River valley, crossed the river, and isolated the Chinese forces to the west, thus liberating Seoul again, but the advance in part was another Chinese ploy to allow the Americans to overextend their forces. When the Eighth Army advanced past the 38th Parallel, Peng Dehuai—on Mao's orders and against his own judgment—committed at least half of his army and began the Fifth Offensive (First Phase) with eleven Chinese armies and two North Korean corps. The attacks occurred along virtually the entire front, but the offensive's weight came against the American and Korean divisions deployed along the Imjin River valley, the tributaries to the upper Han River, Chunchon, and the Hwachon Reservoir. Allied intelligence had provided some warning of the attack, but it came at an awkward moment for the Eighth Army because it had again changed commanding generals. Eleven days before the offensive began on April 22, President Truman, with the support of his civilian and military advisers, relieved Douglas MacArthur of all his commands and ordered him back to the United States for a long-postponed retirement. The change elevated Ridgway to commander in chief, Far East Command and United Nations Command, and brought Lt. Gen. James A. Van Fleet, USA, to Korea to command the Eighth Army. Like Ridgway, Van Fleet had earned wide respect as a division and corps commander against the Germans from 1944 to 1945.

Before Van Fleet could reform the ROK Army and reorganize his own to provide more forces to the central sector, the Chinese struck the ROK II Corps and the shoulders of the U.S. IX and X Corps on either side of the South Koreans. A low point in Korean military history, the battered divisions of the Korean corps gave way, and the American divisions peeled back to protect their flanks and rear, widening the gap between Seoul and Chunchon. The I Corps, however, refused to evacuate Seoul, and the ROK 1st Division, in another of its courageous actions, stopped a Chinese Army from slipping across the vital lines of communication south of the city. The 1st Marine Division held the eastern shoulder of the salient until Van Fleet could commit five American and Korean divisions and a British brigade to halt the two Chinese armies at the point of the attack on April 28.

Mao refused to accept Peng's report that the Chinese People's Volunteers Force no longer held the initiative, and he ordered a second phase offensive, which began on May 16 and lasted another bloody week. The Chinese and Korean attack this time focused against the eastern divisions of the U.S. X Corps and the ROK III Corps in the eastern one-third of the front. The Chinese again gained miles of territory at the expense of the U.S. 2d Infantry Division and two ROK divisions. Once again allied airpower and heavy artillery stiffened the resistance. The corps commander, General Almond, persuaded Van Fleet to let him keep the reinforcing 3rd Infantry Division and 187th Airborne Regimental Combat Team and to mount a major counteroffensive. Almond's counterstrike caught three Chinese armies in a planned withdrawal and created an even larger opportunity for offensive exploitation. Van Fleet even planned a one-corps amphibious assault on the east coast behind the Korean and Chinese armies, but Ridgway vetoed the idea for reasons of time, risk, and the lack of reinforcements. Van Fleet and Almond believed they had lost a chance to recapture the eastern part of the Wonsan-Pyongyang line. Instead, Van Fleet ordered his whole army onto the attack through May and much of June 1951. The United Nations Command once more crossed the 38th Parallel and prepared for further offensives to the north in pursuit of a battered (but not beaten) Chinese expeditionary force.

The Korean War reached another critical turning point in June 1951, with the Chinese last offensive blunted and the United Nations Command poised to advance north. Despite Syngman Rhee's enthusiasm for the October 1950 war of unification, the Truman administration and the United Nations wanted to return to the status quo ante. Intelligence assessments increased their caution. Despite probably 500,000 casualties since November, the Chinese and Korean armies had grown to 1.2 million soldiers. The North Koreans had returned to the war with more tenacity and viciousness than they had shown in 1950. Both Communist armies had received common families of Russian small arms and artillery. Although the Russian MiG-15 force had not expanded its aerial war, it had trained Chinese and North Korean MiG squadrons and seemed ready to allow them to move forward into North Korea. Meanwhile, the United Nations Command had not done badly in keeping in the manpower race. In May 1951, American ground troops numbered 256,000 and the South Korean army 250,000 soldiers, or two times its size the previous year. The allied contingents added 28,000 more soldiers. The British Commonwealth nations had provided sufficient forces to form their own division, but the other brigades, regiments, and battalions remained in their American divisions. All of the Eighth Army had taken its share of casualties, more than 100,000 since the Chinese intervention, but the Department of Defense kept sending replacements. The U.S. Army also ordered the National Guard 40th Infantry Division and the 45th Infantry Division to Japan for eventual use in Korea.

From General Ridgway's perspective, his strongest instrument of war was the Far East Air Forces, composed of Fifth, Seventh, and Thirteenth U.S. Air Forces and reinforcing squadrons from South Africa, Australia, and Canada. The British Commonwealth navies contributed twenty warships, and Colombia, the Netherlands, and Thailand sent four light escorts. Both the South Korean Navy and Air Force became useful adjuncts of the UNC naval and air forces. In addition, the UNC air effort included the 1st Marine Aircraft Wing (based mostly ashore) and the air groups of at least two on-station American carriers. In terms of operational combat aircraft, Far East Air Forces grew from almost 700 aircraft in July 1950 to more than 1,400 in February 1951. As great an air enthusiast as MacArthur, Ridgway viewed an accelerated air campaign against military targets and transportation systems throughout North Korea as a realistic alternative to additional ground offensives.

Another major shift in the war's character came from Washington and Beijing. From the start of the American intervention, General MacArthur had bedeviled the Truman administration in three different ways: he wanted to conduct his own diplomacy with Nationalist China, Japan, and South Korea on strategic issues; except for the Inchon landing, his military assessments had been flawed and out of touch with the fighting; and he had a bad habit of communicating publicly with the press, the enemy, and the Republicans in Congress about American war aims, the untrustworthy nature of the United Nations and his European allies, the importance of defeating Communism in Asia, and his own infallible wisdom. In March 1951, MacArthur interrupted some delicate undercover negotiations about a cease-fire. His interference embarrassed Truman and his foreign allies. The general then followed this gaffe with a letter to Congressman Joseph Martin, the Republican leader in the House of Representatives, that suggested the Truman administration had no intention of winning the war. Backed by

Acheson and Marshall, Truman relieved MacArthur, much to the relief of his own party's liberals and his European allies. This act allowed him, Truman thought, to consider escalating or de-escalating the war without "the MacArthur factor" influencing his judgment. He wanted to examine a range of options from the potential use of nuclear weapons to a major offensive that would take the United Nations Command back to the Pyongyang-Wonsan line at a minimum and might result in an imposed peace settlement.

As the Chinese Fifth Offensive reached its peak, both coalitions of belligerents—except the Koreans—considered the possibility that neither side could impose a peace settlement upon the other through military defeat, at least at an acceptable cost. From Washington's perspective, a negotiated peace, even if it did not come rapidly, offered several advantages. It preempted demands from the "Asia First" lobby in Congress (mostly Republicans) that more direct pressure be directed at China, as MacArthur had argued, through the use of air, naval, and Chinese Nationalist forces. Yet the Truman administration needed to appease the Republicans to some degree—in other words keep fighting—to win their support for the defense build-up then under way and for the creation of an allied defense force for NATO. These same factors made the UN members, even those with troops in Korea, sympathetic to the idea of a negotiated settlement, even for the status quo antebellum, which would abandon the war aims of the General Assembly Resolution of October 7, 1950.

Although the State Department's low-level advances to Soviet diplomats produced no hints of negotiations, members of the Truman administration still bargained among themselves. Truman himself remained fairly bellicose, much relieved to have MacArthur checkmated. His military and civilian advisers, however, moved toward a position they believed would not jeopardize the Atlantic alliance and yet strengthened the American position in north Asia. They sought an alliance with Japan and greater cooperation with the Chinese Nationalists as well as military assistance to the Philippines and for the French in Indochina. Indications were that the United Nations might assist in this policy of "containing" the People's Republic of China. The General Assembly condemned China as an aggressor in February 1951, and in May the Assembly called for its members to join the United States in an economic embargo of China. What was not negotiable was preserving the Republic of Korea with sufficient political legitimacy, economic stability, and military strength to deter another war. Just what its northern border might be, however, was negotiable. The theoretical option of neutralization and demilitarization remained dead. The Joint Chiefs of Staff supported negotiations as long as the talks would not endanger the United Nations Command or restrict General Ridgway's freedom to use his forces to respond to any escalatory threat, particularly an expansion of the air war.

After much deliberation the National Security Council accepted a new policy statement on the Korean War, NSC 48/5, on May 17, 1951, that returned the United States to its original war aim of June 1950—that is, to preserve the Republic of Korea and protect it from aggression. NSC 48/5 committed the United States to seek a unified, democratic Korea but not necessarily one unified by military action and the overthrow of Kim Il-sung. Syngman Rhee could not accept this position because of his personal convictions and for fear of weakening his anti-Communist political base, which was much strengthened by 1951. His only solace was that with NSC 48/ 5, the UN promised to expand and modernize the South Korean Army as rapidly as possible. There would be no second "march north," however, as long as the Chinese expeditionary force remained in Korea and the North Korean Army remained an effective force. When Ridgway received his strategic guidance based on NSC 48/5, the JCS made clear that the defense of Japan, South Korea, and Taiwan could not be endangered by a major offensive against North Korea or an expanded war against China.

The Communist road to a negotiated peace started in Beijing, not Moscow. Although the Russians had no objections to armistice talks or even a cease-fire, they wanted Mao Zedong to bear the burden of any settlement just as he had borne the war's human cost. In fact, Stalin was perfectly happy to keep the Chinese fighting with military assistance and limited air power as long as the war was confined to Korea. Reluctantly, in May 1951 Mao conceded the CPVF could not destroy an American or British division (an achievement of which he attached great psychological importance) and that destroying ROK divisions did not seem to have much effect. Peng Dehuai encouraged Mao to rethink the Chinese strategy of annihilation. The CPVF had lost 50,000 men in just the second phase of the Fifth Offensive and for the first time had experienced the humiliation of a mass surrender by the fragmented, surrounded CPVF 180th Division, the only Chinese unit of its size to surrender during the war.

From late May until mid-June the Chinese leaders discussed their Korean War strategy. None of them wanted to end the war; they just wanted to change their strategy. Mao finally approved an approach Peng and others gently suggested:

hold the ground in Korea, conduct a campaign of attrition against the United Nations Command, and attempt to win limited victories against small allied units with Soviet artillery; sudden, violent night attacks; and infantry infiltration tactics. An extensive system of field fortifications, dug into the Korean mountains, would provide protection from UNC air and artillery attacks; Chinese officers would later proclaim their system of caves and bunkers in Korea was comparable to the construction of the Great Wall. Mao likened this approach to war to eating one of his favorite candies from Hunan province, *niupitang*. This candy, Mao thought, epitomized the new strategy: it took time to devour, was sticky and hard to resist, required patience, and demanded subtle handling. Part of Mao's new approach would involve demanding more modern air and ground warfare weapons from the Soviet Union and encouraging Kim Il-sung to increase his demands of the Russians as well. Moreover, negotiations would be managed by the Chinese, an unparalleled chance to appear as an equal power to the United States in Asia and take a slap at the hated Japanese. The Koreans' fate, on either side, was not a major factor. At the moment Mao wanted to buy some time to build the future power of the Chinese armed forces throughout Asia.

The military realities soon shaped the diplomatic minuet. Suddenly in May an American diplomat at the United Nations learned from his Soviet counterpart that the Russian representative to the United Nations, Jacob Malik, wanted to talk with an important American diplomat about a possible Korean War settlement. The message went to Washington, and Secretary of State Dean Acheson deputized Ambassador George Kennan, a Soviet specialist then on leave, to pursue the tempting offer. Kennan and Malik met privately several times in the

New York area, and Kennan apparently persuaded Malik that the United States would seriously consider a negotiated end to the war. On June 23, 1951, Malik used a radio program sponsored by the United Nations to announce that in the interest of world peace, the Soviet Union would not block a negotiated settlement to the Korean War. What Malik did not say was that the United States would have to deal directly with the Chinese and North Koreans since the Soviet Union was not a party to the war. Instead the Soviets wanted to restore the United Nations as an instrument of peace and to support the candidacy of the People's Republic of China as the Chinese people's legitimate representative in the Security Council.

The United States chose to accept what it liked in Malik's message and to ignore what it did not like simply to see if peace talks in Korea might be initiated. The Truman administration had already alerted Ridgway to the prospect of truce talks and clearly stipulated no issue outside of the combat in Korea was negotiable. The United States would neither discuss any issue that dealt with the Chinese Communist government's legitimacy nor agree to anything beyond halting the fighting in Korea and ensuring the survival of the Republic of Korea. On June 30, 1951, Ridgway issued a public statement that he had been authorized to participate in "a meeting to discuss an armistice providing for the cessation of hostilities and all acts of armed force in Korea, with adequate guarantees of the maintenance of such an armistice." On July 2, 1951, the Chinese and North Koreans issued a joint statement that they would discuss arrangements for a meeting but only at their place of choice, the city of Kaesong. An ancient Korean capital, Kaesong was once part of the Republic of Korea but was now occupied by the Communist forces at the very edge of the current

frontlines north of the Imjin River. The Chinese had just fired
the first salvo of a new war in which talking and fighting for
advantage would someday end the conflict.

Talking and Fighting: Korea,
July 1951–July 1953

From the time the liaison officers of both coalitions met at Kaesong on July 8, 1951, until the armistice agreement was signed
on July 17, 1953, the Korean War continued as a "stalemate."
The stalemate characterization is appropriate in only two ways:
both coalitions had given up unifying Korea by force of arms,
and the movement of the armies on the ground never again
matched the fluidity of the war's first year. Otherwise, the word
stalemate has little meaning. The survival of the two Korean
governments was still at stake. Furthermore, the United States
and the People's Republic of China still had much to gain or
lose in terms of their future ability to shape events in Asia. The
other members of the United Nations Command still had their
relations with the United States to consider. The Soviet Union
also had a great deal at stake. Here was an opportunity to
weaken the United States and Japan, to divert the United States
from NATO, and to increase China's dependency on the Soviet Union. Meanwhile, several UN member nations saw the
negotiations as an opportunity to improve the leverage of "neutral nations" on the American-dominated majority in the General Assembly and to advance the cause of anticolo-nialism.
The line of troops on the ground might not have moved much,
but the stakes in Korea remained high.

    The negotiations had much the same quality as the Japa-
nese dramatic form *bunraku*, in which puppets represent reality

but only as extensions of the darkened humans in the background who manipulate their movements. Each delegation had five military members. That of the United Nations Command was composed of a chief delegate (initially, Vice Adm. C. Turner Joy, USN), three flag officers (one each from the U.S. Army, U.S. Air Force, and U.S. Navy), and a fifth delegate, a general of the South Korean Army who could hardly influence the talks since Rhee opposed them in principle. The Communists' chief delegate from start to finish was Gen. Nam Il, chief political officer of the Korean People's Army and chief of its general staff. The two Chinese delegates were among the most talented and sophisticated generals in the Chinese Army: Xie Fang, chief of staff of the CPVF who spoke English well, and Deng Hua, the CPVF's deputy commander. Both Chinese officers enjoyed the confidence of Mao, Zhou Enlai, and Peng Dehuai. The fourth and fifth delegates were two North Korean generals from that army's political directorate, Lee Sang-cho and Chang Pyong-san. The three KPA generals had Chinese connections. The real leader of the Communist team, however, was Li Kenong, Zhou Enlai's close associate and a senior official in the Chinese foreign ministry and intelligence establishment. A veteran negotiator, foreign ministry official, and propagandist, Qiao Guanhua assisted Li. Neither Li nor Qiao ever sat at the table, but they dominated the negotiations' conduct and controlled communications with Beijing. The United Nations delegation, in turn, answered to General Ridgway. His political adviser, Ambassador Robert Murphy, and an interagency negotiations team in Washington chaired by Assistant Secretary of State Dean Rusk and Ambassador U. Alexis Johnson shaped Ridgway's positions. Representatives of the Washington group met regularly with representatives of the other allied nations and with UN officials. The talkers at Kaesong were but the tip of the spear of diplomacy.

As the negotiations at Kaesong developed, the two coalition armies licked their wounds and prepared for more warfare. Neither Ridgway nor Van Fleet believed the talks would produce anything without more United Nations Command offensives beyond the 38th Parallel. With the onset of the summer rains, however, it would be late August or September before the weather turned benign and allowed a new offensive.

Van Fleet continued to plan for another amphibious envelopment, but Ridgway intended to use air power to carry the offensive for the UNC. Although the Fifth Air Force's two wings of F-86 interceptors had blunted the Soviets' air defense of the Yalu River, American bombers found approved strategic targets hard to find. The most promising targets were troops and supplies flowing toward the Communist front armies, so Far East Air Forces initiated Operation Strangle, a maximum-effort interdiction campaign against the Communist road and railroad supply lines. The strikes of 1951 proved that UNC airpower could reduce the flow of supplies to the Communists by half. Then the Chinese simply doubled their shipments' size, organized thick antiaircraft defenses around the critical bridges and tunnels, and brought thousands of laborers from Manchuria to repair the damage to the roads, tracks, tunnels, and bridges. When the Chinese and North Koreans tried to establish their own air forces on fields within North Korea, the F-86s cleared the way for the UNC bombing attacks that stopped any forward movement of the enemy air base system. Nevertheless, the UNC air effort stretched the outnumbered F-86s wings and again produced unacceptable casualties among the B-29 and B-26 bomber forces.

The first phase of the truce talks quickly confirmed that any agreement, even if confined to Korean military matters, would be difficult to draft. The Chinese were in no hurry since they believed time aided their cause and would bring inevitable friction among the UNC allies and the South Koreans. The Chinese characterized the talks as *tanpan,* or an adversarial process in which victories could be gained and casualties inflicted. The first talks, which covered the negotiating site's security, the admission of the media, the administrative procedures, and the agenda, revealed a high degree of tension and anxiety on both sides. Moreover, the Communists were better prepared to reap the psychological and propaganda benefits of every confrontation and misunderstanding. For example, the Communists inherited responsibility for the security of the negotiating site, defined as a five-mile radius from where the meetings occurred in the center of Kaesong; both sides violated the neutral zone, the UNC by accident and the Communists by intent or to fabricate incidents for which they could blame the UNC. Against this background of distrust, the negotiators took three weeks simply to prepare a format for the talks. A delay occurred in part because of Chinese attempts to introduce issues beyond the Korean War.

The final agenda established the essential issues covered in the Agreement:

ITEM	AGENDA (JULY 1951)	AGREEMENT (JULY 1953)
1	Agenda	
2	Military Demarcation Line, Demilitarized Zone	Article I
3	Conditions for the cease-	Article II

The first substantive issue the negotiators attacked was item 2, with the Communists insisting on a return to the 38th Parallel and with the UNC team maintaining each side should occupy the terrain it held at the time of the cease-fire. Since the Eighth Army had already driven well north of the 38th Parallel except in far western Korea, the UNC's position was understandable. Its stance also reflected Ridgway's conviction that Van Fleet needed to push his army farther north and take the key terrain between the headwaters of the Imjin River and the highest eastern mountain ranges that began in the Kumsong River sector. The terrain between these two regions, hardly flatlands, became known as the "Iron Triangle." Its three angles included the cities of Chorwon (west), Pyonggang (north), and Kumhwa (east). Communist planners were equally convinced that control of the Iron Triangle offered advantages for defending North Korea or for continuing the war with offensives to the south and east. Although the Eighth Army had reached the southern edges of the "Iron Triangle," it had not yet penetrated the area. On August 22 the Chinese negotiators called off the plenary sessions and subcommittee meetings, citing UNC violations of the Kaesong neutral zone, but they probably wanted to test the UNC's resolve on the battlefield and its negotiating stamina. General Van Fleet, however, was equally determined to fight more and talk less. At a minimum, Ridgway wanted enough military pressure to get the Communists to accept a new negotiation site under a joint security administration.

Although the ground war never stopped in the summer of 1951, none of the actions matched the ferocity and frustration of the Eighth Army's offensive of August 31 through November 12, 1951. This campaign marked the high point of the UNC's strategic initiative. The pivotal terrain objective was the Iron Triangle, but much of the effort—certainly on the Chinese and North Koreans' part—was simply to test Mao's niupitang strategy. The North Koreans were especially loath to surrender any more territory since Kim Il-sung and his generals now commanded a bigger and better-armed force, and they feared the Chinese would trade ground for the possibility of luring unsuspecting UNC units into a trap. The result of Kim's "stand or die" order was the North Korean I, III, and VI Corps in the eastern mountains proved especially difficult to dislodge. Both the Chinese and Korean armies also demonstrated their new prowess with artillery and their willingness to mount attacks under the most trying conditions.

Van Fleet's general concept of operations for the autumn 1951 offensive envisioned operations by his two largest corps, the I Corps (five divisions) in the west and X Corps (five divisions) in the central-eastern sector. The ROK 1st Division and the British Commonwealth Division (I Corps) made notable advances beyond the Imjin valley while the 1st Cavalry Division, ROK 9th Division, and 25th Infantry Division advanced past Chorwon and then stalled in heavy fighting. The X Corps, fighting a crack Chinese army and two North Korean corps, pushed northward through the mountains and succeeded only in making names like "Bloody Ridge," "Heartbreak Ridge," "the Punchbowl," and "Kanmubong Ridge" bad memories for the 2d Infantry Division and the 1st Marine Division. The ROK I Corps pushed the KPA VI Corps back through the mountains that now make up Mount Sorak National Park, but it did so at a considerable cost. The most surprising advance occurred in the IX Corps sector, where the 24th Infantry Division, 7th Infantry Division, and two ROK divisions pushed the Chinese back almost ten miles from Kumhwa to Kumsong. Thus, they created a salient but also a strong position to advance west to Pyonggang. The cost of the campaign troubled Van Fleet and Ridgway: 60,000 casualties, 22,000 of them American soldiers and Marines.

The autumn 1951 campaign did not discourage the Chinese leadership, since in their eyes the niupitang strategy had worked. The United Nations Command had given up its offensive operations in October, and the Chinese had actually struck back in local attacks with some success. The Chinese generals argued that they needed more artillery, more antiaircraft protection, and more field engineering equipment and troops to dig ever deeper into Korea's ridgelines. They could maintain an "active defense," and Peng Dehuai recommended his logistical burden would be eased if his army could be reduced by as much as one-quarter in strength. Just how badly the Communists suffered from September through November 1951 is hard to gauge. Chinese commanders misrepresented their own losses to their superiors, and American analysts consistently overestimated enemy casualties when they added up unit reports. Van Fleet claimed his forces had inflicted 234,000 casualties on the Communists, but a more prudent estimate based on actual counted bodies, POWs, and reasonable estimates for the wounded would put Communist losses in the 100,000 to 150,000 range, still significant but not crippling. Their losses certainly did not drive the Chinese to end the war. They only concluded that they should talk more about it.

In late October 1951 the Communists agreed to change the location of the truce negotiations and to restart the subcommittee work on each of the four substantive agenda items. The Truman administration jumped at the opportunity for more diplomacy. Ridgway and Van Fleet did not share Washington's urge to rush to peace. Not only did they want to shift the talks to a more secure area—that is, along an open rural road at a village named Panmunjom—but they also wanted to pressure the Communists to cede Kaesong or at least to strip the city of its protected status, which the Communists used to mass troops. Recovering Kaesong would be a useful sop to Syngman Rhee. The Washington negotiations committee gave Ridgway definitive guidance: go to Panmunjom and settle on the current line of contact.

Within the next two months the negotiating teams made rapid progress on items 2, 3, and 5. The most significant trade-offs were (1) the Communists' acceptance of the line-of-contact concept and related measures for creating a Korean Demilitarized Zone, (2) the UNC's tacit acceptance that there would be no verification activities outside the DMZ or realistic prohibitions on the introduction of new troops and weapons to the war zone, and (3) both sides agreeing to work out a regime for enforcing and further elaborating on the armistice after the shooting stopped. Much work on these items remained to be done, but the outline of a truce agreement became apparent as the year ended—with one major exception.

As another bitterly cold Korean winter congealed ground operations, the political and military leaders of both belligerent coalitions sought ways other than a ground war to pursue their limited political-strategic goals. At the truce negotiations, item 4, or the disposition of the prisoners of war (POWs), became part of a war "conducted by other means." The international conventions governing the handling of POWs, signed after World War II, had already set the foundation for a bitter dispute. Although the Allies had released POWs in their custody in 1945–46, the Soviets did not and held hundreds of thousands of Axis POWs as slave laborers and thousands as war criminals. These POWs' eventual repatriation—still incomplete at the time of the Korean War—brought stark evidence that more than half of the POWs in Soviet custody had died. Moreover, the Soviets demanded that the thousands of former Red Army soldiers and Eastern Europeans who had fought in or with German armed forces be returned by the United States and Great Britain. The Allies complied and sent thousands of men to certain death.

Weighing these two experiences, the United States chose to adhere to a revised third Geneva Convention (1949), which required a nation (or "detaining authority") that held POWs to return all of them to their homelands as rapidly as possible when a war ended. This position reflected American occupation policy, which was to strengthen pro-American political reformers in Germany and Japan and to restore the economic and social fabric of these nations as quickly as possible as bastions against Soviet-Communist revolution. The Communist domination of Eastern Europe and the creation of the Warsaw

Pact military alliance, however, made complete (even forced) repatriation a less appealing position. American internationalists and psychological warfare experts worried that their efforts to create dissention and even rebellion in East Germany, Poland, and Czechoslovakia would have little appeal if mutineers and defectors faced involuntary repatriation. The American armed forces, however, wanted an "all-for-all" policy and a clear obligation by a detaining power to repatriate military personnel completely and quickly. Early reports from Korea of atrocities against POWs and of the conditions in Communist POW camps, reported by German and Japanese survivors, hardened the position of Ridgway and the JCS on "all for all."

From the Communist perspective, the issue also had important implications. The North Koreans might have to answer for murdering and enslaving the South Korean people. The PLA leaders knew some of their soldiers, impressed former soldiers of the Nationalist Army, would refuse repatriation if possible. Even the least political Chinese private also knew that his POW status condemned him to dishonor and abuse in his native land. The Communists had already taken steps in 1951 to infiltrate political officers into the UNC POW camps along the southern coast and to establish a harsh, unforgiving system of Communist control "inside the wire." The two senior KPA representatives at Panmunjom, Nam Il and Lee Sang-cho, had been instrumental in this effort, which linked the POWs with agents within the Korean refugee community and with Communist guerrillas throughout southern Korea.

The issue of POW repatriation—namely, whether it would be voluntary or forced—became the most intractable issue at Panmunjom early in 1952, but it alone was not the sole barrier to an armistice. The subcommittee's initial assumption on item

4, nurtured by the Communists, was that the Geneva Convention would be followed: all for all. It reflected the American military's position, and even the interagency task force in Washington leaned toward that formula. The South Korean government, however, was adamantly opposed to complete repatriation. It knew that thousands of its citizens had been forced into the KPA or were captured and now lived in prison camps; many of these "detainees" might be innocent or at least "reconverted" to loyalty. A vocal minority of Cold Warriors in Washington linked the Korean–Eastern European political issue with the moral distaste of sending unwilling repatriates to certain death, a perspective with a powerful domestic constituency in the United States among European political refugees and immigrant groups as well as an assortment of Protestant groups and the Catholic church. Truman knew the U.S. delegation to Geneva had agreed to complete repatriation, but he also knew Congress had never ratified the treaty because of this provision, among others. Even the JCS began to have second thoughts about the all-for-all policy because of the possible effects upon the ROK Army.

The first serious consideration of the POW issue at Panmunjom in December 1951 and January 1952 immediately brought the all-for-all issue into question. The negotiators agreed both sides should exchange the names of POWs and the numbers held in various categories. The results of the tally shocked all the participants. The U.S. armed forces were carrying 11,500 men as missing in action (MIA), but the Communists reported only 3,198 American POWs in their custody. (There were only 1,219 UNC POWs, mostly British and Turkish soldiers.) The accounting for the South Koreans was even worse; of an estimated 88,000 MIAs, only 7,142 names of ROK soldiers were listed. Some names of Americans and Koreans the Communists had released earlier did not now appear on the lists. The Communists also refused to work with the International Red Cross on POW accounting, something to which UNC had already agreed. American intelligence officers and war crimes judge-advocates thought the numbers confirmed that the murder of POWs, both American and Korean, had been even worse than they suspected from the atrocities they had already investigated. (UNC war crimes investigators had identified more than 800 Koreans and Chinese in UNC custody as indictable for war crimes on the testimony of survivors and other participants.) This assessment, widely shared in Tokyo and Washington, seemed to argue for all for all, but it also meant that the lives still at risk were small. It also meant the Communists would have a great deal to answer for, especially for all the vanished ROK soldiers. In truth, most of the MIAs had died in battle, but a substantial minority numbering in the thousands (perhaps 15,000) had died in Communist hands from torture, execution, starvation, and medical mistreatment.

The Communists, for their part, found little comfort in the names and numbers provided by United Nations Command. Incautious estimates of POWs in UNC custody had been too low—around 90,000 men—and too high, 170,000. The official list produced a different accounting: 95,531 North Koreans, 20,700 Chinese, and 16,243 South Koreans, or 132,474 POWs. Anxious about UNC charges about their own POW handling, the Communists demanded more information about the "missing" POWs. The UNC delegates countered that exchanging 12,000 men for 130,000 men on an all-for-all basis made no sense. They also reported that the "missing"

40,000 men were South Koreans who had already been screened and had passed loyalty investigations; although still in custody, they had become "detainees" under the jurisdiction of the Rhee government and would not count as potential repatriates in any exchange. Against this background, in January 1952 President Truman ruled no POW in UNC custody would be forced to return to North Korea or China against his will, but South Koreans could choose to be exchanged, which opened the door north to captured South Korean Labor Party partisans and intelligence agents. This formula should be administered as a "one-for-one" exchange until all 12,000 allied POWs had been returned. Such a process, however, required extensive screening of individuals about their preferences, a condition that soon created open warfare for the hearts and minds of the Communist POWs. General Ridgway correctly predicted that this screening would further deepen the politicization of the POW issue, but Washington stuck to the "no-forced-repatriation" policy.

The Communists started a war in the POW compounds under joint American–South Korean administration, which included the camps on Koje-do Island and a series of small POW hospitals and camps on the mainland. Overcrowding, limited medical care, and harsh living conditions prepared the groundwork for a POW rebellion, especially when the inadequate numbers of untrained guards demonstrated their fear and indiscipline by beating and shooting the captives first and asking questions later. Moreover, POW camp administration was one of many jobs assigned to the Eighth Army's 2d Logistical Command, whose officers had little appreciation of the camp's explosive conditions and did not heed cautionary advice from intelligence and military police officers. The real catalyst for the POW uprisings of 1951–52 was the repatriation screening process and the orders from Pyongyang to the three senior Korean Communist prisoners (two colonels and a provincial party chairman) to obstruct screening without regard for the loss of life among the POWs, even the most dedicated Communist cadres. These orders made clear that any KPA POW who refused repatriation had signed his death warrant. The more media attention these incidents produced, the better. In fact, Communist gangs held the terrorist ascendancy well before December 1951.

The purpose of the POW uprising was simply to make the POWs so obnoxious that the United Nations Command would gladly return all the POWs as quickly as possible, using force if necessary to send every Korean and Chinese in its custody back to Communist control. From the Communist perspective, the propaganda prospects were irresistible: they would show American and "puppet" troops shooting Asian victims, mass suicides, riots, and protest movements, all played out for a gullible Western media. In fact, from 1951 to 1953, all these incidents occurred. The first battle between POWs and the guard force in December 1951 left fourteen POWs dead and twenty-four wounded. A bigger battle in February 1952 between an American infantry battalion and the POWs left fifty-five POWs dead and 140 wounded at a cost of thirty-nine American casualties (one killed in action [KIA]). Segregating the POWs did not reduce the violence. In the summer of 1952, the UNC resettled the Chinese POWs to Cheju-do Island, but the movement allowed POW organizers to concentrate their most militant supporters in selected camps. Incidents that began in August culminated in an open battle in October between 5,000 Chinese and a reinforced American infantry battalion. When the Chinese demonstrators would not disperse, even after the soldiers used tear gas, the soldiers opened fire. Fifty-six POWs died, and 120 were wounded. The camp commander justified the violence by reporting the demonstration was the prelude to a mass breakout, which may have been true. The Cheju-do revolt strengthened the Chinese resolve to prevent nonrepatriates from defecting and from receiving further political reeducation by Nationalist agents and anti-Communist American missionaries.

Despite Communist intimidation, the screening continued, and the Korean and Chinese death toll mounted. In March 1952, South Korean guards tried to save some nonrepatriates and started a fight, ending in another thirty-eight casualties. Nam Il kept the pressure on at Panmunjom, accusing the UNC screening teams of coercion, yet pressing demands for more and more screening. In May 1952 the cadre at Koje-do pulled its largest coup, taking one American general hostage and persuading another general to sign what amounted to an admission of criminal behavior. After the captive general's release, Gen. Mark W. Clark, who had replaced Ridgway as the UNC commander in May 1952, ordered the execution of a contingency plan, Operation Breakup, to crush the POW revolt. A reinforced American airborne regiment started the operation against the two most violent compounds on Koje-do. It finally broke the resistance with tanks, gas, and bullets at a cost of 150 POWs dead and wounded and one U.S. soldier killed and thirteen wounded. The paratroopers also discovered the bodies of many Koreans who had been murdered by their fellow POWS. Operation Breakup continued throughout the year until the repatriates (75,594) and nonrepatriate (49,920) Chinese and Koreans had more or less been segregated into separate compounds, the refugees resettled, some of the Communist inte-lligence network disrupted, and POW camp administration improved. All the Chinese went to compounds on Cheju-do Island. Vigilantism and gang warfare never ceased entirely. In December 1952 another major revolt on Pongam-do Island produced another 300 POW casualties. Even in UNC hospitals the POWs produced a bewildering series of suicides and murders and even supported guerrilla raids. One hospital served as the central contact site between the POWs and KPA agents.

The Communist POW revolt reflected only one aspect of the other war raging behind the Eighth Army's lines in the same regions where Communist guerrillas had been active in 1948–50. Southern Communist partisans and KPA stay-behind units plagued the UNC lines of communications, rear-area camps, and Korean towns. With established base camps in the mountains of South Korea's four southernmost provinces, about 10,000 partisans and an unknown number of sympathizers presented a force too large and skilled for the available field battalions of the Korean National Police (KNP) to handle. In the autumn of 1951, with the ROK Army expanding and the ground war slowing, General Van Fleet ordered Maj. Gen. Paik Sun-yup—one of the ROKA's most effective officers and a counterpartisan commander in the Manchukuo Army and the Korean Constabulary—to take command of two ROKA divisions and the KNP field forces and to begin Operation Ratkiller. Paik opened his deliberate cordon-and-search operations in December 1951 and concluded the operation in March 1952. During the campaign the ROK security forces killed 11,090 partisans and sympathizers and captured 9,916 more, a ratio that suggests the operation was akin to a "scorched earth, no-quarter" policy. Ratkiller broke the back of extensive guerrilla activity, but the partisans continued to raid camps and roads. Other ROK divisions deployed to the Chiri mountains for counterguerrilla operations, usually as part of their precombat training. A regiment of the ROK 11th Division, which Task Force Paik replaced, conducted one such exercise and perpetrated the war's worst atrocity by a UNC unit, the execution of 800 to 1,000 villagers at Kochang in South Kyongsang Province in February 1951. This incident eventually contributed to a political crisis in 1952.

The United Nations Command attempted to mount a partisan war behind North Korean lines with marginal results. The concept started with an anti-Communist uprising in Hwanghae Province (western Korea) and around Wonsan in the autumn of 1950. When the Chinese and North Koreans swept south in December, the partisans fled, although some small bands simply hid in the mountains. American and South Korean special operations officers gathered the refugee partisans on offshore islands and sent them back into the war as raiders and saboteurs. The Korean guerrillas learned that their mission was to prepare the way for amphibious operations; however, their raids stirred the North Korean security forces' wrath and often led to the slaughter of hostage villagers. The partisans' intelligence operations and distant direction of air strikes and naval gunfire produced better results. The partisans also assisted in rescuing downed UNC pilots and provided the defense force for the electronics intelligence sites that sprouted on the offshore islands. In 1952 two groupings—Donkey and Kirkland—of around 4,000 partisans worked as amphibious raiders from the islands while another battalion, Baker, mounted airborne raids from South Korean bases. The airborne raids proved disastrous since the Communists had captured operatives, radios, and codes and used them to lure rescuers and unwary aircraft. The raids, however, apparently kept the Communists concerned about another Inchon-type landing; their coastal defense forces grew from four divisions in 1952 to eleven divisions in 1953. The partisan force, eventually reorganized as the United Nations Partisan Infantry Regiment—Korea (UNPIRK), expanded beyond 10,000 operatives by the war's end. The group lost much of its effectiveness, however, as the local leaders fell by the wayside, with many suspected of disloyalty to the Rhee regime. Fewer than half of the UNPIRK partisans were northern Koreans by 1953.

Airpower, not guerrillas, gave the United Nations Command its greatest hope to offset the Chinese manpower and increasing firepower. UNC aerial attacks on military and economic targets in North Korea between 1951 and 1953 might actually have forced the Communists to become more pliant at Panmunjom and, at a minimum, seriously limited their ability to mount an offensive campaign. The aircraft wings of the Far East Air Forces could conduct four basic types of air warfare. The first task of the FEAF fighter-interceptor wings was to ensure air superiority, which allowed offensive air operations anywhere in North Korea and protected the Eighth Army from air attack. The F-86 pilots succeeded in their role, although they could not provide perfect protection for those B-29s flying daylight raids into "MiG Alley." More important, the FEAF did prevent the Communists from creating a base system within North Korea that would have allowed Communist air operations against the United Nations Command.

The battle for air superiority over the Yalu pitted fewer than 100 F-86 Sabre jets against Russian, Chinese, and North Korean MiG-15 squadrons that often enjoyed 4:1 advantages in numbers. Nevertheless, the Americans had skilled pilots and durable aircraft in their favor. The Soviets rotated squadrons of their air defense force (PVO) to Korea to fly against the Americans; near the war's end Soviet inexperience resulted in serious pilot losses. The Chinese air forces proved uneven in combat. Some of their pilots were exceptional, but most were too inexperienced and timid. On numerous occasions the senior Soviet air commanders demanded that the Chinese pilots be grounded for more training. Many years after the war, the Russians confessed they had lost more than 200 pilots and 345 MiGs in the air war, but they believed the cost was worth their education in antibomber defensive warfare.

The UNC offensive air operations fell into three broad categories: strategic bombing, interdiction, and close air support, supported by reconnaissance, electronic warfare, intelligence, and logistical operations. The greatest limitation to the air campaign was the lack of air-to-air refueling capability. Thus, FEAF had to develop air bases within South Korea, draining manpower and scarce resources. The strategic bombing campaign, of course, was also limited by policy. Throughout 1951–52 American bombers and fighter-bombers pummeled North Korean cities and military installations until they made the rubble bounce. Pyongyang resembled Hiroshima or Tokyo in 1945. The UNC bombing campaign made little difference because the Communists used war matériel manufactured in China and Russia or underground in North Korea.

The strategic bombing campaign, however, received a new lease on life in 1952 when the Truman administration changed the approved target list. Desperate to increase the pressure on the Communists, the JCS (with Truman's concurrence) authorized FEAF to bomb the power plants and dams along the

Yalu, which provided hydroelectric power to China and Russia. FEAF easily attacked three complexes, but the critical test of Communist resolve and reaction would be the destruction of the Suiho electrical complex, at the time the fourth largest power generator in the world. In four days of attacks, FEAF and naval aircraft struck Suiho in June 1952 and destroyed 90 percent of North Korea's power grid. Neither China nor Russia reacted. In 1953 the strategic bombing campaign sparked again when FEAF received approval to attack North Korea's dams and supporting irrigation systems. The campaign began in May 1953 and continued until the end of the war. The resulting floods disrupted Korean rice production and flooded many underground installations around Pyongyang. Although the North Koreans' pain undoubtedly increased, they still had to follow Chinese and Russian strategic direction, and these attacks hurt the Chinese and Russians very little.

Throughout the war American political and military leaders studied the possible use of nuclear weapons, and on four separate occasions they gave this option special attention. The answer was always the same: the existing nuclear bombs, carried by modified B-29s, would have little effect on already leveled cities. The U.S. Strategic Air Command (SAC) discouraged the use of nuclear weapons since its commander, Gen. Curtis E. LeMay, understood these weapons' deterrent effect on the Soviets depended on *imagined* destruction and not on ineffective strikes against the Koreans or Chinese. Moreover, small nuclear weapons for battlefield use had not yet been developed. In addition, SAC was loath to reveal any of its real nuclear delivery capabilities or its limitations. Although the United States played some nuclear bluff, especially near the end of the war, it did not come close to using nuclear weapons. The one time President Truman suggested he was considering the nuclear option, in December 1950, the British led the allied charge to stop such talk.

The limited success of strategic bombing simply reinforced the U.S. Air Force generals' predisposition to mount an air interdiction campaign. They believed attacks on military installations and the Communist road and railroad system would produce catastrophic shortages for the Communist field armies, rendering their manpower advantages meaningless. The UNC's air forces had the capability for such a campaign: 1,000 to 1,400 aircraft that could put ordnance on ground targets. The UNC air units flew more than a million sorties during the war, far greater than the Royal Air Force (RAF) Bomber Command's sorties in the 1939–45 war against Germany. By World War II standards the UNC's losses in the air offensive were bearable: 2,500 aircraft, divided about evenly between losses to enemy action and operational accidents. About one-third of all air sorties were directed against the Communist supply system.

Although the UNC's air effort was staggering, its effectiveness was quite another matter. A Chinese division used only one-tenth of the supplies each day as an American division did, with the difference being gasoline, artillery ammunition, and creature comforts. Moreover, the Communists had the labor to repair the damage to their lines of supply. They also deployed antiaircraft artillery in hillsides to protect key bridge and tunnels. The Communist labor and air defense forces soon numbered more than 100,000. Both the Chinese and North Koreans still celebrate the defense of their supply lines as a great victory, one they maintain cost the UNC's air forces more than "10,000" aircraft. Essentially, the Korean War repeated some of World War II's lessons: attacking supply lines was costly, dangerous, and only partially effective. Only when the enemy emerged from protected positions to stage an offensive did air power really produce significant losses.

More air interdiction assets might have been used in close air support or aerial attacks integrated with ground combat. Senior officers of all the American services except the air force believed the 120,000 close air support sorties should have been doubled and would have damaged the Communists. While this argument had some validity when the Communist armies were moving, as they had until November 1951, after that point the Communist field fortifications defied air attack. In addition, the U.S. Air Force would not relinquish its control of sortie allocation or release the control of close air support strikes to the ground forces, something the Marine Corps and Navy air commanders did on a routine basis. The close air support issue poisoned air force relations with the other services throughout the war and for years afterward.

Without question the UNC air campaign hurt the Communists, and the Chinese and North Korean leaders (with local Russian collusion) sought various ways to blunt the aerial blitz. For intelligence and psychological purposes, they treated captured air crewmen with special brutality and callousness and often called them "air pirates" who had sacrificed any claim to POW status. Air crewmen made up the largest single group of American servicemen who disappeared while POWs, presumably dying under interrogation in Manchuria or China proper. The Communists also claimed the air war included an effort to spread epidemic diseases among the innocent Chinese and Korean civilian populations of northern Asia.

Whether the Communists actually believed their charges of biological warfare were true, they had many reasons to press them through sympathetic European and Asian governments and media. First, such charges raised the specter of American anti-Asian racism, which the Communists hoped might demoralize the Koreans and Japanese. Germ warfare charges also explained away the serious public health problems of north Asia. Certainly the Chinese used the germ warfare scare as a prod for a massive public health program. Another aspect of the propaganda campaign was directed at the CPVF. When the Americans dropped surrender leaflets and safe conduct passes in canisters, CPVF political officers identified them as carriers of diseased vectors such as insects and mice. The allegations against the United States also pointed to an embarrassing reality; namely, the Americans had not prosecuted Gen. Ishii Shiro, the director of the Japanese medical research program in World War II. He was a reviled villain to the Chinese, who had been his principal victims during germ warfare and biological experiments. The Communists pointed out an unpalatable truth: Ishii had traded the medical findings of his Unit 731 for immunity from prosecution as a war criminal.

The Communists strengthened their germ warfare charges by extracting confessions from captured American pilots. Almost every American air officer—pilots, copilots, and bombardier-navigators—who fell into enemy hands received harsh physical and psychological torture to extract incriminating statements of terror bombing and germ warfare. Although the Chinese handled the principal responsibility for interrogation, they received ample assistance from Russian and Eastern European intelligence officers. Eventually, forty-two American officers confessed to germ warfare operations, and about half were subjected to extreme coercion to extract their so-called confessions. One Marine colonel confessed because he feared his torture had reached the point where he would reveal something really important—that is, the nuclear war plans he had drafted in a previous assignment. Although the germ warfare charges disconcerted the UNC political leadership, they did not influence the conduct of the air campaign.

If air power held the Communists at bay in the near term, the Republic of Korea's eventual security depended not just on American support but on larger and improved Korean armed forces. American planners believed the Korean economy and political system could not bear the costs of a military establishment adequate to deter the Communists, but they saw no choice except to create a modern Korean military establishment, whatever the eventual costs. Only after establishing such a force would the American armed forces, especially the U.S. Army's divisions, be able to leave Korea. When General Van Fleet succeeded General Ridgway as commander of the Eighth Army, one of his principal missions was to improve the Korean armed forces and quickly. A dimension of the program that the U.S. Navy and U.S. Air Force accepted with minimal enthusiasm was to give the Koreans more air and naval capability. The South Korean Navy started the war with 7,715 officers and sailors and twenty-eight surface warships (corvettes and smaller types) and at the war's end had a force of 30,000 personnel and 76 vessels. The ROK Air Force started with one mixed Korean-American F-51 squadron in 1950 and ended the war with eight operational squadrons and the foundation of an air base system. These services, however, remained handmaidens to the South Korean Army.

In structural terms, the ROK Army required major reforms. It needed to increase the number of men in its ranks, to form effective combat divisions that at least matched the

Communists' levels of firepower, and to create an institutional base for educating and training its officers and enlisted men. General Van Fleet understood all these requirements after heading a military mission to reform the Greek Army (1948–49), and he brought to Korea a proven expert in training, Maj. Gen. Cornelius E. Ryan, as chief of the Korean Military Advisory Group from 1951 to 1953. The Korean government was responsible for mobilizing manpower, and through all sorts of coercive measures, it stripped the nation of its young and not-so-young adult males. Some Koreans escaped the army by becoming policemen, UNC employees, interpreters, augmentees to the Eighth Army through the KATUSA program, and bearers in the Korean Service Corps. Most Koreans, however, went into the army, which increased from 284,322 (December 1951) to 568,994 (July 1953). The change in the war's tempo helped; the Korean Army lost 59,132 troops in 1951 but only 22,712 the following year. The manpower numbers allowed the formation of ten divisions in 1951, with eight more added thereafter. Half of the new 1952–53 divisions actually saw combat.

The composition of Korean divisions also changed and influenced the training command's development. The most pressing needs were to provide more and heavier artillery and some tanks for each Korean division. The ROK 1st Division, the only Korean division in 1950 with three artillery battalions and a tank battalion (three of them American), proved so formidable in combat that the Chinese first thought it was an American division. Later they decided it was better than an American division because its infantry fought harder. In 1951 the U.S. Army devised a plan to provide every Korean division with one tank company and at least two artillery battalions and a maximum of four if they could be manned and armed.

The Korean gunners would also trade in their light 105 mm howitzers for the standard U.S. Army M2A1 105mm howitzer and the M-1 155mm howitzer. Van Fleet stressed that the ROK divisions that fought well would get more fire support. His criterion included adequately protecting American artillery groups attached to ROK divisions, a serious problem in 1951. Van Fleet's initial goal was to create an American-style field artillery group of four battalions, plus heavy mortar and anti-aircraft batteries, for the first ten ROK divisions. By the end of 1952 the ROK Army had formed and trained twenty-two additional artillery battalions under American tutelage. By the end of the war each Korean frontline division had a four-battalion artillery group (often attached from other divisions) with corps heavy artillery attached from the Eighth Army.

The ROK Army's future depended on the effectiveness of its training command, which was reorganized and expanded after the 1950 campaign. The U.S. Korean Military Advisory Group, working with its Korean counterparts, organized the training command to mirror American practices. The training program of 1951 had two echelons. The first trained existing Korean divisions when they went into army reserve. A U.S. Army mobile training team with specialists from all the combatant and support branches conducted the division-wide training program. The second echelon was a schools system designed to train or retrain replacements (mostly infantry) and a wide range of specialists. In addition, the Koreans reactivated their military academy as a four-year institution in 1951 and started a system of progressive officer education, enriched by the participation of Korean officers who attended army schools in the United States. Probably the most important change in the training command was the length of its schools: they increased from around three weeks to twelve for basic soldiers with appropriate increases throughout the system to ensure adequate training. Artillery instruction, for example, grew from eight weeks to twelve. By war's end almost 600,000 South Koreans had passed through the new training command, managed by about half of KMAG's 3,000 personnel.

Whether a larger South Korean Army would mean a greater ROK role in the war faced its most severe test in 1952. In that year most certainly the Communists increased their own operations' tempo when a constitutional crisis in the Republic of Korea widened the growing split between the U.S. government, the United Nations, and President Syngman Rhee. For several months it seemed possible that the Rhee regime would collapse, followed by at least part of the army, and lead to a war between different parts of the ROK Army with the presidency at stake. (This doomsday scenario actually occurred in 1980.) At issue were the elections of 1952, which were supposed to produce a new National Assembly that would then vote for a new president. When the year began Rhee and the National Assembly were already at odds over such issues as patronage, corruption, the Kochang village massacre, taxes, inflation, abuses of power by Rhee's cabinet officials and other cronies, and the privileged assignment of the army's generals.

Rhee believed he had an unfinished, divine mission to save Korea from the Communists, the United States, Japan, and itself. Late in 1951 he had started a campaign to reduce the National Assembly's influence and to rewrite the constitution of 1948. He wanted the National Assembly to pass a new electoral law that would allow the general public to elect the president and the vice president (a new office). Although Rhee's challengers had a good chance of replacing him under the existing constitution, they stood no chance under a new law since the government could use every instrument of power at its disposal to ensure Rhee's popular election. For six months Rhee used his most loyal civilian supporters, the mobs of Pusan, paramilitary associations, the police, and parts of the ROK Army that were not under American control to intimidate the assembly. Rhee empowered these army units, which were the internal security forces of the Provost Martial Command, to override the civilian police and courts by declaring that the southeastern provinces of Korea were under such subversive threats that they had to be governed by martial law. Under the pressure of imprisonment, the loss of civil liberties and employment, and political disgrace, the majority of the National Assembly finally voted to reform the constitution in July 1952. Rhee held the election with indecent haste the following month and won a second, four-year term after receiving five million of the six million votes cast.

Neither the United States nor the United Nations regarded Rhee's victory with comfort, but neither wanted to risk the political collapse that might follow Rhee's departure by whatever means. They had few realistic weapons to pressure Rhee to step aside and arrange a peaceful succession. First of all, the likely successors all had disabilities equal to Rhee's and none of his strengths. The leading opposition candidate died of cancer, and the most likely successor was Chang Myon (John Chang), a Christian, educated in the United States, likable, honest, and ineffectual. The Korean economy was a mess with rampant inflation, speculation, and profiteering, but the American money coming to Korea fueled the war effort and could hardly be stopped. Rhee, in fact, promised economic reform if he continued in office. Moral suasion had no influence since Rhee

entertained no doubts about his infallibility, influenced probably by the fantasies of advanced age. In 1952 the president
turned seventy-seven years old. America's greatest fear was that
Rhee's favorite generals would take their parts of the army out
of the war if the United States acted against him. In fact Rhee
ordered the chief of staff, Lt. Gen. Lee Chong-chan, to pull
two regular divisions out of the war and send them to Kyong-
sangnam Province for security duties. Lee refused, and Rhee
relieved him over American protests. After the crisis faded, Rhee
appointed Paik Sun-yup in Lee's place, mollifying Van Fleet.
The Eighth Army staff had prepared a contingency plan for
varied actions if the ROK Army left the war engaged in fac-
tional fighting. One possibility addressed in Plan Everready
and Plan Stand-To was replacing Rhee with an acting president drawn from the South Korean Army. The Americans,
however, could find no coup master and suitable leader willing to take power.

Syngman Rhee's political victory in 1952 had a ripple effect that spread to the armistice the following year and into
the future. In the face of American and domestic opposition,
Rhee had triumphed, and he became even more convinced he
could manipulate the United States into continuing the war,
once again taking the strategic initiative, and reunify Korea by
force. His dogmatic opposition to a cease-fire increased in scope
and vigor, strengthened to some degree by the improvement
of his army. Moreover, Rhee believed his intransigence would
pay additional dividends with the Democratic administration's
defeat in Washington. He welcomed its replacement with a
Republican administration led by two venerable Cold Warriors, Dwight D. Eisenhower and John Foster Dulles, the latter a friend of Rhee's and a fellow Princetonian. He believed

the party of capitalist-internationalists, Asia Firsters, McCarthyites, and representatives of the most anti-Communist Christian churches would not allow American soldiers to "die for a tie." The Russians, Chinese, and North Koreans believed the same thing.

From September until November 1952 the Chinese expeditionary force staged its sixth major offense of the war, designed to drive in the combat outposts of platoon and company size a mile or two in front of the Eighth Army main line of resistance, a cordon of fortified hills and disconnected trails and trench lines. Its purpose was to force the allies back to the 38th Parallel, to inflict unacceptable casualties, and to pin the UNC divisions to their frontline positions. A major consideration for the Chinese high command was the possibility that General Clark would take advantage of the autumn weather window to mount an amphibious envelopment on the east coast and take the first step in a drive to establish the Pyongyang-Wonsan line. Clark had a corps in Japan that could be used for this purpose since he had withdrawn the 24th Infantry Division and 1st Cavalry Division from the Eighth Army and replaced them with the 40th and 45th Infantry Divisions. In addition, the Chinese assumed Clark would withdraw the 1st Marine Division from its new sector, which was only a day's truck ride from Inchon.

The pattern of the ground war that raged from the valley of the Imjin through the Iron Triangle to the eastern mountains followed the same dismal pattern. To avoid air strikes and minimize the allied artillery's effects, the Chinese infiltrated the allied outpost positions at night and then attacked under the support of short, intense artillery barrages. Companies attacked platoons while battalions attacked companies;

companies and battalions disappeared in counterattacks, mounted by both sides. Artillery expenditures reached and exceeded World War II tonnages when measured by the ground they pulverized. To hold captured ground and their own positions, the Chinese and Koreans went underground into tunnels and caves and then stormed out of their burrows at night to continue the war, a war in which submachine guns and hand grenades ruled the trenches. Both sides attempted to catch their foes above ground in artillery storms while they huddled in their bunkers and hoped the shells would not bring their fortifications down and bury them alive. Flamethrowers and demolitions became standard weapons for the best assault units; German special assault units of 1917–18 would have recognized the combat immediately. In the Battle of White Horse Mountain, October 6–15, the ROK 9th Division, assisted by more than 700 air strikes and almost 200,000 shells from almost every artillery battalion in the IX Corps, held off almost three Chinese divisions. The South Koreans lost 3,500 soldiers; the Chinese, 15,000. The key terrain on the ridgeline changed hands twenty-four times. Both sides claimed victory even though the South Koreans still held most of the ground after their counterattack finally routed the surviving Chinese. Similar battles on usually a smaller scale provided obscure hills with memorable names: Bunker Hill, Old Baldy, Sniper Ridge, Capital Hill, Triangle Hill, Pike's Peak, Jackson Heights, and Jane Russell Hill. The Chinese called a series of bloody clashes with the IX Corps in October and November the "Battle of Shangganling" and still celebrate it as a great victory since the IX Corps offensive did not break the Chinese defensive lines. The Eighth Army's losses for October 1952 were 6,500 and the Chinese casualties reached almost 12,000 soldiers. By the time fighting faded in mid-November the Eighth Army had lost another 3,000 men and the Chinese, 7,000. The senior Chinese commanders hoped they had persuaded President-elect Eisenhower to abandon any ambitious plans he might have had for a major offensive in 1953.

The Chinese need not have worried about President-elect Eisenhower's interest in winning the Korean War, for he and Secretary of State–designate Dulles viewed continuing the Korean War as incompatible with American national security interests. Both internationalists, they agreed the Soviet Union was the major competitor, the crucial arena was Europe, and the major tool of containment should be nuclear deterrence and forward, collective defense but at a minimum cost to the American economy. In Asia the People's Republic of China was the enemy and Japan the best future ally, and Japan's security depended in part on a pro-Western Republic of Korea and the preservation of the Republic of China (Taiwan). Korea was but one theater in the struggle against Asian (interpreted as Chinese) Communism. In February 1953, for example, President Eisenhower announced the United States would no longer discourage Chinese Nationalist military operations against the PRC, and the administration strengthened military assistance to French Indochina and the Philippines. Dulles began an aggressive extension of the pro-Western alliance system in the Asia-Pacific area. None of these policy measures saw a role for the United Nations, much to Rhee's relief.

With the truce negotiations at Panmunjom at an impasse over the exchange of POWS, the United Nations attempted to exercise its meager influence and considered several neutral nations' proposals on various exchange formulas. They were unappealing to the United States and unacceptable to the

Republic of Korea because of the intrusion of multinational agencies into Korean-American relations. American resistance, which blunted UN activism, was not complete since Dulles admitted some sort of international involvement in the POW exchange might be acceptable if that was the price of peace. The Communists still had not accepted the principle of voluntary repatriation, so it was not yet a matter for decision. What was clear in Tokyo and Washington, however, was the Communists would never agree to a POW exchange based on U.S.-ROK screening without additional screening done by an international agency. The 1952 screening tabulations showed what a potential political embarrassment voluntarism was for the Communists:

INTERNEES	REPATRIATION	NON-REPATRIATION
Chinese POWs	6,388	14,412
KPA POWs (from DPRK)	62,169	34,373
KPA POWs (from ROK)	4,560	11,744
Civilian internees (from ROK)	9,954	26,338
Total	83,071	86,867

Eisenhower assumed office without a plan to end the war despite hinting during his campaign that he might have such a plan. He admitted privately the key to an acceptable armistice was the economic and military strength of the Republic of Korea, which would require a great deal of long-term American assistance. He and his closest advisers agreed they could not retreat from the principle of voluntary repatriation. Yet Eisenhower wanted some movement in the peace negotiations. After the United Nations and the International Red Cross (IRC) called for an exchange of the sick and disabled POWs as a goodwill gesture, the administration approved this initiative, and General Clark issued such an appeal in February 1953. The plan proved a good test of the Communists' intentions and quite by accident. On March 5, 1953, Marshal of the Soviet Union and Premier Josef Stalin died to the immense relief of much of the world. Within weeks of his death a special meeting of the Politburo, delicately balanced between Stalin's presumptive heirs, voted to end the war in Korea. The Russians communicated their conclusion to Beijing, where Mao Zedong received it with dismay. Mao had to accept a hard fact: his army could not continue the war without Soviet military assistance and that assistance was now at risk. He would end the war if the rearmament and modernization of the People's Liberation Army would continue for the other struggles ahead.

With a speed that amazed the negotiating teams on both sides, the plenary armistice talks began again on the issue of POW exchange. In a message of March 30, Foreign Minister Zhou Enlai in essence accepted an earlier UNC proposal accommodating the principle of voluntary repatriation. POWs who wanted to return to their homelands would be released immediately. Those who chose non-repatriation would go into the custody of a neutral, international agency—not the International Red Cross, which was anathema to the Communists—for noncoercive screening, including interrogations by officers from their national destinations. To demonstrate their good intentions, the Chinese and North Koreans (the latter reluctantly) agreed to Operation Little Switch and exchange sick and disabled POWs. Between April 19 and May 3, both coalitions exchanged POWs at Panmunjom. The United Nations Command accepted back 471 South Koreans, 149 Americans, and 65 allied personnel; it released 5,194 Koreans, 1,030 Chinese, and 446 Korean civilian internees. On April 26 the negotiators at Panmunjom once more discussed a range of formulas that could be applied to exchanging the remaining POWs, the only issue left to be settled before an armistice agreement could be signed.

Peace was not yet at hand. Whatever the Russians, North Koreans, or Americans may have wished, the Chinese and South Koreans still saw much to gain before settling for a cease-fire. In many ways the war had always been a Sino-Korean war as well as a Korean civil war. Syngman Rhee had no use for the Russians and Japanese, but he had always feared the rival Koreans in Pyongyang would hold fast to their Chinese allies (a ploy in the many Korean civil wars of antiquity) and use the Chinese to destroy the Republic of Korea through subversion or direct attack after the Americans left and the United Nations lost interest. The Rhee government had encouraged anti-armistice demonstrations in the autumn of 1952, and these rallies took on a strong hint of anti-Americanism in 1953. In public Rhee never surrendered his "march north and unify" position. In private he hinted he might accept an armistice but only if the United States (not the untrustworthy, neutralist United Nations) agreed to an unambiguous, bilateral mutual security alliance, the continued presence of American air and naval forces in the ROK, a generous economic rehabilitation program of at least $1 billion, sponsorship for the ROK's admission to the United Nations, and a military assistance program to make his armed forces more than a match for the North Koreans. Moreover, he would not accept UN-neutral troops on Korean soil—

meaning the Indian Army—to manage the POW exchange. He would certainly not accept any procedures that denied freedom to the 72,455 Korean men and women still held in UNC custody who chose to stay in the Republic of Korea.

The Chinese saw only one way to encourage the South Koreans and the Americans to make concessions and surrender more territory before a peace agreement: kill more of them on the battlefield. Throughout the spring of 1953 the CPVF had made extensive preparations for a seventh offensive, but it was conceived initially as an attritional campaign. The Chinese attacks opened in the Imjin sector in early May 1953 against the 1st Marine Division and British Commonwealth Division. The battle shifted north and east against other American and ROK divisions deployed in the hills around the Chorwon-Kumhwa base of the Iron Triangle with more success as a series of Eighth Army outposts fell or were abandoned. In early June the Chinese high command decided to focus its attacks on the South Korean Army. As one CPVF general put it, "We mean to kill the chicken so as to scare the monkey." On June 10, the Twentieth Army Group (nine infantry and two artillery divisions) attacked the ROK II Corps (four divisions) but carefully avoided major battles with the two U.S. divisions on either of the Koreans' flanks. Two more ROK divisions were drawn into the battle but not before the Chinese army group (also reinforced) had driven the Koreans back thirty miles from the Kumsong salient and thus improved the Communists' position at the Iron Triangle's western edge. Inept generalship by Chung Il-kwon, the corps commander, rather than poor fighting characterized the South Koreans' defense. American airpower and massive artillery finally halted the Chinese. Nevertheless, at a cost of 15,000 casualties, the Koreans had inflicted at least two to three times that number of losses on the Chinese without involving American infantry divisions. Both sides claimed the Battle of the Kumsong Salient as a great victory, and in a strange way they were both right.

The battle ended the war with some of the same bizarre twists with which it had begun. On May 25 the Panmunjom negotiators had worked out the details on the POW exchange that satisfied them. They had made provisions for neutral nation management of the repatriation process with the United Nations taking custody of the non-repatriates after a ninety-day period. They began to plan for an armistice signing and implementation. Even with Peng Dehuai ready to sign the agreement for the Chinese, Syngman Rhee on June 18 arranged for his military police to allow the 27,000 internees in their custody to escape. The Americans had orders not to fire on the escapees, but a new Marine detachment at one camp and isolated soldiers did not get the word and killed sixty-one anti-Communist Koreans during the escape. Enraged at the breakout, the Chinese ordered further attacks on the ROK Army.

President Eisenhower shared the Chinese fury with Rhee, but Dulles convinced him that Plan Everready—dusted off in April by the current Eighth Army commander, Lt. Gen. Maxwell D. Taylor—was not the answer to Korean stubbornness. Instead, the administration sent a special diplomatic mission to Korea to talk sense into Rhee. Headed by Assistant Secretary of State Walter S. Robertson, the mission also talked compromise and basically convinced Rhee that Eisenhower would meet all his preconditions for accepting the armistice. Robertson told Rhee bluntly the United States could quit the war now with or without an armistice, but it preferred an armistice. His best reassurance, however, was the United States was prepared to renew the war and to consider the possible use of nuclear weapons if the Communists broke the agreement's terms. On July 9 Rhee agreed to accept the armistice (although no ROK representative ever signed it), which meant he had to allow the POW exchange arrangements he found so distasteful. On July 27 General Clark in nearby Munsan-ni, Peng Dehuai at the Communist negotiating camp, and Kim Il-sung in Pyongyang signed copies of the armistice agreement. The same day the shooting stopped (more or less), and the armies began the awkward process of disengagement across what became a four-kilometer Demilitarized Zone and the broad defensive bands beyond the DMZ.

Implementing the armistice took the rest of the year. The parties faced acrimony and a continued propaganda war, mounted especially by the Chinese and North Koreans against the South Koreans. The supervision of the armistice actions fell to the Military Armistice Commission (ten officers representing the belligerents), the Neutral National Supervisory Commission (Sweden, Switzerland, Poland, and Czechoslovakia), and the Neutral Nations Repatriation Commission (NNRC), which included the same four nations and India as the custodial force. Despite continued violence among the POWs under UNC supervision and then Indian custody, Operation Big Switch began on August 5 and ended on September 6. In all, 75,823 Communist soldiers and civilians (all but 5,640 of them Koreans) returned to their most-favored regime, and 7,862 ROK soldiers, 3,597 American servicemen, and 1,377 persons of other nationalities (including some civilians) returned to United Nations Command control. Big Switch became a media event of potent possibilities; the Communist

POWs stripped off their hated capitalist uniforms and marched off singing party-approved songs.

The NNRC's handling of those who refused repatriation turned into a nightmare, especially for the Indians. The relatively few POWs in Communist hands had varied and strong reasons (e.g., criminal collaboration) for not returning home; 21 of 23 Americans, one British Marine, and 347 of 359 Koreans again refused repatriation. The 22,604 Chinese and Korean non-repatriates turned over to the Indians for neutral screening were never completely processed or interviewed since Communist agents among the POWs and Communist interrogators made life miserable for the Indians, who never had enough guards, translators, or administrative personnel to manage their mission. When the Neutral Nations Repatriation Commission admitted final defeat in February 1954, only 628 Chinese and Koreans had changed their minds, and 21,839 remained in NNRC control awaiting final determination of a country of destination. Eighty-six Communist soldiers actually fled Asia and went to India with the custodial force; most of the non-repatriates eventually settled in Korea and Taiwan, where they provided ample testimony to the evils of Communism.

As provided for in the armistice agreement, the United States organized an international conference for all the Korean War belligerents in Geneva, Switzerland, to discuss the political future of Korea and the possibility of unification. The Soviet Union served as cosponsor, and the Chinese and North Koreans sent a high-level delegation headed by Zhou Enlai and Nam-Il. The actual meetings occurred between April 26 and June 15, 1954. While it did not produce an agreement on how the United Nations might supervise elections that would

created a unified Korea, the meeting did result in formal recognition of the Republic of Korea as a UN member and the
legitimate government of all of Korea since only it agreed to
have UN representatives monitor its elections. In sum, all the
belligerents gained something from the Korean War, but the
Korean people had lost the most. Two million of their countrymen were dead; their homes, infrastructure, and economic
system were destroyed; and they would continue to be caught
in the toils of a great power rivalry in north Asia. Yet the Republic of Korea's survival keeps alive the possibility of civil
liberties, democracy, economic development, and eventual unification with the north, even if their fulfillment requires another fifty years or more.

2 THE COMMUNIST ALLIANCE AND THE KOREAN WAR

Intelligence officers and historical pundits label enemy deployments and operations as "the other side of the hill" perspectives. In Korea too many GIs, Marines, and South Korean soldiers found the enemy on *their* side of the hill and wished them elsewhere. The wartime stereotypes of the North Koreans as murderous sociopaths and the Chinese as drug-crazed peasants still prevail among too many veterans and the veterans' admirers who listen to them with suspended disbelief. No doubt the North Korean Army contained fanatics; there were too many victims of atrocities to explain away. No doubt Chinese soldiers behaved in strange ways in battle, but in the 1950–51 offensives they suffered from starvation, dehydration, fatigue, debilitating and terminal illnesses, and general despair. They behaved accordingly. The Communist coalition forces deserve more dispassionate analysis than they have thus far received, and fifteen years of enlarged access to print and archival materials in Beijing and Moscow have produced the most "other side of the hill" perspectives since the allied forces captured some North Korean records in 1950.

The most active area of U.S. and Russian archival contact at the official level concerns the fate of some 262 American airmen missing in action (and presumed dead) who may or may not have been POWs before they disappeared. In 1997, after years of negotiation, the Russian Federation Ministry of Defense allowed researchers of the POW/Missing Personnel Office, Department of Defense (now the Joint POW/MIA Accounting Command) to examine materials in its central archives relating to the Korean air war. Private researchers had seen some of the documents, but the POW/MIA research teams have wider access. Their conclusions shattered a great myth of the air war—namely that U.S. Air Force F-86s had inflicted 10:1 losses on the Communist MiG-15 air forces. The real number is closer to 2.5:1. As consolation to true believers, Russian claims of 1,300 F-86 kills give overestimating a new meaning. Nevertheless, greater documentary transparency of any kind is welcome. In 2005 the Chinese agreed to open their archives to official POW/MIA researchers, with as yet unknown results.

The most useful Russian perspective on the formation of the Democratic Peoples Republic of Korea is the work of Dr. Alexandre Y. Mansourov, a former Russian foreign service officer and Korean specialist and now an analyst for Asian affairs for the U.S. Pacific Command. Mansourov's expertise in the Korean language qualified him to be the archivist-historian who identified, duplicated, and translated the documents from the Soviets' Presidential, Ministry of Defense, and Foreign Ministry archives that were delivered to the Republic of Korea during its period of rapprochement (1989–92) with the Soviet Union. Mansourov used many of these documents in writing "Communist War Coalition Formation and the Origins of the Korean War," his doctoral dissertation. He summarized his study of Soviet-Korean relationships in a mistitled essay, "Korean War Studies in the United States." Valuable parts of Mansourov's manuscript are his appendixes on the Koreans and Soviets in the DPRK government and his comparison of USSR and DPRK intelligence assessments with those of the ROK and U.S. agencies.

Mansourov had no monopoly on access to Soviet archives, and his first work—translation of Russian wartime documents into Korean and published in Seoul in 1994—was soon followed by two other documents-based studies by Russian historians with Foreign Ministry ties. The first manuscript to reach the West came through South Korea: Evgeniy P. Bajanov and Natalia Bajanova, "The Korean Conflict, 1950–1953: The Most Mysterious War of the 20th Century." The Korean Military Academy obtained it in 1998 already in English and ready for backdoor distribution in photocopied form to Korean War experts. The second work was from Anatoly Torkunov, *The War in Korea, 1950–53*. These books both use many of the same source documents and make the similar case that Stalin, Kim Il-sung, and Mao Zedong chose war against the best interests of their countries and their revolutions. They are largely silent on Soviet relations with North Korea until after its independence in 1948. The recent limited release and access to Soviet-era documents does not reduce the value of earlier works, such as Robert Simmons's *The Strained Alliance: Peking, Pyongyang, Moscow, and the Politics of the Korean War,* but the "new scholarship" does correct or enhances such accounts as Vladislaw Zubok and Constantine Pleshkov's *Inside the Kremlin's Cold War* and adds credibility to such suspect accounts as Nikita Khrushchev's memoirs. Odd Arne Westad's anthology of essays on the Soviet-Chinese connection, *Brothers in Arms: The*

Rise and Fall of Sino-Soviet Alliance, 1945–1963, establishes a high standard for collaborative international scholarship.

The central source of printed and translated Russian, Chinese, and North Korean documents related to the Korean War is the *Bulletin* of the Cold War International History Project (CWIHP), sponsored by the Woodrow Wilson International Center for Scholars. Founded in 1991 and located in Washington, D.C., the center is a foundation-sponsored and government-supported institution dedicated to the study of the Cold War. Dr. Kathryn Weathersby, an internationally recognized expert on Soviet foreign policy, directed the CWIHP's Korea Project. The first *Bulletin* appeared in 1992. Of the subsequent issues, numbers 5 (Spring 1995), 6–7 (Winter 1995–96), 8–9 (Winter 1996–97), 11 (Winter 1998), and 14–15 (Winter 2003–Spring 2004) carried Korean War–related documents, annotations, articles, commentary, and bibliography. The fuel for all this scholarly exchange comes from the Russian archives but only as released by Russian archivists. The documents tend to put all Russians except Josef Stalin in a good light and pass responsibility for Communist misjudgments regarding the war's causes, conduct, and consequences to Mao Zedong and Kim Il-sung. A useful dimension to this debate has been the release of documents from former Warsaw Pact nations that no longer feel any fraternal bonds with Russia, China, and North Korea. The *Bulletin* has carried articles and translated documents from the archives of Hungary, the former German Democratic Republic, Bulgaria, and the Czech Republic. The central dialogue, however, is still focused on Chinese-Russian relations, for which the *Bulletin* provides a window for Western scholars. One recent and revealing example is Shen Zhihua, translated by Dong Gil Kim and Jeffrey

Becker, "Sino-North Korean Conflict and Its Resolution During the Korean War."

Thus far, the Russian materials have focused on political and geostrategic issues. The most significant operational source is now Gukbangbu Gunsa Pyeonchan Yeonguso's *6.25 Jeonjaeng Bogoseo*, or *Nachal'niku General'nogo Shtaba SA Generalu Armii Tovarishchu Shtemenko 5.M: Diestviia voisk KNA*. This source, printed thus far only in Russian and Korean, is a series of reports and studies sent to Moscow by Maj. Gen. Vladimir Nikolaevich Razuvaev, the chief of the Soviet military mission to the North Korean Army and a Soviet military attaché in Pyongyang from November 18, 1950, to September 29, 1953. Razuvaev became responsible for conducting a critique of the Korean People's Army's defeat in 1950, arranging its reorganization and retraining in 1951, and reporting on its operations from 1951 through 1953. Razuvaev had served as a common soldier in the civil war and as an officer in the 1939–40 Winter War in Finland. In that war and the Great Patriotic War (1941–45), Razuvaev proved a skilled, diligent chief of staff of Red Army formations up to the army (corps) level. On several occasions he assumed command of armored forces and had success. In 1950 he took command of a dispirited Red Army training cadre that had just abandoned Pyongyang. He also acted as the Soviet ambassador to North Korea until the end of the war. According to custom, Josef Stalin hounded him about his reports, but the general managed to outlive his tormentor and finally retired in 1968 after a series of honorable but marginal commands and school directorships.

The Razuvaev *Reports,* of course, are collective works by the military mission, so determining who wrote what is impossible without a working familiarity with the entire mission.

What is more important to know is that Russian historians now cite the Razuvaev *Reports* as a definitive history of the war and as contemporaneous "lessons learned," Red Army style. Volume 1 is a history of the war in 1950 with a special emphasis on both sides' artillery and armor operations. It includes a continuing commentary on the U.S.-ROK lack of ability in night operations and scathing criticism of the KPA for its lack of combined arms coordination and minimal ardor in exploiting opportunities. The Russian analysis remains heavily weighted toward artillery employment. Volume 2 continues the operational analysis of the 1950 war and then covers the 1950–51 KPA reforms. Each arm and service of the army rates a chapter as does the navy and air force. The analysis includes statistical tables and inspection reports. Only one chapter deals with the Chinese People's Volunteers Force. The volume concludes with a summary of the 1951–53 operations, again emphasizing KPA artillery and engineering employment compared to U.S.-ROK operations. Volume 3 deals with nonmilitary aspects of the war: POWs, economic recovery, the air war, and post-armistice policies. Making the Razuvaev *Reports* available in English would be the most significant contribution to Korean War studies until the USSR and DPRK political and military communications become fully available.

The perestroika policy concerning Korean War documents has faded in Moscow, and the Pyongyang archives remain as closed to Western researchers as most of the rest of the country is. As I said to seven inscrutable Chinese officer-historians of the People's Liberation Army's Academy of Military Sciences during a visit to Beijing in July 1998, the Chinese and Russians hold the key to greater understanding of the Communists' conduct of the war. Actually, the archives that the U.S. Eighth Army captured in Pyongyang in October 1950 offer some useful evidence on the DPRK military affairs before its temporary exile from the capital. The books, memoranda, and pamphlets swept up in Operation Indianhead and other intelligence special operations are now available and accessible (and have been for years) in the National Archives' Collection of Foreign Records Seized, Record Group 242, National Archives and Records Administration, Washington, D.C. However, since the North Korean political and military leaders had about ten days to evacuate Pyongyang, which South Korean and American soldiers captured on October 16, 1950, the most significant DPRK archives went north with their custodians to the temporary capital of Kanggye. The city became a rallying point for the North Korean Army and a rendezvous with the headquarters of the Chinese People's Volunteers Force (Renmin Zhiyuanjun). Masses of military, party, and governmental documents fell into UNC hands in Pyongyang, Wonsan, and smaller cities, but these documents, organized by location of capture, are either not very revealing or unexploited. The Russian materials are innocuous, mostly published technical books and pamphlets. It is analogous to capturing Washington and seizing the Library of Congress, some Capitol Building offices, the National Archives, and the Old Executive Office Building, but finding the White House, the Pentagon, the State Department, and CIA headquarters empty and abandoned. Record Group 242 also includes translations of DPRK documents, almost all military, by the Allied Translator and Interpreter Service (ATIS), part of the Far East Command's Military Intelligence Service (MIS) and directed by the assistant chief of staff (G-2). (ATIS became the Military Intelligence Service Group–Far East in 1951 and the 500th Military Intelligence Service Group in 1952.) The

ATIS translated and distributed documents it judged useful to ongoing operations.

The North Koreans have not yet deviated from their line that South Korea attacked them as part of a Japanese-American plot to restore the Japanese Empire. Heo Jeong-ho, Kang Sok-hui, and Pak Tae-ho, in *The U.S. Imperialists Started the Korean War*, identify the villainous instruments of imperialism as a clique of South Korean generals, who actually invaded the North Korea in June 1949. The doctoral work of Kim Kook-hun, a retired general in the South Korean Army, provides a more balanced picture of North Korea's dependence upon its Soviet advisers and Russian-controlled support system in "The North Korean People's Army: Its Rise and Fall, 1945–1950." Just from materials held in the West, such as POW interrogation reports and the personal memoirs of non-repatriated North Koreans, more comprehensive studies of North Korean military affairs from 1945 to 1955 could be written now and provide new insights into the 1948–50 guerrilla war in southern Korea and the conventional war that followed. The government-approved *Imperialists* volume is a model of sophisticated analysis compared with two other English-language books on the North Korean side of the war: *The Heroic KPA: The Invincible Revolutionary Armed Forces* and *The Victorious Fatherland Liberation War Museum,* a guide to the Korean War Museum in Pyongyang. The North Korean version of the war is notable for the immense casualties inflicted on the United Nations Command (1.5 million) and the number of aircraft destroyed (5,729) and warships sunk or destroyed (564). There is no mention of UN POWs and little acknowledgment of the Chinese participation in the war.

The Chinese accounts of the Korean War could use a big dose of the South Koreans' "sunshine policy." The official history is the Shen Zonghong and Meng Zhoahui et al. book for the Academy of Military Sciences, *Zhongguo Renmin Zhiyuanjun Kangmei Yuanchao Zhanshi* (*The Chinese People's Volunteers Force in the War to Resist America and Aid Korea*). It has appeared in several forms through 2000 and can be found in two basic versions, one meant for internal use within the People's Liberation Army planning and education staffs and the other designed for a wider audience. There is also a shorter volume on the Chinese participation in the multivolume *Zhongguo Junzhi Baike Quanshu* (*Encyclopedia of the Chinese Military Experience*). Also untranslated are histories of each Chinese army (corps) and selected units such as the air defense forces and railway forces. The best introduction to the Chinese perspective on the Korean War, written by historians still resident in China, are the essays of Song Zhongyue and Han Gaoyun. These senior researchers work for the China Society for Strategy and Management, Beijing, which publishes occasional pieces in English in its journal.

In China the official function of Korean War literature and museum exhibits is to remind the Chinese people of the great sacrifices of the Generation of the Revolution and their requirement to remain ever vigilant against counterrevolutionary histories. The stories of the heroic victory of the Chinese People's Volunteers Force (the nom de guerre the People's Liberation Army expeditionary force in Korea adopted) over the firepower of United Nations Command are sanctified in the writings of Wei Wei. A journalist, novelist, and propagandist in Korea, his most famous essay, "Who Are the Most Beloved People?" remains a classic. The continued popularity of *A Volunteer Soldier's*

Diary (Beijing: Foreign Languages Press, 1961) reflects the PLA's stress on honorable service. Over time, the official line has emphasized the Chinese soldiers' endurance under the most severe combat conditions. The event of choice for patriotic emphasis is the Battle of Shangganling. The battle is part of the October and November 1952 campaign along several ridges and mountains between Chorwon and Kumhwa. The most violent clashes involved the U.S. 7th Infantry Division's and ROK 9th Division's defense of Triangle Hill, Sniper Hill, and Paekmasan or White Horse Mountain. Beyond boosting the Chinese forces' morale, the Battle of Shangganling deserves more analysis as the first test of the rearmed and retrained CPVF in a set-piece battle with the reformed American and South Korean armies and was, perhaps, a major effort to preempt a feared UNC amphibious turning movement.

Behind the PLA's official history and the literature of national sacrifice and heroic service that shapes the Chinese image of the Korean War—images reinforced by the museums in Beijing and Dandung—there is a growing body of memoir literature from the Chinese generals who fought the war. Their writings provide more realistic views of the war. One afternoon in late July 1988 several retired generals gathered for tea. Their host was retired Lt. Gen. Chai Chengwen, head of the People's Republic of China's military mission to Pyongyang in 1950 and a senior liaison officer for the Chinese negotiating team at Panmunjom. That day's conversation focused on the Chinese intervention in the Korean War. When Chai reminded his guests it was the thirty-fifth anniversary of the signing of the Korean cease-fire agreement, the excited and nostalgic generals talked freely about their wartime experiences. As Chai prepared to record the conversation, some wanted to remain

anonymous, but others insisted that "now that we all are retired and carry no responsibility for any government units, we
shall voice our opinions freely." The first result of that
afternoon's meeting—and many others—is the memoir,
Banmendian Tanpan (*Panmunjom Negotiations*), an insider's
account of the armistice negotiations. Chai stresses the leadership of Li Kenong, deputy foreign minister and intelligence
director of the Central Military Commission. Li never sat at
the negotiating table and thus remains invisible in Western
accounts. In Chinese photographs of the negotiating team, a
uniformed Li Kenong is seated in the center of the front row.

Chai's reminiscences and others that followed offer an
important source of information and opinions on the war's
many aspects, including combat operations, logistics, political
control, field command, and communications. Most of these
high-ranking officers relied not only on their personal papers
but also on still-classified archives. Moreover, they cite such
important documents as *Mao Zedong Junshi Wenxuan—
Neibuban* (*Selected Military Works of Mao Zedong*), *Jianguo Yilai
Mao Zedong Wengao* (*Mao Zedong Manuscripts Since the Foundation of the PRC*), *Peng Dehuai Junshi Wenxuan* (*Selected
Military Works of Peng Dehuai*), *Nie Rongzhen Junshi Wenxuan*
(*Selected Military Writings of Nie Rongzhen*), the four volumes
of *Kangmei Yuanchao Zhanzheng Houqin Jingyan Zongjie* (*A
Summary of the CPVF's Logistical Service Experience in the War
to Resist the United States and Aid Korea*), and the two volumes
of *Zhongguo Renmin Zhiyuanjun Kangmei Yuanchao Zhanzheng
Zhengzhi Gongzuo Zongjie* (*A Summary of the CPVF's Political
Work in the War to Resist America and Aid Korea*).

Some personal accounts predated General Chai's party.
As the commander in chief and political commissar of the

Chinese forces in Korea, Marshal Peng Dehuai gives detailed personal information on the major battles he commanded, important decisions made at the front, his daily communications with Mao Zedong, cooperation with Kim Il-sung, and his visit with Stalin in Moscow. Peng wrote his autobiography during the decade when he was under arrest during the Cultural Revolution, so his recollections were not part of official China's propaganda for its "glorious war" in Korea, but confessional. Others excluded Peng's name even from the Korean War literature for more than two decades, and his memoir, *Peng Dehuai Zishu*, was not published until after his posthumous rehabilitation. An abridged version of Peng's memoir is available in English as *Memoirs of a Chinese Marshal*.

Acting chief of staff of the PLA and Marshal Nie Rongzhen's account of how the top Chinese Communist Party (CCP) leadership debated and then decided to intervene in Korea is invaluable: *Nie Rongzhen Huiyilu* (*Nie Rongzhen Memoirs*). In charge of the war mobilization in 1950–52, Nie in particular recalled the difficulties the new regime faced in financing the Chinese intervention. Chief of Staff and Marshal Xu Xiangqian, who resumed the leadership of the PLA Headquarters of the General Staff late in 1952 after a two-year sick leave, reflected on the subtle and sometimes difficult PRC-USSR relationships in his memoir, *Lishide Huigu* (*Remember History*). His vivid description of his 1952 trip to Moscow for more material assistance will enhance one's understanding of that "special relationship." Gen. Yang Dezhi's memoir, *Yang Dezhi Huiyilu* (*Yang Dezhi's Memoirs*), reveals the thinking of Chinese Communist officers on strategy and tactics. As the vice commander responsible for CPVF operations in 1951 and commander of the Nineteenth Army Group in 1952, Yang

discussed in great detail how the CPVF designed and organized each offensive and defensive battle. Another CPVF vice
commander, Gen. Hong Xuezhi, who took charge of the
CPVF's logistics during the war, provides a comprehensive account of CPVF's rear service problems and performance in
*Kangmei Yuanchao Zhangzheng Huigu (Recollections of the War
to Resist America)*. Only during the Korean War, Hong explained, did the Chinese Communist forces realize the importance of a standardized and efficient logistics system. Hong
also explains how the CPVF countered the air raids on its supply lines. Gen. Du Ping describes the war from the perspective
of the CPVF's principal political officer in two versions of his
memoir, *Zai Zhiyuanjun Zongbu: Du Ping Huiyilu (My Days
at CPVF Headquarters: Du Ping's Memories)*.

The recent release or leakage of Chinese sources, especially
the wartime correspondence of Mao Zedong, has also resulted
in a new wave of scholarship by Hao Zrifan, Shen Zhihua,
Zhai Zhihai, Chen Jian, Zhang Shu Gang, Zhang Xiaoming,
Yu Bin, and Michael Hunt in both article and essay form. These
scholars add texture to the earlier works of Joseph Camilleri
(*Chinese Foreign Policy: The Maoist Era and Its Aftermath*), Tang
Tsou (*America's Failure in China: 1941–1950*); and Melvin
Gurtov and Hwang Byeong-mu (*China Under Threat: The Politics of Strategy and Diplomacy*). One result of international collaboration on exploring the conflict between the United States
and China is Harry Harding and Yuan Min's *Sino-American
Relations, 1945–1955*. A critical view of the People's Liberation Army and Mao is found in Zhang Shu Gang's *Mao's Military Romanticism: China and the Korean War, 1950–1953,* based
largely on the PLA's sources, but this work should be matched
with Chen Jian's *China's Road to the Korean War: The Making of*

the Sino-American Confrontation. Zhang and Chen evaluate the role of Maoist ideology and self-delusion in the Chinese intervention differently, reflecting a continuing debate over the strengths and weaknesses of the chairman's politico-strategic domination of Chinese policy. Chen gives greater attention to the Central Military Commission–People's Liberation Army tensions over functional issues. Yu Bin's much-cited and re-printed essay, "What China Learned From Its 'Forgotten War' in Korea," which first appeared as a journal article in 1998, reinforces Chen's arguments. Two Western works of lasting value on the Chinese intervention are Allen Whiting's *China Crosses the Yalu: The Decision to Enter the Korean War* and Walter Zelman's *Chinese Intervention in the Korean War.*

Access to Russian and Chinese sources by scholars with the linguist skills and infinite patience to plumb these sources has created a growing body of significant work on the Soviet-Chinese relationship and the Cold War. The Korean War is a major part of this collaboration. Published in English, the leading works in this category are Sergei Goncharov, John Lewis, and Xue Litai, *Uncertain Partners: Stalin, Mao, and the Korean War*; Gordon Chang, *Friends and Enemies: The United States, China, and the Soviet Union, 1948–1972*; Chen Jian, *Mao's China and the Cold War*; John Lewis Gaddis, *The Cold War*; and Odd Arne Westad, *The Global Cold War.* These works' most notable aspect is that they do not see international politics as just the domain of the American government or from a Eurocentric historical perspective.

When based on translated documents and professional intelligence assessments, the Western perspective on the Communist armies has considerable value. For a face-of-battle account of Chinese struggles in the winter of 1950–51, see Russell

Spurr, *Enter the Dragon: China's Undeclared War Against the U.S. in Korea, 1950–1951,* which is based on interviews with veterans. Patrick Roe, in *The Dragon Strikes: China and the Korean War, June–December 1950,* sees the intervention from the field military intelligence perspective. In *Communist Logistics in the Korean War,* Charles Schrader provides an able introduction to a critical limitation on Sino-Korean operations.

The most significant point of Chinese-Russian military collaboration and coalition tension is in the conduct of the Korean air war. From American air intelligence sources and the interviews with Russian air veterans by Jon Halliday, the depth of the Soviet air force's involvement in Asia is now public knowledge in the historical sense. It was no secret to Far East Air Forces pilots that their MiG-15 adversaries were Russian pilots, augmented with Chinese and North Korean aviators. For the Soviets the Korean War provided an unparalleled opportunity to assess American air operations and technology as long as the U.S. Air Force did not attack the Russian air bases in Manchuria and the Maritime Province. If the Russians had not provided for the air defense of Chinese bases in Manchuria—which they were obligated to do under the terms of the Treaty of Friendship, Alliance, and Mutual Assistance of February 1950—the Chinese might not have intervened in Korea in October 1950.

The continued complexity of Sino-American relations (with Korean history subsumed in this fatal and enduring attraction) continues to draw serious scholars to intricate and elusive issues. See, for example, Thomas Christensen, *Useful Adversaries: Grand Strategy, Domestic Mobilization and Sino-American Conflict, 1947–1958*; Alfred Wilhelm, *The Chinese at the Negotiating Table*; and Stephen Endicott and Edward Hagerman, *The United States and Biological Warfare.*

Western studies of the North Korean and Chinese armed forces are founded on the wartime studies and reports of FECOM intelligence staffs and United Nations Command's major ground, naval, and air forces components. At the center of the process was the Allied Translator and Interpreter Service, which published summaries of individual POW interrogation reports. Numbering in the thousands by the end of 1950, the ATIS published them for internal distribution in groups of a hundred. The debriefs, or *Interrogation Reports*, cover the entire war. Obviously, the POW debriefings' value varies, but all are illuminating on issues of North Korean and Chinese military affairs. The ATIS also used the individual POW debriefs and other materials to publish a series called *Research Supplements* (the first is from October 19, 1950) that include the short histories of the services, divisions, and other agencies of the North Korean armed forces. They also prepared research supplements on the Chinese forces, but the limited range of sources reduces their value. A third ATIS series, *Enemy Documents,* covers translated KPA and CPVF written materials. As with other armies, these forces published all sorts of guidebooks, technical manuals, and training instructions. Such writings in any language could cure insomnia, but there are some real gems in the bureaucratic mines. My favorite is from the Renmin Zhiyuanjun Headquarters, "Combat Experiences Against U.S. and ROK Forces" (January 1951), which was translated and distributed by G-2 ROKA and MIS, FECOM, the same year.

The Far East Command had no monopoly on using POW interrogations, captured documents, and other operational evidence, such as shell reports or observation post (OP) sightings, to produce material on enemy forces. The intelligence staffs of the Eighth Army, its corps, and its division headquarters published documents variously called "Combat Information Bulletins," "Combat Notes," and "Periodic Intelligence Reports." Similar reports on enemy forces were produced by the Far East Air Forces, the Fifth Air Force, Naval Forces Far East, and the commander in chief of the Pacific Fleet, who retained administration responsibility for the deployed task forces of the Seventh Fleet. There are three potential sources for such relevant intelligence assessments. The consumers often kept these reports, especially those they deemed important. Not surprisingly, the private papers of Generals Douglas MacArthur, Charles A. Willoughby, Matthew B. Ridgway, Edward M. Almond, and James A. Van Fleet contain such collections. In addition to profiting from the generals' screening, these documents are declassified and often easier to access than the same documents still held by official repositories.

Collections of ATIS documents may be found in catalogued groups in the libraries of the U.S. Army Military History Institute and the U.S. Air Force Historical Research Agency. The Far East Command sent ATIS documents to wide distribution lists, so sets of studies and reports might appear in many record groups of the National Archives and Records Administration (NARA) at the NARA II facility in College Park, Maryland. The first place to look, however, is in Record Group 319, Records of the Army Staff. The responsible office in 1950 through 1953 was the Assistant Chief of Staff (G-2) whose retired files are called the "Records of the Document Library Branch." The Korean War materials are in the "P" file of reports and messages (491 feet), "ID" file (4,495 feet) of documents, and the Intelligence Documents File Publications (503 feet). Fortunately, these collections have indexed folder lists.

These intelligence studies have been exploited in a limited fashion. One example of their possible use is found in Kevin Mahoney's *Formidable Enemies: The North Korean and Chinese Soldier in the Korean War,* which provides sketches of North Korean and Chinese divisions drawn from ATIS *Research Supplements*. Also utilizing the ATIS materials are the special studies by the U.S. Army's Center of Military History and those under contract by the Operations Research Office, Johns Hopkins University, which maintained field offices with Far East Command, Far East Air Forces, Fifth Air Force, and Eighth Army. Another user was the Human Resources Research Office of George Washington University, which did human factors analyses of the Communist forces.

THE KOREANS' WAR, 1945–1954

Even on the brightest days in Seoul, a spiritual pall still hangs over the Republic of Korea, a blanket of memory that connects almost every Korean older than forty years of age to a war from fifty-five years ago that has not faded away fast enough. The memories don't end with the familiar sorrows of modern war: young servicemen dead in battle, families killed in a rain of bombs, starvation, disease, degradation, and the destruction of homes and dreams. Koreans north and south experienced all these horrors and more. As Koreans themselves assert, their national experience parallels the twentieth-century history of the Poles and Jews. The Koreans' ordeal includes a diaspora in their flight to avoid living as Japan's colonial subjects after 1910, a flight that took Koreans to Hawaii and Kazakhstan, to Chungking and Washington, D.C. Within Korea survival under Japanese rule required duplicity and collaboration of some sort during the increasing oppression of the 1930s. The Koreans then died by the tens of thousands in the failed foreign war (1937–45) to "civilize" China, to end European imperialism in Asia, and to build a Japanese empire that would last for a thousand years.

After Japan's surrender in September 1945, Korea endured two occupations on either side of the 38th Parallel. Both the U.S. and Soviet occupations, designed to repatriate the Japanese, set off a wave of Korean immigration out of Japan, Manchuria, and the Soviet zone and into the American zone. As it ended elsewhere, World War II came directly to Korea, with a wave of political killings, arson, confiscation, theft, and extortion violence by Koreans against Koreans, much like the conflicts in Yugoslavia, Malaya, China, Indochina, and the Philippines.

The best way to understand the Korean War is to see it as a three-phase Maoist war of national liberation in which two competitive, parallel political movements, neither strong enough to eliminate the other, started their struggle to prevail in 1945. Unlike French Indochina and Malaya, for example, the liberation struggle in Korea took place in collaboration with two clumsy neo-colonial powers, the United States and the Soviet Union, and not as a war against a colonial regime and its local successors. Through 1948, the Communists in Korea won the early organizational war hands down. In North Korea the Soviet occupation authorities brought their man with them, a minor guerrilla-patriot with the nom de guerre of Kim Il-sung, who was in reality Kim Sung-ju. More established and battle-worn Communist organizers such as Kim Tu-bong and Pak Hon-yong occupied places in Kim's inner circle, but they were not in his plans for the future. What the Korean Communists had in common in 1945–48 was a shared desire to eliminate their potential rivals. In the Russian zone they used their control of the police and the party structure to arrest, isolate, beggar, and drive away northern Koreans with any competitive political power by virtue of family, military service, wealth, Christian leadership roles, learning, and character. The

Soviet occupation's rapacious nature made creating refugees easy; official confiscations and unchecked banditry along the 38th Parallel made certain that much wealth and some people never made it to the south. The Communists very quickly jailed their foremost rival, Cho Man-sik, a Christian lay leader, patriot of national reputation, and chairman of the People's Committee of Pyongyang.

In the southern occupation zone the U.S. Army Military Government in Korea (USAMGIK) carried out its task of disarming and repatriating the Japanese with speed, efficiency, and little loss of life. The Koreans may have let the Japanese depart without a wave of retributive vigilantism because they wanted no confrontation with the Americans in order to devote their time and energy into organizing competitive political organizations. Street violence and political assassinations started almost immediately. As in northern Korea the quickest way to tarnish an adversary leader or group was to accuse them of collaborating with the Japanese; however, in truth, except for a handful of nationalist and Communist militants, all the Korean elite had made accommodations of some sort for personal or their families' economic advantage and to have access to educational and occupational opportunities. Only some degree of accommodation had allowed Christianity to survive in Korea. The American military authorities found no easy way to encourage the development of a centrist coalition, because all the strong political factions sought confrontation and polarization.

The political division of post-liberation Korea involved far more than an arbitrary geographic line. It grew from the pressures of forced modernization, directed agricultural development, colonial industrialization, and the collapse of traditional value and behavioral systems. The immediate rivalries arose, however, from the struggles of Korean exile and underground factions for political power through cooperation or opposition or both to the dual foreign occupations. The stresses on Korea after the liberation from Japan (officially, August 15, 1945) may have made a civil war unavoidable. The major social factors certainly point to conflict: the return of over a million exiles and refugees, the Japanese empire's economic collapse, the urbanization of the desperate, community and familial disruption, the increase of property crimes, resentment over collaboration with the Japanese, and opposition to foreign military occupation, whether Russian or American. These themes are developed in detail by Bruce Cumings in his seminal two-volume work, *The Origins of the Korean War*. Cumings then extended his analysis of modern Korean history in *Korea's Place in the Sun*, which argues that ill-conceived American influence simply exacerbated Korea's political ills. He believes the displacement of the extemporized "people's committees" of 1945 and the stillborn "People's Republic of Korea" destroyed any chance for a reformed, postcolonial, authentic Korean government. Just how this change would have come about above the 38th Parallel is unclear. As Cumings acknowledges, much of his inspiration comes from an earlier (1968) book by the late Gregory Henderson, who served in Korea as an idealistic junior foreign service officer in the late 1940s and early 1950s. Henderson's *Korea: The Politics of the Vortex* establishes that American policy, consciously or not, empowered a pro-Japanese, antidemocratic, economically privileged Korean elite that doomed Korea to continued division and political violence. A nuanced exploration of this perspective, carefully documented and argued, may be found in Carter J. Eckert's biography of Kim Sung-su of the Kochang Kims, a nationalist entrepreneur and founder of the Korean Democratic Party. The "frustrated revolution" theme with the United States as the designated villain found full expression in Vietnam War–era anthologies intellectually shaped by Cumings, Henderson, Frank Baldwin, and James Palais, which might collectively be called the University of Washington's "school of revisionist Korean studies."

The analysis of modern Korea's political troubles and the history of American involvement in Koreans' affairs has other expert interpretations that counterbalance the revisionists. Two long-time residents and scholars of Korea, George M. McCune and Arthur L. Grey, attempted to explain Korean culture in *Korea Today*. Essential readings on postliberation Korea are the books of the late Donald Stone Macdonald, who served with notable success in Korea as a military government officer and diplomat after 1945. He then became a leader of Korean studies at several Washington-area universities and the Foreign Service Institute. His summative book is *The Koreans*. The most authoritative work on Korea's cultural development is a book by a distinguished Korean-American academic, Andrew C. Nahm, whose work *Korea, Tradition and Transformation* is essential reading. The introduction to Korean-American relations can begin with the anthology *U.S.-Korean Relations, 1882–1982*, a group of scholarly essays edited by a team that included Shannon McCune, like his father, a lifelong student of Korea.

The specialized works on the American military government period and the Republic of Korea's early years are distinguished by their sympathetic but critical view of American policy and their effort to gauge Korean "liberation politics." The most notable are James Matray, *The Reluctant Crusade: American Foreign Policy in Korea, 1941–1950*; Allan R. Millett, *A House Burning, 1945–1950*, volume 1 of *The War for Korea*;

Bonnie Oh, ed., *Korea Under the American Military Government, 1945–1948*; John Merrill, *Korea: The Peninsular Origins of the War*; William Stueck, *The Road to Confrontation: American Policy Toward China and Korea, 1947–1950*; Charles Dobbs, *The Unwanted Symbol: American Foreign Policy, the Cold War, and Korea, 1945–1950*; Lisle Rose, *Roots of Tragedy: The United States and the Struggle for Asia, 1945–1953*; and Grant Meade, *American Military Government in Korea.*

Treatments of the war written by Koreans and published in English reflect a common sense of victimization. Among the South Korean sources one finds various degrees of outrage over intervention, remorse over the role of the Koreans themselves in encouraging foreign intervention, deep sadness over the war's consequences, pride and contempt over the Koreans' military performance, a tendency to see conspiracy everywhere, and a yearning for eventual unification. There is no consensus on how unification might have been accomplished, only the certainty that the war blighted Korea for the rest of the century. Among the more insightful works by Korean scholars are Kim Myung-ki, *The Korean War and International Law*; Pak Chi-yong, *Political Opposition in Korea, 1945–1950*; Kim Joung-won, *Divided Korea: The Politics of Development, 1945–1972*; Kim Gye-dong, *Foreign Intervention in Korea*; and Cho Soong-sung, *Korea in World Politics, 1940–1950.*

Syngman Rhee is protean in his failures and his successes, including keeping America involved in Korea, more or less on his terms. He succeeded where Chiang Kai-shek, Ferdinand Marcos, and Ngo Dinh Diem failed. Robert T. Oliver, a university professor of communications and Rhee's American media adviser, wrote two admiring books noted for their conversations, letters, and speeches: *Syngman Rhee: The Man Behind the Myth* and *Syngman*

Rhee and American Involvement in Korea, 1942–1960. Henry Chung, Rhee's personal secretary, wrote a memoir, *Korea and the United States through War and Peace, 1943–1960.* A less sympathetic view is found in Richard Allen's *Korea's Syngman Rhee: An Unauthorized Portrait.* Rhee's political contemporaries, who often shifted between being rivals and supporters, left extensive memoirs. These Koreans included Cho Pyong-ok, Yi Pom-sok, Yo Un-hong, and Louise Yim. The Institute of Modern Korean Studies at Yonsei University has published eighteen volumes of Rhee's correspondence in Korean and Chinese.

The contemporaneous creation of South Korea's revolutionary rival, the Democratic People's Republic of Korea, remains befogged with "Great Leader" mythology and anti-Communist demonizing. Nevertheless, perceptive digging in Western and Japanese sources made it possible for first-generation studies that predated the era of partial openness in Chinese and Russian studies. The pioneering work, stressing the growth of Korean Communism, includes Robert Scalapino and Chonsik Lee's *Communism in Korea* and Suh Dae-sook's *The Korean Communist Movement, 1918–1949* and *Kim Il-sung: The North Korean Leader.* With some access to Soviet materials and expatriate North Koreans' accounts, the next wave of scholarship focused on the Russian version of trusteeship: Eric Van Ree, *Socialism in One Zone: Stalin's Policy in Korea, 1945–1947,* and Sydney Seiler, *Kim Il-sung: The Creation of a Legend, the Building of a Regime.* Seiler's work is especially valuable because it includes a translation of the memoir of Gen. Yu Song-chol, the KPA's former director of operations and a Soviet citizen purged in 1959 by Kim Il-sung. Written by a Soviet-trained officer and Kim's Russian-language interpreter and originally published in nineteen installments in Seoul's *Hanguk Ilbo* in November

1990, General Yu's *Testimony* provided intimate and damning details of Kim Il-sung's subversion of true socialism and Korean independence. The leading studies of the second-wave histories have stressed the Korean origins of Korean Communism. They combine Russian materials with the greater exploitation of the North Korean documents collected in 1950: Andrei Lankov, *From Stalin to Kim Il-sung: The Formation of North Korea, 1945–1950,* and Charles Armstrong, *The North Korean Revolution, 1945–1950.* Professor I. G. Kim's *Historical Dictionary of North Korea* is shallow on the 1945–50 period as well as the "big war" of the 1950s. It has some useful information on places and policies, but it omits many key personalities of North Korea's early years, such as Pak Hon-yong, Kim Mu-chong, Kim Tu-bong, Kang Kon, Nam Il, O Jin-u, Kim Tal-sam, and Oh Kai-i. The dictionary also does not have an entry for the Kangdong Institute. A team of international scholars needs to revise this book.

Although it is not exactly a black hole in Korean historiography, the Communist-lead insurgency of 1948–50 against the creation of the Republic of Korea still requires more study. A great deal about the partisan war discouraged honest reporting by all the belligerents. The survivors of that war and their descendents will continue to avoid the truth of the Cheju-do revolt, the Yosu-Sunchon rebellion, and the terrorist-guerrilla war that swept much of South Korea with two years of massacre, execution, arson, and betrayal. The South Korean government's investigation in the 1990s of Cheju-do's pacification only discredited the official 1948–52 ROK reports.

The bitter divisions and polarization of 1948–50 may have been driven by Korean passions, but only Russian and Chinese sources will shed additional light on the level of external support for the rebel South Korean Labor Party. Until that day, the most comprehensive way to follow that conflict and the internationalized civil war that followed is through the history of the Korean Constabulary, which was transformed into a national Korean army, navy, and air force from August to December 1948. The key studies, all "official history," describe the Constabulary's travails from 1946 to 1948 and the ROK Army's growing pains. In many ways more revealing are the memoirs and biographies of the first officers of the South Korean Army, especially members of "the First Class," or the first 110 officers commissioned into the Korean Constabulary in 1946. Four of these officers' memoirs—books by Gen. Paik Sun-yup, Brig. Gen. Lee Chi-op, Brig. Gen. Song Hyo-soon, and Gen. Choi Duk-shin—are available in English.

General Paik, a legendary figure to Americans who have served in ROK since 1945, set off a flurry of interest in the Korean War's history from the Koreans' perspective and has continued in a less hurried form since the Korean War's fiftieth anniversary. General Paik's memoir is only an abridged version of the book originally published in Korean, *Gun Kwa Na* (*The Army and I*). The literature by other senior ROK officers, not yet translated into English, is substantial and includes the memoirs of Generals Chung Il-kwon, Choi Young-hee, Lee Hyong-kun, Song Yo-chan, Chang Do-young, and Yu Jae-hung.

Much of the Korean memoir literature on the 1945–50 era appears as evidence in several studies by ROK Army officers who have received graduate degrees in the Unites States: Huh Nam-sung, "The Quest for a Bulwark of Anti-Communism: The Formation of the Korean Army Officer Corps and Its Political Socialization, 1945-1950," Ph.D. dissertation, The

Ohio State University, 1987; Lee Young-woo, "The United States and the Formation of the Republic of Korea Army, 1945–1950," Ph.D. dissertation, Duke University, 1984; and Chung Too-woong, "The Role of the U.S. Occupation in the Creation of the South Korean Armed Forces, 1945–1950," Ph.D. dissertation, Kansas State University, 1985. Their work, however, only establishes the foundation for additional studies of the history of the ROK armed forces.

The most influential U.S. Army adviser of the pre-1950 period, the late Lt. Col. James H. Hausman, USAR, drew more than his share of historical interest and was demonized by Bruce Cumings in his books and by Jung Il-hwa in *Daetongryeongul Omkin Migun Daewi* (*The U.S. Army Captain Who Moved Presidents*). Hausman's stature as both a hero and a villain stems from his long service in Korea, 1946–51, and his return in 1956 as an army officer and civilian employee until 1980. Harvard University's Korea Institute is building a collection of documents on U.S.-ROK military relations based on Hausman's papers. In my own, "Captain James H. Hausman and the Formation of the Korean Army, 1945–1950," *Armed Forces and Society* 23 (Summer 1997): 503–539, I compare Hausman to other military reformers who played instrumental roles in creating new non-Western armies. My interviews with Colonel Hausman identified many other American officers whose advisory careers might be useful vehicles for examining the South Korean Army's development. Colonel Hausman died in 1996.

The South Korean accounts of the big war rapidly improved in the 1990s and will continue to do so for several reasons. One is the publication in 1998–2000 of a three-volume revised, translated, and annotated English-language version of the War History Compilation Committee's nine-volume *Hankuk Jeonjaengsa*

(*The Korean War*). This history should not be confused with the War History Compilation Committee's six-volume *History of the United Nations Forces in Korea*, which is valuable for its organizational and operational histories of the various non-Korean, non-American UNC contingents. It also includes short histories of the South Korean and American armed forces and the war. Some of the statistical and operational information, however, should be checked against more recent official histories published by the participating armed forces.

The new English-language *The Korean War* is an improvement over the 1967–70 *Hanguk Jeonjaengsa* because the researchers used a wider variety of American, Chinese, and Korean sources than they had consulted for the first version. They also supplemented the materials with personal interviews, POW interrogation reports, and ATIS studies of the North Korean and Chinese armies. Another useful source—now also fully exploited by TV documentary crews—are former North Korean and Chinese POWs who refused repatriation in 1953. Had the South Korean Army kept and maintained better records, especially from 1950 and 1951, the book's research would be more complete, but the authors did consult the parallel reporting system created by the members of the U.S. Army's Korean Military Advisory Group and other U.S. Army reports and studies. Although the rediscovery and cataloging of military records by the Korean government's new archival service might produce new and important evidence, it is unlikely *The Korean War* will require major revision. The hardback, English-language, Ministry of National Defense edition is now on limited distribution, but all three volumes are still available in a paperback edition published by the University of Nebraska

Press. These volumes are worthy companions to the three volumes of the U.S. Army's operational history of the war.

The list of official, semiofficial, and private books and articles written in Korean for a Korean audience is large and growing, with the titles ranging from glossy museum guides to illustrated simple histories designed to help the reader learn English. The central bibliographical point of contact is the library of the Institute for Military History Compilation (IMHC), the War Memorial, Yongsan-gu, Seoul. The IMHC is also the administrative home of the Korean War Society (KWS), a successor to the Korean War Studies Association. The KWS has begun an ambitious series of annual conferences with mainland Chinese scholars since 2000 and has published two anthologies from four conferences (2000–2004), *Talnaengjeon Sidaeui Hanguk Jeonjaengui Jaejonyeong* (*Illuminating the Korean War From the Post–Cold War Era*) and *Hanguk Jeonjaenggwa Jungguk* (*The Korean War and China*).

The war's fiftieth anniversary and the speed of academic-intellectual liberalization in South Korea since the 1990s has encouraged Korean scholars to examine the republic's early years in more searching terms. Whether this new freedom produces something more than "counter history"—in other words, debunking the official histories of the Ministry of National Defense—remains to be seen. Another peril (not unknown in the United States) is that the war's history will be used to justify or even sanctify some current defense policy issue such as conscription or the acquisition of tactical nuclear weapons. Thus far, the official historians have proven more objective about the "hard war" in the rear areas than have been the historians with a political and academic base.

4 THE KOREAN WAR AS AN INTERNATIONAL CONFLICT, 1950–1954

Whether the Korean War was an "international" or "civil" conflict is a minor issue. Civil wars are seldom, if ever, fought in a vacuum. Established regimes and insurgents search for external sponsors to enlarge their strengths and to compensate for their weaknesses. When analyzing the twentieth cen-tury's wars of decolonization, that complex web of client-patron and exploiter-exploited relations, they must be measured by ideology, class and ethnic conflict, money, military forces, leadership, foreign support, personalities, and social reform. The Korean War should be treated as one of several Asian wars of decolonization that began during World War II and continued during the Cold War. A reference that puts the Korean War in its Cold War context and provides some guidance for research, Michael Kort's *The Columbia Guide to the Cold War* combines history, encyclopedia entries, bibliographical assessments, and other reference tools. Its Korean War and Korean-U.S. relations entries represent much Western scholarship on Asia: insensitive, erroneous, superficial, and limited. It focuses almost completely on U.S.-USSR conflict and accommodation. Bruce Cumings's work gets one citation and no discussion in the annotated bibliography. There is no mention of Korean scholarship on the war. It reveals all the limitations of the Eurocentric Cold War paradigm as the framework for understanding the wars of decolonization.

Although many scholars now view the Korean War as an internationalized civil war, they surrender the legitimacy argument to the anticolonial revisionists. The urge to blame the Americans and the Korean political elite for all the subsequent ills of Korean politics at least puts Korean politics back into the causes of the war. For an indictment of U.S. and UN intentions and the conduct of the war, Jon Halliday and Bruce Cumings's *The Unknown War: Korea* set the pace. Their sympathy for Korea's plight is admirable, but their tilt toward leftist Koreans as helpless victims is not. Several British authors have written significant books also critical of the American conduct of the war: David Rees, *Korea: The Limited War*; Callum MacDonald, *Korea: The War Before Vietnam*; and Max Hastings, *The Korean War*. Rosemary Foot's *The Wrong War: American Policy and the Dimensions of the Korean Conflict* continues with selective detail the British tradition of special criticism of American policy. Gavan McCormack, in *Cold War, Hot War*, gives the anti-U.S. account an Australian twist. In *The Korean War*, Peter Lowe provides an account of the war's origins and gives the United States low marks for dealing with Korea. To put the British critique in historical perspective, however, one should consult the contemporaneous reports of the British diplomatic mission to the Republic of Korea—now preserved in the Foreign Office File 371 (Korea), Public Record Office, London—as printed in Robert Jarman, ed., *Korea: Political and Economic Reports, 1882–1970*. In this new (2005) fourteen-volume document collection, volumes 10 and 11 cover the 1945–53 reports. The collection also includes U.S. documents and a selection of Parliamentary Papers. As one would suspect, the professional diplomats' reports are balanced, judicious, qualified, and accurate, especially as critiques of American and ROK relationships. On the ground, British diplomats agreed that inaction often seemed preferable to such "action options" as overthrowing Syngman Rhee.

Although the British revisionists appear to hold the historical field in criticizing the American political and strategic direction of the Korean War, they do not displace the British government's official two-volume history of the war prepared by Gen. Sir Anthony Farrar-Hockley, GBE, KCB, DSO, MC with Bar, *The British Part in the Korean War.* A model of its type, this encyclopedic work covers coalition decision making at the highest levels to combat on the Korean battlefields with ease and clarity. Its only limitation is its scant attention to the South Korean perspective. Farrar-Hockley, however, provides exceptional insight into the North Korean and Chinese view of the war, rooted no doubt in his unhappy stay with the enemy as a POW (1951–53) while serving as an officer in the ill-fated 1st Battalion, the Gloucestershire Regiment. Although sympathetic to the United Nations Command, Farrar-Hockley is no apologist for American military and political leadership, but he does not treat the allies as dim-witted or malevolent. Both volumes—*A Distant Obligation* and *An Honourable Discharge*—are especially noteworthy for their maps, photographs, and appendixes.

The first significant American jeremiad is I. F. Stone's *The Hidden History of the Korean War, 1950–51.* He discovers an unholy alliance of "Asia Firsters" in Washington, Asian tyrants abroad, economic royalists everywhere, and power-crazed diplomats and soldiers in every important capital except Moscow and Beijing. His thesis finds more sophisticated restatement in Michael Hogan's *Cross of Iron: Harry S. Truman and the Origins of the National Security State, 1945–1954*, which argues that Truman's "national security state" made the war inevitable since it needed a crisis to militarize containment and assert its authority. The military companion to Stone's work is T. R. Fehrenbach's *This Kind of War: A Study of Unpreparedness*, a critique of what Fehrenbach considered "permissive" American societal effects on the postwar army. The U.S. Army reprinted this book in 1993 with its errors and misrepresentations intact. More recent books in a similar genre—Bevin Alexander, *Korea: The First War We Lost*; Joseph Goulden, *Korea: The Untold Story*; and Stanley Weintraub, *MacArthur's War: Korea and the Undoing of an American Hero*—are all written by veterans who remain unhappy with the war. Richard Thornton, in *Odd Man Out: Truman, Stalin, Mao, and the Origins of the Korean War*, circles back to I. F. Stone's position, internationalized. Thornton argues Stalin and Truman entrapped Kim Il-sung and Mao Zedong in a grand scheme to start and sustain a war in a region where both the superpowers would not risk a larger war but could advance their global agenda for hegemony at China's expense. Thornton's barrage of assertions range from penetrating to confusing to laughable, but his book is worth some willing suspension of disbelief—but not much. To put the Korean War in its regional context, see Rosemary Foot's *The Practice of Power: U.S. Relations with China Since 1949* and editors Warren Cohen and Akira Iriye's *The Great Powers in East Asia, 1953–1960*.

Two recent studies of American security policy establish a more detailed, measured, and sympathetic scholarly basis for examining the Truman administration's Asia policy before and during the war: Melvyn Leffler's *A Preponderance of Power: National Security, the Truman Administration, and the Cold War* and William Stueck's *The Korean War: An International History*. Probably influenced by the Soviet Union's disintegration, Leffler and Stueck maintain America's commitment to Korea is essential to making forward collective defense a credible part of containment. They also believe the Truman administration hoped the United Nations would be influential in managing the inevitable wars of decolonization of the 1950s. Stueck extends and refines his analysis in *Rethinking the Korean War: A New Diplomatic and Strategic History* and in an edited anthology of conference papers, *The Korean War in World History*. Neither Leffler nor Stueck is an apologist for the Truman administration, and both find little to admire in its China policy. Like most American diplomatic historians, they attribute to the United States more power and responsibility than most administrations believe they exercise. Burton Kaufman's *The Korean War: Challenges in Crisis, Credibility, and Command* and *The Korean Conflict* are useful guides to the Truman administration's conduct of the war. Though Glenn Paige now denounces American intervention, in *The Korean Decision: June 24–30,* he dependably reconstructs the decision to save the Republic of Korea.

Anthologies of informed essays and personal testimony also introduce the causes and conduct of the Korean War. The best are Francis Heller, ed., *The Korean War: A 25-Year Perspective*; James Matray and Kim Chull-baum, eds., *Korea and the Cold War*; Nagai Yonosuke and Akira Iriye, eds., *The Origins of the Cold War in Asia*; Korean War Research Committee, comp., *The Historical Reillumination of the Korean War*; James Cotton and Ian Neary, eds., *The Korean War as History*; Lee Chai-jin, ed., *The Korean War: 40-Year Perspective*; William Williams, ed., *A Revolutionary War: Korea and the Transformation of the Postwar World*; Daniel Meador, ed., *The Korean War in Retrospect: Lessons for the Future* (papers from a University of Virginia 1990 conference); and "The Impact of the Korean War," from a special issue of *The Journal of American-East Asian Relations* 3 (Spring 1993). *America's Wars in Asia: A Cultural Approach to History and Memory*, edited by Steven Levine and Jackie Hiltz, is a collection of essays that tries to find links in America's Asian wars and the perceptions of the Japanese, Koreans, and Chinese.

As Stalin and Mao recognized, Japan, technically still an occupied supplicant for a peace treaty, served as an undeclared belligerent in the war as America's junior partner for basing and logistics. Japanese historians have been explaining this role ever since, usually from a critical position. The basic studies are Masao Okonogi, *Chosen Senso: Beikokee no Kainyu Katei (The Korean War: The Process of U.S. Intervention)*; Ryo Hagiwara, *The Korean War: The Conspiracies by Kim Il-sung and MacArthur*; and Wada Haruki, *Chosen Senso (The Korean War)*, which is available in Korean but not in English. For a short but comprehensive discussion of Japan and the war, see William F. Nimms, ed., "The Occupation of Japan: The Impact of the Korean War," symposium, *Proceedings*, October 16–17, 1986, MacArthur Foundation, Norfolk, Virginia. The scholarship is reviewed in Sakurai Hiroshi, "A Survey: Studies on the Korean War in Japan," *Social Science Japan Journal* (1998): 85–99.

Assuming the fullness and openness of American official documents and the major collections of the Harry S. Truman and Dwight D. Eisenhower papers at their respective presidential libraries, one might conclude the American conduct of the war has been covered. Certainly the body of Korean War literature from the American perspective is impressive. Truman's own selective version of events is found in his two-volume *Memoirs*. Truman biographies are uneven in their treatment of the war: David McCullough, *Truman*; Robert Donovan, *Tumultuous Years: The Presidency of Harry S. Truman*; Richard Haynes, *The Awesome Power: Harry S. Truman as Commander in Chief*; Robert Ferrell, *Harry S. Truman and the Modern American Presidency*; Donald McCoy, *The Presidency of Harry S. Truman*; Alonzo Hamby, *Man of the People: The Life of Harry S. Truman*; and Dennis Wainstock, *Truman, MacArthur and the Korean War*. Arnold Offner, in *Another Such Victory: President Truman and the Cold War, 1945–1953*, gives the president low marks as a diplomat and unfairly accuses him of ignoring his advisers. None of these books exhausts the subject of Truman and the war.

The impact of the Korean War on American politics is important but elusive because of the influence of other Cold War events with tenuous connections to the war. Some of the more successful efforts to link Korea to American domestic life are Lisle Rose's *The Cold War Comes to Main Street: America in 1950*, Paul Pierpaoli's *Truman and Korea: The Political Culture of the Early Cold War*, Paul Edwards's *To Acknowledge a War: The Korean War in American Memory*, and Robert Caridi's *The Korean War and American Politics*.

Secretary of State Dean Acheson provided his personal interpretation of the war in *Present at the Creation* and in an abridged account, *The Korean War*. The standard biography of Acheson is Gaddis Smith's *Dean Acheson*, which is the sixteenth volume in the American Secretaries of State and Their Diplomacy series, but it should be supplemented with Ronald McGlothlen's *Controlling the Waves: Dean Acheson and U.S. Foreign Policy in Asia*. Other diplomats' accounts include memoirs by U. Alexis Johnson, Harold J. Noble, Dean Rusk, Ellis Briggs, John M. Allison, Charles E. "Chip" Bohlen, Robert Murphy, Paul H. Nitze, and George Kennan.

The Department of State's institutional participation may be gleaned from documents published in *The Foreign Relations of the United States* series, a standing though controversial publications program. National Security Council declassified documents are contained in the National Security Archive at George Washington University, Washington, D.C., as well as at the Truman Library in Independence, Missouri. The Truman papers provide some interesting materials that scholars have not fully exploited in examining Washington's diplomacy during the war because they are not published in the appropriate volumes of *Foreign Relations*. The key figures in building a historical record for the war's conduct were Dean Acheson and George M. Elsey. Preparing to write his memoirs after leaving office, Acheson had his private staff collect documents (some of them originals) on the Korean War. Not surprisingly, the Truman-MacArthur controversy, dealings with the allies and the Rhee regime, and the armistice negotiations get the most attention. This special "Korean War file" also served Truman in writing his memoirs. Acheson then conducted a running debrief of his closest associates in a seminar conducted at Princeton University from 1953 to 1955, and his papers contain their complete transcripts and supporting documents. In addition, Acheson had his former staff members screen the drafts of his memoir chapters for security and discretion problems, which were many. The commentary, omitted excerpts, and more documents are found in Acheson's book notes. Although Acheson's papers contain no surprises, they reveal a president who had grave difficulty in making decisions, who often said and did things that required extensive damage control, and whose reputation for strong leadership should be shared by his personal and executive department staffs.

George Elsey spent World War II (1942–47) as a navy officer assigned to the White House map center and operations room then remained as a presidential special assistant until 1951. Winning President Truman's complete confidence, he became the president's personal administrative assistant from 1949 to 1951 and became the human "fly on the wall" for Truman's Korean War decision making. Elsey's documents and conversation records were matched only by those of Acheson's Boswell, Ambassador Philip Jessup, a famous international lawyer and accomplished historian. Elsey maintained the White House's Korean War subject files, some in his own papers, but most are preserved in the various collections associated with President Truman's personal office. Elsey also assembled the Korean War documents from the State and Defense Departments. He also supervised the creation of the NSC's files (1947–53) for the president's use. They were transferred to the CIA in 1953 but recovered in 1981. Elsey also ensured that the Psychological Strategy Board, established in 1951, kept complete records.

For personal and procedural reasons, Truman felt overwhelmed in dealing with the collective expertise and experience of the Joint Chiefs of Staff and their service staffs. Truman solved part of the problem by appointing General Marshall as

Secretary of Defense Louis Johnson's replacement, teamed with Robert A. Lovett as deputy secretary and who later became Marshall's able replacement (1951–53). Truman attacked the problem of analysis from the field by sending to the Far East a personal representative, Maj. Gen. Frank E. Lowe, a reserve officer whom Truman trusted from their World War II association. Lowe's reports, which covered August 1950 to March 1951, are preserved at the Truman Library and provide telling commentary of the U.S. Army's problems in the Far East. Lowe also collected and saved detailed reports for all the Far East Command's service components. Lowe's critical reports are verified by independent assessments by teams from the U.S. Army Field Forces headquarters and the Defense Department's Weapons Systems Evaluation Group.

The Eisenhower administration brought considerably more military experience to the Oval Office, but it also brought considerable historical baggage that Eisenhower and Secretary of State John Foster Dulles did their best to obfuscate. In 1950 both of them—on the record—had endorsed the Korean intervention, and both of them had served the Truman administration in 1950–51 when the war took its basic shape. In truth, they had no better solution to the war than Truman's options: build up the Republic of Korea with military and economic assistance, maintain the United Nations Command's military pressure, string out the armistice negotiations, and hope something would turn up. The definitive account of the Eisenhower security policy may be found in *Waging Peace*, written by Robert Bowie and Richard Immerman, the State Department's policy planning director and NSC representative (1953–57) and the biographer of John Foster Dulles, respectively. Although both administrations periodically examined the theoretical option of using nuclear weapons, they found little to gain in nuclear escalation and much to lose, a view supported by the Joint Chiefs of Staff. The supposed influence of the fuzzy nuclear threats of 1953 were largely imagined but still useful in supporting the strategic concept of massive retaliation and the deployment of new tactical nuclear weapons to NATO. Although recent books on airpower in Korea touch the nuclear issue, the most complete accounts are in journal literature: Daniel Calingaert, "Nuclear Weapons and the Korean War," *Journal of Strategic Studies* 11 (June 1988): 177–202; Roger Dingman, "Atomic Diplomacy During the Korean War," *International Security* 13 (Winter 1988–89): 50–91; Rosemary Foot, "Nuclear Coercion and the Ending of the Korean Conflict," *International Security* 13 (Winter 1988–89): 92–112; and Edward Keefer, "President Dwight D. Eisenhower and the End of the Korean War," *Diplomatic History* 10 (Summer 1986): 267–89.

The dialogue between the Eisenhower administration and Syngman Rhee can be found in the two *Foreign Relations* volumes for *Korea, 1952–1954*, and in the correspondence files in the Eisenhower Presidential Papers at Abilene, Kansas, and the John Foster Dulles papers at the Princeton University Library. The private letters restore the influence of personality and contingency to the politics of armistice making in 1953. Dulles, for example, emerges as a key conciliator between Rhee and Eisenhower. So, too, does General Clark, Eisenhower's friend and the UN and American theater commander in 1952–53. Although Clark preferred an imposed settlement, he recognized the military costs would be exorbitant and that a pre-armistice security arrangement with Rhee was essential to ensuring a workable armistice. He insisted it should be part of a postwar alliance system in north Asia that included Japan. Clark's correspondence on Korea is preserved in the Eisenhower Library as well as in the Clark collection at The Citadel in Charleston, South Carolina. Of course, Eisenhower's National Security Council secretariat maintained copious relevant records, and although some intelligence and nuclear matters remain classified, at least some are subject to review for declassification.

Regarding the Korean War's conduct, the official histories now offer a relatively consistent and detailed account of the war as viewed from the United Nations Command and the Far East Command, with the first being a coalition headquarters, the second the joint American theater command, and both almost interchangeable. These histories provide what cultural historians call "the agreed-upon narrative" or a consensus history. See, for example, three key works: Doris Condit, *The Test of War, 1950–1953*, which is the second volume in the *History of the Office of the Secretary of Defense* (OSD) series; James Schnabel and Robert Watson, *The Korean War*, which is the third volume in *The Joint Chiefs of Staff and National Policy*, reissued in 1998 by the JCS Joint History Office in a more polished format; and Schnabel, *United States Army in the Korean War: Policy and Direction—The First Year.*

Examinations of American military leadership in the Korean War tend to focus on General MacArthur and his disagreements with Harry Truman over the conduct of the war. The focus shifts in 1951 to General Ridgway's dynamic leadership in putting the fight back in the U.S. Eighth Army. In *The Forgotten War: America in Korea, 1950–1953*, Clay Blair plumbs the problems of command in the Eighth Army and X Corps, but the quality of American military leadership deserves more searching analysis. Walker's accidental death in December 1950 ensured he would be a scapegoat—and was so identified by

MacArthur's staff and Ridgway, as mean-spirited an American officer as ever wore stars when it came to criticizing his peers. Moreover, JCS chairman Omar N. Bradley and U.S. Army chief of staff J. Lawton Collins wore Teflon uniforms for much of the war and put the onus of misjudgments on MacArthur and Walker. As commander in chief Far East (CINCFE), MacArthur, in fact, seldom planned any major operation without Washington's prior knowledge, although he sometimes started an operation before he received formal approval. Neither Bradley nor Collins wanted to challenge him, as he knew.

Douglas MacArthur stands in the center of American military leadership, and his definitive biography is D. Clayton James's *The Years of MacArthur.* See especially James's third and final volume, *Triumph and Disaster, 1945–1964,* but supplement it with Clayton James and Anne Sharp Wells's, *Refighting the Last War: Command and Crisis of Korea, 1950–1953,* and with Roy Flint's "The Tragic Flaw: MacArthur, the Joint Chiefs and the Korean War," a doctoral dissertation. MacArthur's charismatic personality and Victorian style drew a share of hypnotized admirers, among the first rank the general himself. MacArthur's own *Reminiscences* carries on the hagiographic tradition established in Courtney Whitney's *MacArthur: His Rendezvous with Destiny.* On the side of responsible demythologizing, the place to start is Michael Schaller's *Douglas MacArthur: The Far Eastern General* and Trumbull Higgins's *Korea and the Fall of MacArthur.* Hugh Baillie, the UP bureau chief for Asia, had ample opportunity to observe MacArthur since he shared some of CINCFE's political views and thus received special access to "El Supremo." His memoir included sharp commentary on MacArthur's lifestyle and habits of command. In his classic *The Truman-MacArthur Controversy and the Korean War,* John Spanier believed he saw a civil-military relations problem that transcended personalities in the inevitable conflict between a theater commander and Washington. Several more regional wars have produced more tensions and personality conflicts but have prompted no fundamental change in civilian control of the armed forces.

Other army leaders tell their stories in various mixes of biography, autobiography, and history. See, for example, J. Lawton Collins, *War in Peacetime*; Matthew B. Ridgway, *The Korean War*; Forrest Pogue, *George C. Marshall,* vol. 4, *Statesman, 1945–1959*; Omar Bradley and Clay Blair, *A General's Life*; Wilson Heefner, *Patton's Bulldog: The Life and Service of General Walton H. Walker*; Paul Braim, *The Will to Win: The Life of General James Van Fleet*; and Mark Clark, *From the Danube to the Yalu.* One essential review of MacArthur's generalship and American policy from 1950 to 1951 is found in U.S. Congress, Senate, Committees on Armed Forces and Foreign Relations, *Military Situation in the Far East* (5 vols. ["parts"], 82d Cong., 1st sess., 1951), available through the Government Printing Office and reproduced as a five-volume commercial publication by Arno Press in 1979.

Convinced of the value of their historical studies during and after World War II, the American armed forces mounted field history programs, interviewed senior officers, and produced documentary and internal-use histories that served as the foundation for the official history publications series and private authors' unsponsored histories. Scholarly Resources, Inc., has published on microfilm four sets of documents: U.S. Army historical studies and supporting documents done during the war over virtually every aspect of the conflict, the interim evaluation reports done for the commander of the Pacific Fleet and the Marine division and aircraft wing, documents and reports preserved by the Department of State on Korea from 1950 to 1954, and the documents that the UN military observers and the Military Armistice Commission collected from 1951 to 1954. University Publications of America has produced a similar collection on microfiche of unpublished histories and after-action reports the Far East Command's military history office, directed by Dr. Gordon Prange, collected during and shortly after the Korean War. These studies' sources are largely the participants themselves, and the office supplemented their interviews with U.S. Army records.

The international scope of the UN effort included combat service by units from fifteen UN member nations in addition to that of the United States. In addition to General Farrar-Hockley's history of British participation in the Korean War, almost all the members of the United Nations Command published histories. Of the European participants, only the French Army (somewhat distracted by a war in Indochina) did not produce an official history of its battalion's participation. The archives of the Service Historique de l'Armée de Terre in Vincennes, however, hold many relevant reports, including "lessons learned" reports from Col. Ralph Monclar, who was in actuality Général de Corps d'Armée Raoul Charles Magrin-Vernerey, an officer of the Foreign Legion and a former Free French combat commander. "Monclar" went to Korea to oversee French participation. By October 1951 he had submitted 809 separate reports. The British Commonwealth's military experience provides the most accessible account of service with the Eighth Army with muted criticism of the high command. The newest treatment is Michael Hickey's *The Korean War: The West Confronts Communism, 1950–1953*, which also provides an overview of the whole war. It complements C. N. Barclay, *The First Commonwealth Division: The Story of British Commonwealth Land Forces in Korea, 1950–1953.* Other accounts include Robert O'Neill, *Australia in the Korean War*; Herbert Wood, *Strange Battleground: The Official History of the Canadian Army in Korea*; Historical Section, General Staff, Canadian Army, *Canada's Army in Korea*; and Jeffrey Grey, *The Commonwealth Armies and the Korean War.* An ambitious and successful effort to integrate national history and the war is Ian McGibbon, *New Zealand and the Korean War.* In *The Diplomacy of Constraint: Canada, the Korean War, and the United States,* Dennis Stairs offers a Canadian perspective on the conduct of the war. David Bercuson, in *Blood on the Hills: The Canadian Army in the Korean War,* fuses operational history with extensive interviews and research with personal papers into a definitive account of Canadian operations.

The official histories of the European ground forces are History Section, Department of the Army, *The Greek Expeditionary Force in Korea (1950–1955)*; History Division, General Staff, *The Battles of the Turkish Armed Forces in the Korean War, 1950–1953*; M. D. Schaafsma, *The Dutch Detachment of the United Nations in Korea, 1950–1954*; and J. P. Gahide, *Belgium and the Korean War*, which complements the history-memoir from B. E. M. Crahay, the first battalion commander. The experience of the Philippine Battalion Combat Team (actually four different teams rotated to the Eighth Army) is scattered in reports on file with the Military Historical Activities Division, Office of the Adjutant General, Army of the Philippines; in the memoirs of Gen. Dionisio S. Ojeda; and in Lily Ann Polo's *A Cold War Alliance: Philippine–South Korean Relations, 1948–1971.* Other unit histories include Alberto Ruiz

Novoa, *El Batallion Colombia en Korea, 1951–1954*; Thor Thorgrimsson and E. C. Russell, *Canadian Naval Operations in Korean Waters, 1950–1955*; Kimon Skordiles, *Kagnew: The Story of the Ethiopian Fighters in Korea*; and Snit Satyasnguan et al., *The Thai Battalion in Korea*. These volumes provide a human dimension by including several oral histories and individual memoirs.

The U.S. Eighth Army appreciated its allied soldiers, and foreign veterans often participate in reunions held by their parent regiments and divisions. However, a study based on interviews of U.S. senior officers revealed persistent problems. According to the foreign soldiers' complaints, the major issues were unsuitable clothing and food, strange weapons, and tactical practices, while the U.S. officers observed poor maintenance, too much radio chitchat, and officer overstaffing. These issues are discussed in Military History Section (MHS), Headquarters, Far East Command, "History of the Korean War—Interallied Cooperation During Combat Operations" (1952, Dean Historical Center), and Benjamin Franklin Cooling III, "Allied Interoperability in the Korean War," *Military Review* 63 (June, 1983): 26–32.

Senior officers of the allied contingents left their own personal accounts and private papers in their central national military archives, at least in the English-speaking world. These records are the most accessible. A partial sample is:

Imperial War Museum (London, England)
Gen. Sir Michael M. A. R. West
Maj. Gen. Basil A. Coad
Maj. Gen. J. F. M. MacDonald
Maj. Gen. J. H. S. Majury

Kings College, University of London (London)
Adm. Sir William G. Andrewes
Lt. Gen. William G. H. Pike
Rear Adm. A. S. Bolt

Canadian National Archives (Ottawa, Ontario)
Gen. Jacques Dextraze
Gen. J. V. Allard
Maj. Gen. J. M. Rockingham
Maj. Gen. J. R. Stone

Australian War Memorial (Canberra, Australian Capital Territory)
Gen. John G. N. Wilton

Alexander Turnbull Library (Wellington, NZ)
Sir Sidney G. Holland, prime minister

Part of the United Nations Command's mission included supporting the Korean economy or at least attacking its worst problems. Most American civil affairs work had to focus on relief and refugee problems, not long-term developmental issues. Jurisdictional disputes between the Far East Command and the United Nations Korean Reconstruction Agency (UNKRA) did not help. Gene Lyons, in *Military Policy and Economic Aid: The Korean Case, 1950–1953,* introduces the problems from the perspective of the UNKRA, whose records are held by the United Nations. The United Nations Civil Assistance Command Korea (UNCACK), part of the Eighth Army's records (Record Group [RG] 338), holds records of the U.S. military's perspective. Covering 1950–51 and written in

1952, the command history is History Section, FECOM Head-quarters, "Civil Affairs/ Civil Assistance Problems," in volume 3 of *History of the Korean War,* and continued by J-5, FECOM/ UNC, *United Nations Command Civil Assistance and Economic Affairs—Korea* (1953). UNCACK's work is assessed in two studies by the Operations Research Office (ORO): Henry A. Kissinger and C. Darwin Stolzenbach, "Civil Affairs in Korea, 1950–1951," TM ORO-T-184, 1952; and Jo Fisher Freeman and Ralph McCabe, "Economic Support of Military Operations in Underdeveloped Countries," TM ORO-T-329, 1955.

To the degree the Korean economy survived and the UNC war effort succeeded depended on the logistical expertise of the U.S. Army. The definitive study—a four-volume manuscript history—is from Headquarters, FECOM and Eighth Army (Rear), "Logistics in the Korean War Operations," 1955, and is available in army libraries in the United States and Korea. The Yongsan copy is File 500.004. This work extends Headquarters, Eighth Army, "Logistical Problems and Their Solutions," 1952, and combat service support command reports that are available in the Frank Lowe Papers in the Truman Library. The Operations Research Office contributed Robert O. Shreve et al., "Combat Zone Logistics in Korea," TM ORO -T-15 (FECOM), November 1951; and R. B. Black, W. A. Taylor, and William Neilson, "An Evaluation of Service Support in the Korean Campaign," ORO TM-T-6 (FECOM), March 1951. Although logistical matters are integrated into all the services' general histories of the Korean War, the army is the only service to focus on the matériel aspects of the war. The best place to start the study of the Korean War's matériel mobilization is in Terrence Gough's *U.S. Army Mobilization and Logistics in the Korean War.* The medical experience may be found in Albert E. Cowdrey, *The Medic's War*. Logistics are described in James Huston, *Outposts and Allies: U.S. Army Logistics in the Cold War, 1945–1953*. Huston also wrote a more detailed account of the combat theater, *Guns and Butter, Powder and Rice: U.S. Army Logistics in the Korean War*. In an earlier study, *Combat Support in Korea,* John Westover collects case studies of varied logistical challenges.

Of all the residual issues that emerge from Korean War history, none is more incendiary than the related subjects of casualties, prisoners of war, atrocities, and missing-in-action cases. Despite the fact that American accounting becomes more precise all the time through the outstanding work of the U.S. Joint POW/MIA Accounting Command, the MIA issue festers on in the public mind, fed by demagogy, hope, and delusion. Except for the Russians, the Communist side is still not helpful. Formal interim reports, such as *Personnel Recovery and Accounting* and *The Effort to Account for U.S. Servicemen Missing From the Korean War*, are available from the Defense POW/Missing Personnel Office (Department of Defense, 2000). The National Archives and Records Administration scooped the services with *American Prisoners of War and Missing-in-Action Personnel From the Korean War and During the Cold War Era* (NARA, 1997). The breakthrough study was Paul Cole's *POW/MIA Issues;* volume 1 is *The Korean War* (RAND/National Defense Research Institute, 1994), which set off a closer scrutiny of the official statistic that 54,000 Americans died (all causes) in the Korean War. In 2000 the Department of Defense confessed this number, habitually used on monuments and in books and speeches, was wrong. The total number of deaths in the North Asia theater, for all services and all causes, was actually 36,616 as tallied in 2000. This figure gets annual adjustments; it is now 36,574.

Statistical realism started with a forgotten source of the forgotten war: the Office of the Surgeon General, Department of the Army, *Battle Casualties and Medical Statistics: U.S. Army Experience in the Korean War,* which is available on-line at koreanwar-educator.org. For another detailed analysis, see also Frederick W. Cleaver, "U.S. Army Battle Casualties in Korea," TM ORO-T-71 (AFFE), 1956. The other services' casualties were not a statistical issue.

Because it became linked to war crimes—charged by both sides—the POW issue poisoned the 1951–53 armistice negotiations and remains contentious. The terms of the armistice (July 27, 1953) rendered the issue moot. POWs eventually chose repatriation or non-repatriation, allowing them to escape prosecution. Basically, then, each belligerent coalition could prosecute its own service personnel for misbehavior but not hold enemy POWs for trial. For all the ink spilled on the POW and MIA issue, no book provides the wealth of information and clear-headed analysis as the unpublished histories: MIS, Headquarters, UNC and FECOM, "The Communist War in POW Camps," January 1953, copies, Van Fleet Papers and RG 550; Headquarters, U.S. Army Pacific, "The Handling of Prisoners of War During the Korean War," June 1950, File 350.209, Eighth Army Reference Files, Dean Historical Center, Yongsan; U.S. Army Security Center, "U.S. Prisoners of War in the Korean Operation," 1954, File 350.207-2, also in RG 550; and War Crimes Division, Judge Advocate General (JAG), Communications Zone Korea, "Final Historical and Operational Report," 1954—with extensive appendixes on war crimes, crime sites, suspects, victims, witnesses, and investigative reports— Records of the Judge Advocate General Section, Eighth Army, RG 338. Most printed and on-line Korean War bibliographies have extensive POW and MIA listings, especially memoirs, which must be used with care.

The United Nations' role tends to be unappreciated since American money and forces—joined to the people of South Korea—certainly shaped the UN participation. Nevertheless, the General Assembly and Security Council, especially after June and July 1950, did not rubber-stamp American initiatives. Some nations exercised influence well out of proportion to their national power, including India, Canada, Australia, France, Sweden, Switzerland, and Great Britain. The Soviet Bloc of the USSR and its Warsaw Pact allies also made Lake Success, New York—the Security Council's home until 1951— a battleground of sorts. Meanwhile, UN political, military, and relief workers on the ground provided parallel reporting that did not grant the United Nations Command immunity from accountability. The place to begin assessing the United Nations' role is Rosalyn Higgins, ed., *United Nations Peacekeeping, 1946–1967: Documents and Commentary,* but the original documents (bound or on microfilm) may be found in the UN's *The Official Records: General Assembly,* organized by session. Each assembly session also published reports, which, for Korea, included the report of the United Nations Commission on Korea. The UN Department of Public Information also published *Weekly Bulletin* and the bimonthly *Bulletin,* as well as an annual *Yearbook.* The U.S. Department of State also published UN documents through an International Organization and Conference series. For secondary works, consult Tae-ho Yoo, *The Korean War and the United Nations: A Legal and Diplomatic History* and Leon Gordenker, *The United Nations and the Peaceful Unification of Korea: The Politics of Field Operations, 1947–1950.* UN secretary general Trygve Lie wrote a memoir, *In the Cause of Peace,* that centered on the Korean War. More interesting than often assumed, the UNC commander (CINCUNC)—meaning Generals MacArthur, Ridgway, and Clark—submitted reports to the United Nations (through the State Department) twice a month. As might be expected the *Foreign Relations of the United States* series for 1945 through 1954 contains many UN-related documents in its Korean War–related volumes.

On the surface the armistice negotiations had little to do with the United Nations, but as the State Department hammered out negotiating positions in Washington, the diplomats carried on tutorials and discussions that included UN representatives as well as the diplomats accredited to the United States. Often their focus is too tight on Kaesong and Panmunjom. Sydney Bailey, in *The Korean Armistice,* helps adjust for this distortion as does Rosemary Foot in *A Substitute for Victory: The Politics of Peacemaking at the Korean Armistice Talks.* The UN shaped the "greater sanctions" and POW issues and eventually determined much of the POW repatriation process. The best-known American perspective on the armistice talks is *Negotiating While Fighting: The Diary of Admiral C. Turner Joy at the Korean Armistice Conference* edited by Allen Goodman. Joy hated his assignment, however, and made little effort to develop an appropriate negotiating style or to master the issues, as he revealed in *How Communists Negotiate.* A better guide is *Panmunjom: The Story of the Korean Military Armistice Negotiations,* written by William Vatcher, an army reserve officer and academic political scientist who became part of the UNC delegation. Even more definitive is the expert analysis of the staff judge advocate for the delegation and legendary expert in international law, Col. Howard S. Levie, JAG, USA

(Ret.), "The Korean Armistice Agreement and Its After Math," *Naval Law Review* 41 (1993): 115–33. Michael Schmitt and Leslie Green memorialized Colonel and Professor Levie in a collection of his works, *Levie on the Law of War,* which includes essays on POWs and war crimes.

The armistice negotiations, of course, opened a gap in the cooperation between the United Nations Command and Syngman Rhee, whose politics still included the "march north for liberation" strategy. Whether Rhee really wanted more war or just wanted to be bought off to accept an armistice remains uncertain, but Rhee's experience is reconstructed from the archival sources of Yonsei University's Institute for Modern Korean Studies in Stephen Kim, *Master of Manipulation: Syngman Rhee and the Seoul-Washington Alliance, 1953–1960.* Rhee's foreign minister, the aggressive Pyun Yong-tae, left a memoir of his part in Rhee's resistance movement, *Korea: My Country.* His role is also reconstructed in Barton J. Bernstein, "Syngman Rhee: The Pawn as Rook—The Struggle to End the Korean War," *Bulletin of Concerned Asian Scholars* 10 (1978): 40–45. Another comprehensive analysis appears in Donald W. Boose, Jr., "The Korean War Truce Talks: A Study in Conflict Termination," *Parameters* 30 (Spring 2000): 102–116.

An extensive, highly detailed, and competently annotated history of the armistice negotiations that seems to have escaped Korean War historians' attention is part of the theater command's "History of the Korean Conflict," which is the work of FECOM/UNC's Military History Section. The manuscript, "Korean Armistice Negotiations," is divided into five volumes of narrative with many messages and letters reprinted in full: armistice negotiations, July 1951–May 1952, in two volumes; armistice negotiations, May 1952–July 1953, in two volumes;

and a separate volume on U.S.-ROK relations, May 1952–
July 1953, perhaps the study's most interesting part. It also
includes three volumes of documents, photographs, and maps
from the UNC negotiating staff and FECOM intelligence
sources. The history begins as a contemporaneous account of
the 1951–52 negotiations, the account completed in September 1952. In June 1953 General Clark, as CINCUNC, ordered that the MHS assume control of the 1952–53 history.
The study was completed in March 1955, classified "top secret," and reproduced in six complete copies. In 1977–78, at
least the copy in the historical office of the chairman of the
Joint Chiefs of Staff (CJCS) was declassified. The principal
author of the 1951–52 volumes, James F. Schnable, became
the coauthor of the JCS official history of the Korean War,
drawing on the manuscript and the JCS-CINCUNC message
traffic. The manuscript history is still more useful because it
includes critical documents from the White House, the State
Department, the ROK government, and CINCUNC-UNC
negotiating chief, Lt. Gen. William K. Harrison, USA. Many
of these documents appeared in abridged form in the State
Department's official history: *Foreign Relations of the United
States, 1952–1954,* volume 15 (in two parts) *Korea* (Government Printing Office, 1984). The most accessible copy of "Korean Armistice Negotiations" is in the NARA archival files of
the Joint Chiefs of Staff, RG 218.

The post-armistice actions, dictated by the agreement, fell
into several categories. The Demilitarized Zone's creation has
received the least attention, but it can be reconstructed from
1953–54 reports of the Swiss and Swedish members of the
Neutral Nations Supervisory Commission (NNSC) and preserved as part of the United Nations' document archival

system. The controversial system of POW exchange can be seen from the UNC perspective in "The UNCREG [UNC Repatriation Group] Story," a 1954 manuscript history with supporting documents written and collected by Sgt. Jack Tykal, USA (1952–54), a historian for UNCREG, Panmunjom, September–December 1953. Tykal donated all his UNCREG records to the U.S. Army Military History Institute in 1999. The experience of the Custodial Force India—the "protecting power" in legal language and the key member of the five-nation Neutral Nations Repatriation Commission—may be found in the account of its commander, Gen. K. S. Thimayya, *Experiment in Neutrality* (New Delhi: Vision Books, 1981), the core of which is General Thimayya's report and personal notes on his service with the NNRC. S. N. Prasad also wrote an official history: *History of the Custodian Force (India) in Korea, 1953–1954.*

As provided by the armistice agreement, the war's major belligerents met in Geneva, Switzerland, in April through June 1954 for a "political" negotiation on the divided Korea's future. Although not official "participants" in the war, the Soviet Union and India sent representatives, with the first group considered essential and the second was a tolerated nuisance because of India's leadership of the "neutral nations" bloc. Of the combatant nations, only South Africa did not send someone to the diplomatic-propaganda circus in Geneva. Since the United States and the Republic of Korea refused much contact with the Chinese and North Koreans, most of the conference's meetings were organized by British foreign minister Sir Anthony Eden and Soviet foreign minister V. I. Molotov. The issues, however, proved intractable, even to the diplomatic elite of 1954. The conference tried to link an all-Korea, UN-supervised election and the withdrawal of foreign troops, anathema to the South Koreans. The U.S. account of the conference is the State Department's *Korean Problem at the Geneva Conference, April 26–June 15, 1954,* but Bailey's and Foot's books provide sound chapters on the conference. Conference documents may be found in volumes 15 and 16 of the 1952–1954 edition of *Foreign Relations of the United States* and a British Foreign Office publication, *Documents Relating to the Discussion of Korea . . . at the Geneva Conference.* For a competent treatment that stresses Canada's role, consult Graeme Mount and André Laferriere's *The Diplomacy of War: The Case of Korea.* The Geneva Conference, which shifted to dealing with the French defeat in Indochina, marked the unfinished end of the Korean War. The divided Korea remained the site of future international crises.

5 FIGHTING THE KOREAN WAR

Fought so close behind the hecatomb of World War II and pitting opponents of different levels of technological sophistication, the Korean War became hard to distinguish from its global predecessor. From the allied perspective, the weapons and uniforms looked the same—as indeed they were or appeared so. The strategic context, however, could not have been more different. For China and the two Koreas the war became "total," with the issue being one of national survival. For the United States, the Soviet Union, and the UN coalition forces, national survival was not at risk unless the political leaders miscalculated and allowed their allies to draw them into escalated fighting that spilled over into the Soviet Union, China, and Japan. The fighting, therefore, counted, but it became difficult to assess when the only measures of success were body counts and blighted hills. A distance of more than fifty years has frozen the understanding of the war's conduct at the private first class (PFC) level—a constricted vision of danger, futility, hope, and despair. This position limits assessments of the belligerents' relative combat efficiency. The war's conduct reflected the belligerents' varied stakes in the war's outcome. A war that took more lives than any other twentieth-century conflict except the world wars deserves to be taken seriously at the operational and tactical level.

At the operational and organizational level, the U.S. armed forces' historical divisions produced official histories of the Korean War that, within their self-defined missions, remain useful as factual and interpretative sources. Their drawbacks are common to the genre. They are muted regarding institutional and personal shortcomings and guarded about interservice conflict and intelligence matters. These official histories, however, have spawned complementary books that fill the candor gap. These works describe personal and interservice conflict and take strong stands on everything from Douglas MacArthur's generalship to cold-weather field gear. One often overlooked factor in the American official military history program is that the documentation, along with the critiques of the draft manuscripts by the participants, becomes unclassified and open to independent researchers. The "book notes" are sometimes more valuable than the original operational reports. The official history program collects private papers and unofficial document collections used by participants in the field.

The official histories of the U.S. armed forces in Korea meet the same high standards the service historians in World War II established. The U.S. Army's Office of the Chief of Military History's three operational-chronological volumes are Roy Appleman, *South to the Naktong, North to the Yalu*, which covers the Eighth Army and X Corps from June until late November 1950; Walter Hermes, Jr., *Truce Tent and Fighting Front*, on the October 1951–July 1953 period; and a much-delayed third volume by Billy Mossman, *Ebb and Flow*, covering November 1950 to July 1951. The U.S. Air Force history is found in Robert Futrell's *The United States Air Force in Korea, 1950–1953*, which has been revised once. The Marine Corps history is Lynn Montross et al.'s five-volume *U.S. Marine Operations in Korea*. The navy published an official history—James Field's *History of United States Naval Operations Korea*—but two officers, Malcolm Cagle and Frank Manson, produced an earlier and more opinionated account: *The Sea War in Korea.*

The first year of the ground war in Korea offers ample evidence of shared hardship, valor, combat skill, operational ineptness, and battlefield failure at every level. The official histories are always the best place to start, but not to end, a study of the Korean War. For the American experience for July–September 1950, Uzal Ent's *Fighting on the Brink: Defense of the Pusan Perimeter* offers a wealth of operational detail and personal testimony, supported by a treasure trove of documentary evidence General Ent collected and donated to the U.S. Army Military History Institute. Another new classic is Col. Harry J. Maihafer's *From the Hudson to the Yalu,* a memorial to the men of West Point class of 1949 who fought and fell in disheartening numbers in 1950 and 1951. Among the army division histories that are notable for their photographs and vagueness, one exception, albeit a regimental history, is Michael Slater, *Hills of Sacrifice: The 5th RCT in Korea.* The Marines of 1950 receive ample credit for their combat success in Andrew Geer's *The New Breed: The Story of the U.S. Marines in Korea.* Morgan Brainard, in *Men in Low Cut Shoes,* and Randy Mills and Roxanne Mills, in *Unexpected Journey: A Marine Corps Reserve Company in the Korean War,* describe the Marine reservists' role in filling the ranks of the 1st Marine Division.

No more star-crossed unit served in the U.S. Eighth Army than the 24th Regimental Combat Team, a racially segregated force of African American enlisted men and white and black officers. Responding to the black veterans' protests that the U.S. Army's official history of the 1950 campaign unfairly stained the regiment's reputation with charges of cowardice and indiscipline, the U.S. Army Center of Military History sponsored a complete regimental history. It selected a three-man team for their historical skills and their sympathy for the black GIs' plight in a racist army: William Bowers, William Hammond, and George MacGarrigle. In writing their book, *Black Soldier, White Army: The 24th Infantry Regiment in Korea,* they found the charges of poor performance justified but also found many examples of inspired leadership and admirable fighting skills. The issue of reliability, however, remains open. Lt. Col. Charles M. Bussey, USA (Ret.), a Korean War veteran of the 24th Infantry and an officer of unquestioned professional competence, cannot quite change the regiments' image with his memoir, *Firefight at Yechon;* nor does *With a Black Platoon in Combat,* the autobiography of Lyle Rishell, a white platoon commander. The navy's less controversial experience with integration is described in a commemorative pamphlet.

As a great strategic coup (it wasn't) or operational miracle (close enough), the Inchon-Seoul campaign has received more than ample analysis—and special pleading. The portal account is still Robert Heinl's *Victory at High Tide: The Inchon-Seoul Campaign.* More opinionated than the Marine Corps' official historians (volume 2), Heinl was an accomplished Marine officer who understood Operation Chromite's operational challenges. Complementing Heinl's work are two Marine-sponsored fiftieth-anniversary histories, also written by veteran Marine officers: Edwin Simmons, *Over the Seawall: U.S. Marines at Inchon,* and Joseph Alexander, *Battle of the Barricades: U.S. Marines in the Recapture of Seoul.* The navy produced a similar commemorative book with Curtis Utz's *Assault From the Sea: The Amphibious Landing at Inchon.* The X Corps, the landing force headquarters commanded by Maj. Gen. Edward M. Almond, has its experience told in Shelby Stanton's *America's Tenth Legion: X Corps in Korea, 1950.* Of the nonexpert entries in a crowded field, Walt Sheldon's *Hell or High Water: MacArthur's Landing at Inchon* is the best.

The exploitation campaign of October 1950 and the Chinese First and Second Offensives lack a celebratory literature—except in Beijing and Pyongyang—but the dark days of the Chinese intervention have a Thucydides in Roy Appleman. After his retirement from federal service, Appleman turned his considerable talent to reconstructing the nadir of the United Nations Command's operational history. Appleman began with the X Corps' crisis: *East of Chosin: Entrapment and Breakout in Korea* and *Escaping the Trap: The U.S. Army X Corps in Northeast Korea, 1950.* He widened his domain with two essential books: *Disaster in Korea: The Chinese Confront MacArthur* and *Ridgway Duels for Korea.* At the tactical level, S. L. A. Marshall used his World War II experience and exaggerated reputation to access the Eighth Army's reports and the worst nightmares of personal recollections of its November defeat. He then wrote a true classic, *The River and the Gauntlet.* Marshall's two internal reports for the army on infantry operations in cold weather are equally impressive and of lasting value.

As Appleman recognized, the X Corps' escape from northeast Korea remains the stuff of legends—or at least tales of brave deeds and sacrifice. Much of the focus then and now remains on the 1st Marine Division's march out from the Changjin (Chosin) Reservoir. Volume 3 of *U.S. Marine Operations in the Korean War* covers the campaign in detail. A participant, Edwin Simmons, produced a shorter and equally professional history for the Marine Corps' commemorative program: *Frozen Chosin: U.S. Marines at the Changjin Reservoir.* Many authors of mass commercial books about Korea—including Eric Hammel and Martin Russ—have written a Chosin Reservoir book, but Robert Leckie's *March to Glory* remains the best blend of glory and grimness. Of the memoir literature, see William Hopkins, *One Bugle, No Drums: The Marines at Chosin Reservoir,* and Joseph Owen, *Colder Than Hell: A Marine Rifle Company at Chosen Reservoir.* The X Corps–U.S. Navy partnership to evacuate North Korea is described in Richard Stewart, *Staff Operations: The X Corps in Korea, December 1950,* and Glenn Cowart, *Miracle in Korea: The Evacuation of X Corps From the Hungnam Beachhead.* Part of the story of evacuating Korea refugees from Hungnam appears in Bill Gilbert's *Ship of Miracles.*

Except to veterans and professional soldiers, the Ridgway–Van Fleet campaign of 1951 is relatively unknown, which is unfortunate since the campaign includes some of the Americans' hardest fighting and sound leadership in the entire war. Among the best works are Kenneth Hamburger's *Leadership in the Crucible: The Korean War Battles of Twin Tunnels and Chipyong-ni*; J. D. Coleman's *Wonju*; A. L. Hinshaw's, *Heartbreak Ridge: Korea, 1951*; and Russell Gugeler's *Combat Actions in Korea.* Although the Eighth Army's battles with the CPVF from January to June 1951 produced few dramatic victories and defeats, the Ridgway–Van Fleet campaign, which forced a change in Chinese war aims and strategy, has been studied less than it deserves. The exception is Kelly Jordan's doctoral dissertation, "Three Armies in Korea: The Combat Power of the U.S. 8th Army in Korea, 1950–1952."

The last year of the Korean War (1952–53) brought intensive fighting between the two coalitions' ground forces in two major extended engagements, October–November 1952 and March–July 1953. The official histories of the American armed forces, the ROK Army, the British Commonwealth forces, and the Chinese People's Volunteers Force all cover this "outpost" war in detail with good operational assessments. In broad strategic terms the fighting had several purposes. In geographic terms both coalitions sought to hold or seize terrain that would make defending both South and North Korea after the armistice easier. This reasonable goal became complicated by judgments about symbolic objectives (the city of Kaesong) and terrain critical to a renewed war should the armistice negotiations fail or be broken at a later date, that is, after the Chinese and American armies departed. Although both sides understood they would withdraw two kilometers from the line of contact, or the military demarcation line, when the armistice was signed, limited evidence shows objectives were attacked or defended not just to influence the Panmunjom truce talks. The exception was the Chinese offensive to eliminate the Kumsong salient (July 1953), which served as a direct warning to Syngman Rhee and the ROK Army that South Korea had better accept its dependence on American military power and abide by the armistice terms.

The combat literature, often autobiographical or historical, focuses then on the UNC divisions most engaged in these two periods and two operational areas. For the western front, or roughly the watershed of the Imjin River, the histories deal principally with the U.S. 1st Marine Division and the 1st British Commonwealth Division. The classic Marine memoir, Martin Russ's *The Last Parallel*, is iconic and sarcastic, but it has been ably complemented by other Marine veterans' books—Lee Ballenger's two books on the outpost war and former lieutenant James Brady's memoir of his service as a platoon commander. The same experience can also be found from a different perspective in the letters of Richard and Gerald Chappell, brothers who served as navy corpsmen with the Marines, and Roger Baker's memoir-history of Marine tank operations in a decidedly nonmobile war.

The classic account of World War I–style trench warfare in the U.S. I Corps' (western) sector is A. J. Barker's *Fortune Favors the Brave: The Battle of the Hook, Korea, 1953*. It is principally about the 1st Commonwealth Division, but Barker includes the experience of the U.S. 7th Marine Regiment. The defense of this tortured position, actually part of the main trench line, is also described in books about the 3rd Battalion, Princess Patricia's Canadian Light Infantry; the 1st Battalion, the Black Watch; and the 3rd Battalion, the Royal Australian Regiment. To remind us that no war is humorless, however bizarre, see the memoir of Dan Raschen, a Royal Engineers captain who specialized in mine warfare and pheasant hunting.

The battles on the "central front" or the Iron Triangle region of Korea's midsection are most familiar through S. L. A. Marshall's *Pork Chop Hill*. Memorialized in a respectable movie, the U.S. 17th Infantry's defense of this low-lying outpost resembled the stubbornness of Captain Ahab. The book also covers other small unit actions and patrols but not the same hill's defense by the Thai battalion and the U.S. 31st Infantry in 1952 and 1953. The last battle of Pork Chop Hill is rescued by Bill McWilliams, *On Hallowed Ground: The Last Battle for Pork Chop Hill.*

Combat actions in the same area serve as the central focus of memoirs by Lieutenants John A. Sullivan (17th Infantry) and William D. Dannenmaier (15th Infantry). For a UNC ally's jaundiced view of Korean service, see Basri Danisman's *Situation Negative,* the memoir of a Turkish officer. The continuing issue of combat effectiveness in infantry units, however, may best be understood in a 1952–53 study of 310 GIs who were identified by at least two noncommissioned officers (NCOs) as "fighters" or "non-fighters" in three central front U.S. Army infantry divisions. "Fighters" fired their weapons, carried ammunition and the wounded, and exercised informal command. "Non-fighters" shirked their duty in all forms. "Fighters" tended to be older extroverts who were known for their soldierly skills, physical prowess, intelligence, maturity, masculinity, self-confidence, and secure social relationships. They also outnumbered the "non-fighters" 2:1 except among African American GIs. Whatever their feelings about an imminent cease-fire, the GIs kept fighting until July 27, 1953.

The common soldier's experience in combat has always proved irresistible to the readers of military history, and even the Korean War has provided oral historians and vicarious consumers of war with ample material. The genre has limitations beyond faulty memories and vivid imaginations. The largest pool of interviewees and autobiographers are now aging infantrymen, cannoneers, and armored vehicle crewmen. Statistically, many soldiers (and airmen and sailors) are veterans of administrative and service units and thus appear to be unappealing storytellers to "war lovers." While combat veterans tend to have repetitive experiences, service specialists may actually have more unique experiences and important perspectives to offer. Amateur oral historians, however, seldom collect the testimony of participants in critical wartime events, unless (as with dropping the two atomic bombs in 1945) the events have undeniable importance and are so recognized at the time. The most important memoirs have been collected by the services' official historians while writing their books or by authors of great energy and journalistic bent, such as the late Clay Blair, John Toland, and Sir Max Hastings.

These reservations aside, the oral histories and memoirs of the Korean War provide the personal, human dimension that narrative histories cannot easily accommodate. Among the oral history anthologies, the most accessible are: Louis Baldovi, *Foxhole View: Personal Accounts of Hawaii's Korean War Veterans*; Kim Chull-baum, ed., *The Truth About the Korean War*; Donald Knox, *The Korean War: An Oral History* (2 volumes); Richard Peters and Xiaobing Li, *Voices From the Korean War*; Rod Paschall, *Witness to War: Korea*; Rudy Tomedi, *No Bugles, No Drums: An Oral History of the Korean War;* and Henry Berry, *Hey, Mac, Where Ya Been? Living Memories of the Korean War.* In my own *Their War for Korea: American, Asian and European Combatants and Civilians, 1945–1953*, I attempted to illuminate unique aspects of the Korean War through the experiences of forty individuals and small groups. The opposite approach, to focus entirely on American heroes, may be found in Edward F. Murphy, *Korean War Heroes*.

For personal accounts that explore the war's special aspects, the more interesting accounts are by a Marine infantry battalion commander (Robert Taplett, *Dark Horse Six*), an army preventive medicine physician (Crawford Sams, *Medic!*), an acting division commander and division artillery commander

(G. Bittman Barth, *Tropic Lightning and Taro Leaf in Korea*), an army lieutenant who commanded anti-Communist North Korean partisans (Ben Malcom and Ron Martz, *White Tigers*), a British medical officer (John CadmanWatts, *Surgeon at War*), a U.S. Army surgeon (Otto F. Apel Jr. and Pat Apel, *MASH: An Army Surgeon in Korea*), a Marine platoon commander (James Brady, *The Coldest War*), a ROK conscript (Donald Chung, *The Three-Day Promise*), a navy reconnaissance expert (Eugene Clark, *Secrets of Inchon*), a Marine mortar officer (C. S. Crawford, *The Four Deuces*), a ranger officer (Robert Black, *A Ranger Born*), an F-86 pilot (Douglas Evans, *Sabre Jets Over Korea*), a navy air crewman (Jack Sauter, *Sailors in the Sky*), a Korean American newsman (Bill Shin, *The Forgotten War Remembered*), an army artillery forward observer (Addison Terry, *The Battle of Pusan*), and a Protestant minister turned F-51 pilot and father of the South Korean Air Force (Dean Hess, *Battle Hymn*). The range of Korean War memoirs, many cited elsewhere, is wide, but most of these personal accounts appear from obscure publishers and have limited historical value except as individual testimony. This shortcoming is inherent in the genre, not in the authors' character or service.

The U.S. Army National Guard's experience, fighting as Eighth Army units, began in early 1951 and covered the rest of the war. It is described in William Berebitsky, *A Very Long Weekend: The Army National Guard in Korea*. Sgt. William W. Day IV, a "cowboy cannoneer" who later became a university president, tells the story of one esteemed Guard unit in Korea, the 300th Armored Field Artillery Battalion, Wyoming National Guard. Among the unsung heroes of the Korean War are the nine artillery battalions of the National Guard that arrived in Korea in time to become corps artillery in the 1951 campaign and to provide a decisive increase to the Eighth Army's artillery support.

The British Commonwealth troops' combat experience appears in the regimental histories. It may also be sampled in Adrian Walker's *A Barren Place: National Servicemen in Korea, 1950–1954,* a collection of personal testimonies from "other ranks." Two of the best memoirs come from two "diggers" of 3d Battalion, Royal Australian Regiment (RAR): Ben O'Dowd, *In Valiant Company: Diggers in Battle, Korea 1950–1951,* and Jack Galloway, *The Last Call of the Bugle.* The Australians also have solid tactical studies of their great 1951 battles of Kapyong and Maryang-san. Neil C. Smith, ed., *Home by Christmas: With the Australian Army in Korea, 1950–1956,* is a collective memoir as well as a 3d RAR narrative history. The British tradition of regimental history, lived and written, also continued in Korea. The regimental histories not only celebrate combat service but provide unique perspectives on the U.S. Eighth Army. The regimental histories cover the service of battalions of the Gloucestershire Regiment, the Middlesex Regiment ("the Die Hards"), the Royal Ulster Rifles, the Royal Marines, the Argyll and Sutherland Highlanders, and the Black Watch (the Royal Highland Regiment). Individual British soldiers' accounts form the heart of several anthologies: Eric Linklater, *Our Men in Korea*; David Smurthwaite, *Project Korea: The British Soldier in Korea, 1950–1953*; and Ashley Cunningham-Boothe and Peter N. Farrar, *British Forces in the Korean War.*

The UNC's ultimate success in coping with the Chinese and North Korean armies and suppressing the serious rear-area security threat posed by Communist partisans depended on reforming the ROK Army. The overview of rear operations provided is in Andrew J. Birtle's *The U.S. Army Counterinsurgency and Contingency Operations Doctrine, 1941–1975.* In

Korea, rear-area operations fell to the South Korean Army, the Korean National Police, and their KMAG advisers. A four-volume manuscript history of the KMAG, written by army historians (1950–58), was published eventually in a sanitized, abbreviated form as Robert K. Sawyer's *KMAG in War and Peace*. The KMAG left the required historical reports, operational logs, and manuals for preservation in Record Group 554, the GHQ FEC/SCAP/UNC archives, and in Record Group 334, Records of Interservice Agencies, which in practice was a KMAG-only collection. Much of the documentation serves as the base for Bryan Gibby's "Fighting in a Korean War: The American Advisory Missions from 1946–1953," his doctoral dissertation at The Ohio State University, 2004.

The KMAG's major task, of course, was to train an expanding South Korean Army to fight its North Korean rival and the Chinese. Much of this experience can be reconstructed in the correspondence of General Van Fleet and Maj. Gen. Cornelius E. "Mike" Ryan, USA, the KMAG chief for most of the 1951–53 reforms, that is held in the Van Fleet Papers, George C. Marshall Library, Lexington, Virginia. Generals Ridgway and Van Fleet corresponded regularly with the senior officers of the South Korean Army, or at least with those whom they trusted, such as Chung Il-kwon, Paik Sun-yup, and Lee Chong-chan. Their common struggle to create an adequate army is covered by Alfred Hausrath in both *Problems of the Development of a Local Army (ROKA)* and *The KMAG Advisor: Roles and Problems of the Military Advisor in Developing an Indigenous Army for Combat Operations in Korea*. Reforming the ROK Army is recounted in Park Il-song's doctoral dissertation, "The Dragon From the Stream: The ROK Army in Transition and the Korean War, 1950–1953," The Ohio State University, 2002.

The United Nations Command depended on its air superiority to keep it in the war at an acceptable human cost. The American air war's official histories will merely get a student off the runway since the number of scholarly analyses grows like bomb tonnage statistics. The leading study is now by Conrad Crane, *A Rather Bizarre War: American Airpower Strategy in Korea, 1950–1953*. Shorter studies that stress joint air operations are Allan R. Millett's "Korea, 1950–1953," in *Close Air Support,* edited by Benjamin Cooling; Thomas C. Hone's "Strategic Bombing Constrained: Korea and Vietnam" in *Strategic Bombardment,* edited by Cargill Hall; and Eduard Mark, *Aerial Interdiction in Three Wars.* All three books provide extensive citations to archival sources. In another genre, the Office of Air Force Museums and History published a sound, short, updated air war history—Wayne Thompson and Bernard C. Nalty, *Within Limits: The U.S. Air Force and the Korean War*—the centerpiece of five more specialized short histories of air superiority, close air support, strategic bombing, combat cargo operations, and air-sea rescues. The same series provides a chronology and almanac of campaigns, units, and stations.

The newest studies of the belligerents' campaign for air superiority are expanded by complementary studies of the F-86 versus MiG-15 battles, especially as remembered by the pilots. They are memorialized in John Bruning's *Crimson Sky: The Air Battle for Korea* and William Y'Blood's *MiG Alley: The Fight for Air Superiority*, part of the air force's Korean War commemorative series. In Jennie Chaucey and William Forstchen's *Hot Shots: An Oral History of the Air Force Combat Pilots of the Korean War*, the American pilots tell their own "wild blue" stories, tempered by their recognition that the Soviet pilots they fought were more skilled than the Chinese and North Korean pilots were. Far East Air Forces pilots knew their MiG-15 adversaries were Russian pilots, gradually augmented with Chinese and North Korean aviators. For the Soviets the Korean War provided an unparalleled opportunity to assess American air operations and technology as long as the U.S. Air Force did not attack the Russian air bases in Manchuria and the Maritime Province.

The Korean air war's conduct continues to generate controversy, even though open accounts from Chinese and Russian sources add greater transparency to the debate. The official histories have fallen behind the document-based books of independent scholars and collections of oral memoirs. The air superiority issue, defined as FEAF F-86 interceptors pitted against the Communist coalition's MiG-15 force, remains an argument over the jet fighters' kills and losses. All sides' official claims are exaggerated, as revealed in *Sabres Over MiG Alley: The F-86 and the Battle for Air Superiority in Korea*, a careful study by professional historian and former air force pilot Kenneth Werrell. Two other studies agree: Zhang Xiaoming, *Red Wings Over the Yalu: China, the Soviet Union, and the Air War in Korea*, and Mark O'Neill, "The Other Side of the Yalu: Soviet Pilots in the Korean War—Phase One, 1 November 1950– 12 April 1951," a doctoral dissertation written from Russian sources. Using only self-confessed air-to-air combat losses, the American F-86 still holds a 5:1 kill advantage over its Chinese and Soviet opponents, with North Korean air losses unreported. The USAF internal records identify an estimated 101 F-86 losses in air combat, contrasted to Communist pilots' claims of 1,300. American pilots of all services claimed 792 MiG kills, but the Communists reported only 498 MiG losses. In his memoir, former North Korean pilot No Kum-sok reports many reasons for exaggerated claims, and a composite oral history of USAF pilots produces similar evidence of honest and less so overreporting. The commemorative history of the 4th Fighter-Interceptor Wing, one of two F-86 wings, remains celebratory but realistic while the candid memoir of Col. Walker M. Manhurin, USAF, retains its status as the classic tale of a fighter ace turned POW-confessor.

The battle for air superiority had important effects because the MiGs could not be driven off from attacking B-29s, whose missions ideally would have been run in daylight and flown in tight formation. Unacceptable losses after the MiG attacks forced the FEAF Bomber Command to switch to nighttime raids with small groups of planes, reminiscent of the RAF "bomber streams" over Germany. Precision attacks on such fixed targets as tunnels, bridges, and road choke points became the mission of fighter-bombers of three American services and the squadrons of the Royal Navy and from the South African and Australian air forces. American pilots, however, flew the majority of interdiction and close air support sorties. The nature of the offensive (but not strategic) air war is recreated in the official histories and wing histories, but the operational flavor may be found in David McLaren's *Mustangs Over Korea: The North American F-51 at War, 1950–1953* and William Cleveland's *Mosquitos in Korea*. These books fuse personal experience with technical explanations of how sorties were run.

The air war conducted by naval aviation squadrons (U.S. Navy and U.S. Marine Corps) is integrated into both services' official histories. The best of the "nonofficial" accounts is Richard Hallion's *The Naval Air War in Korea* and Lynn Montross's *Cavalry of the Sky: The Story of U.S. Marine Combat Helicopters*. At the personal level, the "cruise books," when upgraded with documentary research, are essential. As an example, see Paul Cooper, *Weekend Warriors,* the history of a navy reserve squadron (VF-871) embarked on the carrier U.S.S. *Princeton.* The war's fiftieth anniversary stirred the Naval Historical Center and Marine Corps History and Museums Division to revisit the naval aviators' war in authoritative form. See, for example, Richard Knott, *Attack From the Sky: Naval Air Operations in the Korean War,* and John Condon, *Corsairs to Panthers: U.S. Marine Aviation in Korea.*

The navy's Korean War commemorative series produced two notable operational studies: Joseph Alexander, *Fleet Operations in a Mobile War, September 1950–June 1951,* and Malcolm Muir, Jr., *Sea Power on Call: Fleet Operations, June 1951–July 1953.* To personalize the long hours of blockade duty, see two junior officers' memoirs: Charles F. Cole, *Korea Remembered: Enough of a War,* and James Alexander, *Inchon to Wonsan: From the Deck of a Destroyer in the Korean War.* The Royal Navy and its Fleet Air Arm receive credit for their contribution in John R. P. Lansdown, *With the Carriers in Korea, 1950–1953: The Fleet Air Arm Story.* The Canadian blockading squadron also rates a history of its service as does the Australian navy. The most challenging aspect of the UNC naval forces' operations was the threat of Communist mines, tethered and free, magnetic and contact. The extemporized mine clearance effort is described in Arnold Lott, *Most Dangerous Sea: A History of Mine Warfare and an Account of U.S. Navy Mine Warfare Operations in World War II and Korea.* As part of the USN mine warfare force, U.S. Coast Guard ships participated in unheralded, dangerous inshore operations.

Other than the shared unpleasantness of captivity, the experience of POWs and civilian internees varied widely by time and place of capture, rank, unit, intelligence value, age, physical condition, and nationality. The common condition for all POWs was their fate as pawns in the fierce competition for relative advantage at the Panmunjom negotiations. The British studies of their POWs resulted in a collective portrait in Cyril Cunningham's *No Mercy, No Leniency: Communist Mistreatment of British Prisoners of War in Korea.* The most exhaustive study of the American POWs' experience remains unpublished: Army Security Center, Ft. Meade, Maryland, "U.S. Prisoners of War in the Korean Operation," 1954, a manuscript history. A copy is in the Historical Files, Dean Center, U.S. Army Base, Yongsan, South Korea. The best published exploitation of the POW debriefings after repatriation is Albert Biderman's *March to Calumny: The Story of American POWs in the Korean War.* His work is shaped as a critique of Eugene Kinkead's *In Every War But One,* a scathing and exaggerated condemnation of GI "collaboration." The first attempt to put GI POWs in a favorable light was William White's *The Captives of Korea.* Extensive debriefings of repatriated POWs collected mass personal testimony and data and produced a postwar POW studies industry among the services and defense contractors. One major study by the army's provost marshal general provided guidelines for safeguarding POWs and foiling POW resistance. The army's Human Resources Research Office (HUMRRO) and the air force's Behavioral Sciences Division, Office of Scientific Research produced studies that led to service programs for POW survival and resisting brainwashing techniques and collaborationism. The U.S. Army's Surgeon General's Office investigated dietary and related health problems associated with captivity.

In the meantime, former POWs wrote books that began to reach commercial audiences and created a whole Korean

War POW genre. Among the captives' classics are the accounts of an American general, a USAF copilot of a special operations B-29 who went to China and returned in 1955, a Greco-British correspondent accused of spying, an army "turncoat," a Protestant clergyman, a Catholic priest, a sergeant "reactionary," and a navy pilot. The most gripping story tells how U.S. Army chaplain Emil Kapuan died for his faith and humanitarianism. Among the anthologies, see also Harry Spiller's sixteen POW accounts by American GIs.

The Communist prisoners created their own hell as they struggled to follow orders to make life miserable for UNC camp authorities and to intimidate those of their countrymen who chose non-repatriation. Harold Vetter's *Mutiny on Koje Island* remains the standard, if dated, account. Stanley Weintraub's *War in the Wards* is a participant account of how Communist patients used UNC hospitals as key elements in their resistance movement. The ordeal of the non-repatriates is described in Kenneth Hansen's *Heroes Behind Barbed Wire.* Not as well publicized as the Communists' educational coercion of POWs is the program by the FECOM Civilian Indoctrination and Education Division, a refuge of displaced missionaries and teachers who believed that Christian vocationalism would wean the Korean and Chinese POWs from their socialist loyalties. A dreamy account of good intentions spawning harm is Harold Voelkel's *Behind Barbed Wire in Korea.* The U.S. Army POW camp's administrative system provided ample evidence of its shortcomings in its simple custodial functions, let alone its screening of the POWs as intelligence and propaganda assets, war criminals, political converts, and shadow POW commanders. The short account is from the Military History Office, U.S. Army Pacific, "The Handling of Prisoners During the

Korean War," June 1960. Reflecting the exceptional research done by the historical staff of U.S. Army Far East Command and the Eighth Army (Rear), *Logistics in Korean Operations* (4 volumes, December 1955) contains much useful POW material. Both of these studies may be found in the U.S. Army Military History Institute's library. HUMRRO added Samuel Meyers and William Bradbury's *The Political Behavior of Korean and Chinese Prisoners of War in the Korean Conflict.* To see UNC camp administration as purposeful oppression rather than ineptness, there is Wilfred Burchett and Alan Winnington— the poet laureates of British socialism and fellow-traveling— and their book *Koje Unscreened*, which reads suspiciously like the report of International Association of Democratic Lawyers. This group visited North Korea to investigate UNC war crimes and the Communist-run camps' conditions.

As the years pass, the individual stories fall back into the collective experience as the demographics of the ex-POW community become more homogeneous—that is, most were former army enlisted men, all relatively young when captured and innocent of any intelligence value and improbable converts to Communism. The more interesting collective accounts remain those of downed pilots, for example, Clay Blair's *Beyond Courage: Escape Tales of Airmen in the Korean War.* The Communist position remains that trumpeted by the Chinese People's Committee for World Peace in 1953: the United Nations Command's POWs received humane and considerate treatment that exceeded international standards. This generalization might have applied to an army private first class (PFC), captured in 1952 or 1953, but it most certainly did not apply to UNC pilots (called "air pirates"), technicians, intelligence personnel, high-profile ground officers, and "reactionaries."

The issue of war crimes, which the UNC defined as "the killing of POWs and civilian hostages," poisoned the armistice negotiations and reflected the murderous competition between the two Koreas. The Communists leveled three war crimes charges against the UNC: arbitrarily executing suspected southern Korean Communists, conducting biological warfare against Chinese and Korean civilians and soldiers in Manchuria and North Korea, and bombing civilians in North Korean cities. Both sides held "war crimes" suspects as POWs and used them as hostages until the belligerents reached a tacit agreement that these "war criminals" would be repatriated if they chose to return to their original military force. For the UNC this agreement meant returning or releasing more than 800 POWs (almost all Koreans) who could have been tried for murder. As with many aspects of Korean War history, the war crimes issue is best explained in an unpublished history with accompanying documentation: Military History Office, War Crimes Division, JAG Section, Korean Communications Zone, "Final Historical and Operational Report," 1954. Its appendixes list victims, witnesses, suspects, and case summaries. The one effort to examine the atrocity issue writ large is superficial and naive: Philip Chinnery, *Korean Atrocity! Forgotten War Crimes, 1950–1953*. As war crimes investigators were aware and as reported by Col. James Hanley, the principal JAG officer for war crimes prosecution, the Korean National Police and the South Korean military police of the Martial Law Command had committed their share of summary executions, and they were often abetted by paramilitary "youth" associations of terrorist bent. Nevertheless, the Korean People's Army won the slaughter-of-innocents prize hands down. American culpability has thus far focused on the murky No Gun Ri Incident of July 1950. The

Associated Press team of Charles J. Hanley, Choe Sang-hun, and Martha Mendoza produced a sensational and flawed account that set off an OSD-sponsored investigation. It concluded some GIs killed some Koreans, but numbers and command responsibility remain vague. A book by Lt. Col. Robert L. Bateman successfully exploded the credibility of some of the AP team's sources and conclusions, but the army admitted some refugees had died in a nighttime shoot-out. In truth, as the AP team is now investigating, air strikes and artillery barrages after the fall of Taejon were not carefully targeted. Groups of GIs and ROK soldiers headed for the Taegu-Pusan-Pohang perimeter as well as refugees were killed.

Looming behind the history of Korean War operations, intelligence history remains unfocused, at least in terms of the intelligence data and analysis used by policy makers in Washington, Moscow, Beijing, Seoul, and Pyongyang. The framework of the American intelligence effort can be reconstructed with some confidence from the daily intelligence summaries and teleconferences between the Far East Command and an intelligence committee in Washington that represented all the relevant intelligence agencies. These documents are declassified and found in the papers of Maj. Gen. Charles Willoughby, the FECOM G-2, at the Douglas MacArthur Library in Norfolk, Virginia. American and British intelligence agencies worked in close association in Asia, even after Nationalist China's defeat, which created a natural division of effort. The British would spy on the Communists, the Americans on the Nationalists, and (no doubt) vice versa. The United States moved a major signals intelligence unit from Shanghai to Taipei and placed another on Okinawa while MI-6 ran a wide range of human intelligence operations out of the British Embassy in Beijing. The most senior intelligence officers may have talked in London and Washington; certainly their joint offices in Hong Kong did. Furthermore, the British spies of the "Cambridge Six" most likely ensured the Soviets received the intelligence evaluations.

In World War II the American intelligence services became too dependent on intercepting and decoding foreign radio communications, so much so that words such as "Ultra," "Magic," and "Enigma" are now as familiar as "Roosevelt," "Stalin," and "Churchill." Efforts during the Korean War duplicated the phenomenon. The detailed intelligence summaries in Willoughby's papers, done in both Tokyo and Washington, are best when they are based on signals intelligence and less positive on questions of inner-circle decision making by Kim, Mao, and Stalin in face-to-face meetings. Some source close to the Chinese Central Military Commission reported one critical meeting in July 1950, but the unknown voice did not speak again. The Communists, of course, had the same sort of problem. They had plenty of information from open and clandestine sources but limited success in predicting American intentions.

The history of intelligence operations during the Korean War still is held hostage to the need to protect sources and collection processes, but some relaxation of classification requirements has helped recent scholars. The National Security Agency used the war's fiftieth anniversary to release four in-house histories of cryptological operations. The Central Intelligence Agency has been equally guarded; however, its declassified materials are very useful because they provide a full picture of what Washington officials thought they knew and not necessarily what the reality was. On microfilm in the United

States and Korea, these collections center on the work of the Office of Research and Estimates / National Intelligence Estimates (ORE/NIE) and the Office of Current Intelligence, which produced daily summaries, current reports, and personality profiles. Many of these reports are also available in the Truman Papers' extensive intelligence files of the President's Secretary's Files. The State Department's Korean mission also performed extensive reporting of South Korean affairs pertaining to politics, refugee policies, economics, internal security, and personalities, and these reports are in the general records of the Department of State (RG 59) and the records of the Foreign Service Posts of the Department of State (RG 84). Accessing the Willoughby Papers simplifies the problem of digging through the Eighth Army and Far East Command's intelligence archives (RG 554), but these files are useful and accessible.

For an introduction to Korean War intelligence, the best place to start is Matthew M. Aid, "HUMINT and COMINT in the Korean War," in Richard Aldrich, Gary Rawnsley, and Ming-Yeh Rawnsley's *The Clandestine Cold War in Asia*. Aid extended the study as "American COMINT in the Korean War (Part II): From the Chinese Intervention to the Armistice," *Intelligence and National Security* 15 (Spring 2000): 14–49. In "Only Half the Battle: American Intelligence and the Chinese Intervention in Korea, 1950," *Intelligence and National Security* 5 (January 1990): 129–49, Eliot Cohen examines the reasons the United States misread the Chinese intervention. Another useful study is John P. Finnegan, "Intelligence Operations in the Korean War," *Studies in Intelligence* 44 (2000): 1–15. Although they reek of self-defense, Willoughby's 1951 explanations of two predictive miscalculations are worth reading, especially for their supporting documentation: "North Korean Pre-Invasion Build-Up" and "Chinese Communist Potential for Intervention in the Korean War." The real jewel, however, is a detailed paper on 1950 intelligence affairs by a participant: Lt. Col. Leonard Abbott, USA, "Korea Liaison Office Report," May 15, 1951, RG 23, MacArthur Papers. Maj. Peter Knight, in a doctoral dissertation on the performance of FECOM's G-2, provides the most comprehensive account to date.

The complex and largely futile special operations mounted by Far East Command and the South Korean intelligence services obscured the intelligence history of the Korean War. In *Apollo's Warriors: United States Air Force Special Operations During the Cold War,* Michael Haas shows just how hard it is to sort out intelligence collection from other special operations mounted by the Combined Command for Reconnaissance Activities (Korea); Detachment 2, 6004th Air Intelligence Service Squadron; the Special Activities Group; and the 581st Air Resupply and Communications Wing, to name a few FECOM agencies. Haas tried to deal with the larger intelligence picture in *In the Devil's Shadow: U.N. Special Operations During the Korean War.* Special operations units create special problems, with the conflict between intelligence collection and direct action being only one of the causes of fog and friction. The Korean War had them all: excessive compartmentalization, interservice rivalry, greed, jealousy, duplicity, personal ambition, and betrayal. And then there was facing the enemy, no slouch at internal security and population control. Some efforts to tell this story of great effort and sacrifice and limited success are Ed Evanhoe's *Dark Moon: Eighth Army Special Operations in the Korean War* and William Breuer's *Shadow*

Warriors: The Covert War in Korea. At one end of the excitable scale is Ellery Anderson's *Banner Over Pusan*, a British officer's tales of derring-do and didn't-do; and at the other, the sober, careful Frederick Cleaver et al.'s *UN Partisan Warfare in Korea, 1951–1954* and the Aerospace Studies Institute's *Guerrilla Warfare and Air Power in Korea, 1950–1953.*

6 LOOKING FOR THE KOREAN WAR

Having fielded Korean War questions for twenty years, I am keenly aware of how broad or narrow such questions can be and how continuing or short lived a searcher's interest can be. A researcher's first line of sources are the encyclopedias and reference books that are most likely to be available in libraries and bookstores in the English-speaking world and the Republic of Korea.

Of the published aids to researching and understanding the Korean War, four hold the high ground. *The Korean War: Handbook of the Literature and Research,* edited by Lester Brune, contains essays not only on the war but on the Cold War history of all the belligerents. Each essay includes an extensive bibliography. The book also covers some aspects of the Korean unification conflict since the 1950s, and it includes materials on Russian and Chinese sources and publications. The collection's focus, however, is heavily slanted to American perspectives and concerns. Of the existing almanacs, dictionaries, and reference works on the Korean War, the latest is also the most comprehensive: the three-volume *Encyclopedia of the*

Korean War. Edited by Spencer Tucker, the encyclopedia is the work of several members of the Virginia Military Institute's History Department and more than a hundred international contributors. Its weaknesses, as those of its predecessors, are the limited number of entries on Chinese, North Korean, and Russian subjects and the inevitable errors of fact written by inexpert authors. Nevertheless, many entries are comprehensive essays on such critical aspects of the war as casualties, germ warfare, prisoners of war, special operations, and the air war. A companion piece, *Conflict in Korea: An Encyclopedia* edited by James Hoare and Susan Pares, also includes subjects from Korean history before 1945 and after 1953. The fourth guide is probably the best, if American military participation is not the central concern. Steven Hugh Lee's *The Korean War* is part of a British-published series, Seminar Studies in History, aimed at teachers and college students. The strength of Professor Lee's work is his ability to balance the civil conflict in Korea with the different types and timings of international involvement. Lee tends to take the position favored by Anglo-Canadian Korean area specialists: a curse on all your policies and historical interpretations, especially those that favor the United States. Lee's book, however, is informed and reflects the author's expertise in Korean studies.

Other Korean War guides have varied strengths. Although dated, *The Korean War: An Annotated Bibliography* edited by Keith McFarland is comprehensive but Western-defined. James Matray's *Historical Dictionary of the Korean War* is especially good on Korean and Chinese entries and remains the best one-volume encyclopedia of the war's Asian aspects. If information on the U.S. military participation is the only object of the search, then the books to consult are Harry Summers's *Korean*

War Almanac and Stanley Sandler's *The Korean War: An Encyclopedia*. Paul M. Edwards, founder and director of the Center for the Study of the Korean War in Independence, Missouri, assembled *The Korean War: A Historical Dictionary*. It contains entries on military units, squadrons, and ships not usually found in such books and reflects the interests of a Korean War veteran. Professor Edwards has also assembled detailed bibliographies on other Korean War subjects. Other guides focus on military data. See, for example, Gordon L. Rottman's *Korean War Order of Battle*, which provides information on the air, ground, and naval units of all the belligerents, including the Soviet Union. A similar military guidebook is Michael Varhola, *Fire and Ice: The Korean War, 1950–1953*. The title of Richard Ecker's *Korean Battle Chronology: Unit-by-Unit United States Casualty Figures and Medal of Honor Citations* describes its focus and usefulness, but the sheer amount and level of statistical detail suggests care in its use.

The books that fall in between professional references and coffee table photograph books are actually improving in accuracy and usefulness. For the Korean War, these works are heavy on aircraft and tanks. On the basis of usefulness and accuracy, three Osprey books are of note: Nigel Thomas, Peter Abbott, and Mike Chappell, *The Korean War, 1950–1953*; Donald Boose, *U.S. Army Forces in the Korean War, 1950–1953*; and Carter Malkasian, *The Korean War, 1950–1953*. Boose, a retired U.S. Army colonel, is a Korea specialist, and Malkasian has a recent Oxford University history doctorate. As always, Osprey books are excellent for maps and photographs. For photographs alone Christopher Anderson's *The War in Korea: The U.S. Army in Korea, 1950–1953,* is outstanding in a crowded field. Reference books on Korean War aviation focus predominantly on aircraft types and their performance. The principal books come from Motorbooks International, Osprey Aviation, Osprey Frontline Colour, Schiffer Publishing, Aerofax (Midland Publishing), and Squadron/Signal Publications. A point of contact for advice on Korean War aviation publications is the U.S. Air Force Museum's bookstore, Wright-Patterson Air Force Base, Dayton, Ohio.

Before becoming absorbed in F-86 nose art and similar military arcana, the Korean War student should remember the "Korea" in the conflict. For general appropriateness, there are several essential reference books: Jennifer Milliken, *The Social Construction of the Korean War: Conflict and Its Possibilities*; Hermann Lautensach, *Korea: A Geography Based on the Author's Travels and Literature*; John Koo and Andrew Nahm, *An Introduction to Korean Culture*; Korean Overseas Information Service, *A Handbook of Korea*; Sheila Mioshi Jager Kim, *Narratives of Nation Building in Korea*; and Keith Pratt and Richard Rutt, *Korea: A Historical and Cultural Dictionary.*

Korean War bibliographies on-line provide researchers with a wide variety of citations. "Korean History: A Bibliography" is compiled by Kenneth Robinson and sponsored by the prestigious Center for Korean Studies at the University of Hawaii–Manoa. It has eighty-six pages on books and articles (in English) on the Korean War and is available at www.hawaii.edu/korea/bibliography/korean_war.htm. The entries are listed alphabetically, by author or title, which is a drawback. The other professionally posted and managed Korean War websites that provide bibliographies are maintained by the agencies of the U.S. armed forces:

U.S. Army Military History Institute, Carlisle Barracks: http://www.carlisle.army.mil/ahec/. Then go to "Resource Guides/Finding Aids," and go on "Reference Bibliographies," then "Subject Bibliographies" to the "Korean War" subject directory.

The U.S. Air Force Historical Research Agency, Air University: http://www.au.af.mil/au/afhra/Korean_war/korean_war.html.

The U.S. Navy Historical Center, Washington Navy Yard: http://www.history.navy.mil/biblio/biblio6.htm for "Korean War Naval Operations: A Bibliography."

There is a listing of Korean War websites at the end of this chapter. None of these websites are endorsed as reliable unless they are posted by a presidential library or some other monitored public agency. Private websites may be legitimate and trustworthy, but no mechanism of review ensures their accuracy. Many websites are established by amateur oral historians whose interest has been stirred by friends and family members. Their intentions are admirable and their energy commendable, but their historical product is marred by limited background research in archives and the flawed memories of their interviewees. Those who interview GIs seem unaware of the protocols and questionnaires developed by U.S. Army historians since World War II. Now the Library of Congress manages a similar mass oral history program for veterans, and it provides extensive guidelines and guidance to aspiring oral historians. The "collectors" are, however, amateur volunteers. Let the user beware and be cautious in using websites.

For those who still prefer to read words on real paper, the first stops should be the National Archives II, College Park,

Maryland, and several presidential and other personal libraries. The National Archives and Records Administration has published an extensive, definitive guide to its organizational records: see Rebecca Collier, comp., *The Korean War*, Reference Information Paper 103. The Harry S. Truman and Dwight D. Eisenhower Presidential Libraries are also mother lodes of Korean War documentation, because the presidents' closest associates also bestowed their papers to the libraries. The next critical stop is the George C. Marshall Library in Lexington, Virginia, which offers not only the papers of the secretary of defense, 1950–51 and his successor, Robert Lovett, but also those of two Eighth Army commanders—Generals Walton H. Walker and James A. Van Fleet. The U.S. Army Military History Institute (MHI) in Carlisle Barracks, Pennsylvania, holds Korean War documentation beyond imagination, but the foundation collections are those of Generals Matthew B. Ridgway and Edward M. Almond. The MHI has many other collections: senior officer papers and oral memoirs, unit collections, special studies (such as the Operations Research Office studies), maps, intelligence reports, and the famous Korean War veterans questionnaire collection created by MHI's oral historians. MHI's riches include the book files created by three historians of the war: Roy Appleman, Clay Blair, and Uzal Ent. Their research files include papers from the principals (e.g., Bradley and Collins) and extensive correspondence from participants, who were asked to comment on Appleman's five Korean War books (all on the 1950–51 campaigns). Blair, of course, wrote books with Bradley and Ridgway as their central figures, as well as his own Korean War book.

The MacArthur Library is a treasure trove of documents for Far East Command covering 1945 to 1951. In addition to

CINCFE's private correspondence, MacArthur's message files are exceptional, as are the teleconference transcripts and intelligence summaries collected by the theater G-2, Maj. Gen. Charles A. Willoughby. The G-2, who served MacArthur for ten years, gave loyalty a new meaning. MacArthur's personal staff provided more papers and memories, but his formal staff members—Willoughby excluded—were not Pacific war veterans and thus not court fixtures. The FECOM G-3, Maj. Gen. Edwin K. "Pinky" Wright, left papers and a very candid autobiography. The MacArthur collection is available on microfilm.

The U.S. Air Force Historical Research Agency (HRA) at Air University holds many of the same Far East Air Forces and Fifth Air Force papers that eventually went to NARA II because the Air University had an honored place on FEAF's distribution list. Moreover, HRA holds the papers of FEAF's "Big Three": Generals George E. Stratemeyer, Earle Partridge, and Otto Weyland. Just as the Strategic Air Command became the bomber generals' Shangri-la, Far East Air Forces became the laboratory for tactical offensive air war. The principal FEAF staff officers and commanders reads like a "who's who" of the U.S. Air Force's next generation of Pacific Air Forces and Air Forces Europe commanders: Generals James Ferguson, Edward J. Timberlake, Gilbert L. Meyers, and Jacob Smart. Having been converted to the cold logic of operations analysis in World War II, the air force produced studies of almost everything, which at least reports what FEAF was trying to do and with what level of effort and resources. Thus, the HRA is the intellectual mecca of airpower students. A place to start a search in personal papers is at the USAF Historical Research Center (now the HRA), *Personal Papers in the United States Air Force Historical Research Center* (5th ed., USAF HRC).

The Naval Historical Center (NHC), the Washington Navy Yard, and the Marine Corps History Division of the Marine Corps University in Quantico, Virginia, are the official archivists and reference experts for their services. As with the U.S. Navy, its historical community has three parts. The Operational Archives, NHC, hold the Pacific Fleet's consolidated reports and studies on Korean War naval operations. The library at the U.S. Naval Academy manages collections of individual naval officers (almost all admirals) and an oral history collection that is sponsored by the U.S. Naval Institute. The library of the Naval War College has a large Korean War book collection as well as other pertinent documents and private papers. For the Marine Corps the library and the archives stress personal papers and oral memoirs, in the case of the Korean War, of the commanders of the Fleet Marine Force Pacific, the 1st Marine Aircraft Wing, and the 1st Marine Division. Of special importance are the papers of Lemuel C. Shepherd and O. P. Smith.

Although somewhat dated—the proceedings of a 1994 international conference—*International Cold War Military Records and History* edited by William Epley provides a useful review of archival research possibilities in North American and European official archives.

One of the ironies of seeking American documents on the Korean experience is that it is often easier—and faster—to find them in Seoul, Republic of Korea, than in the United States. The most comprehensive library and archive of American books, collections, and documents is maintained by the ROK Institute for Military History Compilation, a Ministry of National Defense agency roughly analogous to a combination of all the historical agencies of the American armed forces and the Department of State. The IMHC representatives have collected documents from libraries and archives throughout the United States. Its principal sources are the National Archives, the Harry S. Truman Library, the Douglas MacArthur Library, the Dwight D. Eisenhower Library, and the Library of Congress. The holdings on microfilm and microfiche are exhaustive—and exhausting—covering, for example, U.S. Army special studies, the historical reports and documents of the Korean Military Advisory Group, and twelve reels of documents (15,000 pages) from the Combined Command for Reconnaissance Activities (CCRAK), a joint military-CIA agency. The guide to this collection is Gukbang Gunsa Yeonguso (Institute for Military History Compilation) *Gunsa Saryo Mokrokjip Hoioi Sujip Jaryo—1* (*List of Military History Materials—Overseas No. 1*) Seoul, ROK: IMHC, 1995. Although most of the book's citations are in Chinese and Korean, it does include entries in English for English-language materials.

The major public archives may be the mother lode of treasured Korean War materials, but small pockets of archival gold are scattered elsewhere. Professor Edwards's Center for the Study of the Korean War has a self-defined mission to collect veterans' papers and oral memoirs, especially those of enlisted men. The Korean War Veterans National Museum and Library in Tuscola, Illinois, is also a local initiative with an uncertain future. The Pritzker Military Library in Chicago, Illinois, will become an electronic clearinghouse for Korean War books and articles, especially privately published memoirs of veterans. Unlike other private initiatives, it is well funded.

Many of the printed and on-line bibliographies also list commercial and documentary movies, many now available on VHS or DVD. There is a megaguide to all the celluloid, Robert Lentz's *Korean War Filmography*.

For a "forgotten war" the Korean War has become "re-membered" enough in print—outside Korea—to become a subject for cultural contemplation. What does the war mean? Three anthologies can begin the journey: Gerrit W. Gong, ed., *Remembering and Forgetting: The Legacy of War and Peace in East Asia* (Center for Strategic and International Studies, 1996); Michael A. Barnhart, ed., "The Impact of the Korean War," a special issue of *The Journal of American-East Asian Relations* 2 (Spring 1993); and Kim Hong-nack, ed., "The Korean War (1950–1953) and Its Impact," a special issue of the *International Journal of Korean Studies* 5 (Spring/Summer 2001).

More assessments of the literature are found in Rosemary Foot, "Making Known the Unknown War: Policy Analysis of the Korean Conflict in the Last Decade," *Diplomatic History* 15 (Summer 1991): 411–31; Judith Munro-Leighton, "A Postrevionist Scrutiny of America's Role in the Cold War in Asia, 1945–1950," *Journal of American-East Asian Relations* 1 (Spring 1992): 72–98; Hakjoon Kim, "International Trends in Korean War Studies," *Korean War Studies* 14 (Summer 1990): 326–70; Philip West, "Interpreting the Korean War," *American Historical Review* 94 (February 1989): 80–96; Yasuda Jun, "A Survey: China and the Korean War," *Social Science Japan Journal* 1 (1998): 71–83; and Philip West, "The Korean War and the Criteria of Significance in Chinese Popular Culture," *Journal of American-East Asian Relations* 1 (Winter 1992): 383–408. See also Steven M. Goldstein and Di He, "New Chinese Sources on the History of the Cold War," *Cold War International History Project Bulletin* 1 (Spring 1992): 4–6; James Z. Gao, "Myth of the Heroic Soldier and Images of the Enemy," in *America's Wars in Asia,* edited by Philip West, Steven I. Levine, and Jackie Hiltz (M. E. Sharpe, 1998), 192–202; Man Ha-heo, "From Civil War to International War," *Korea and World*

Affairs 14 (Summer 1990): 303–325; and James I. Matray, "Civil Is a Dumb Name for a War," in the proceedings of the Korean War: An Assessment of the Historical Evidence conference, Georgetown University, July 24–25, 1995.

Selected Korean War Websites

Online Reference Sites

The Columbia Encyclopedia, Sixth Edition, "The Korean War": http://www.bartleby.com/65/ko/KoreanWa.html.

Infoplease, "Korean War": http://www.infoplease.com/ce6history/A0828118.html.

MSN, "Korean War": http://encarta.msn.com/encnet/refpages/RefArticle.aspx?refid=761559607.

RAP News FAQ Museum movies Features Trivia Links, "Soviet Pilots in the Korean War": http://aeroweb.lucia.it/~agretch/RAFAQ/SovietAces.html.

Snowcrest, "Korean War": http://users.snowcrest.net/jmike/koreamil.html.

Wikipedia, "Korean War": http://en.wikipedia.org/wiki/Korean_War.

General Sites

AII POW-MIA Korean War Casualties, "AII POW-MIA Site Search": http://www.aiipowmia.com/koreacw/kwdia_menu.html.

American Battle Monuments Commission, "Korean War Casualties": http://www.abmc.gov/wardead/listings/korean_war.php.

Army Quartermaster Corps, "Army Quartermaster Corps' 50th Anniversary Commemoration: Korea War, 1950–1953": http://www.qmmuseum.lee.army.mil/korea/.

Chinese Military Forum, "Korean War FAQ": http://www.centurychina.com/history/krwarfaq.html.

The Cold War—1917–1953: http://libraryautomation.com/nymas/nymascoldwar1917_1953.htm.

Communists PSYOP Against American Troops During the Korean War, Communist North Korea War Leaflets: www.psywarrior.com/links.html.

Documents on the Korean War, "The Korean War": http://www.mtholyoke.edu/acad/intrel/korea/korea.htm.

The Dwight D. Eisenhower Library: http://www.eisenhower.utexas.edu/.

Evanhoe, Ed., *The Korean War,* General Information: http://www.korean-war.com/.

Examining the Korean War: http://mcel.pacificu.edu/as/students/stanley/home.html.

15th Field Artillery Regiment: http://www.landscaper.net/korean.htm.

The "Forgotten" Korean War: http://members.aol.com/TeacherNet/Korean.html.

The Forgotten War . . . Korea: http://home.earthlink.net/~woll/Bills-Page.htm.

Historycentral.com, "The Major Events of the Korean War": http://www.multied.com/korea/.

The Historynet.com, Col. Harry G. Summers, Jr., U.S. Army (Ret.), "Korean War: A Fresh Perspective": http://www.historynet.com/mh/blthekoreanwar/.

Hofsiss, James, "The Korean War: Forgotten No More": http://members.aol.com/hoffam/hofpage3.html.

International Historic Films, "Korean War Films on Videocassettes": http://www.ihffilm.com/ihf/korean-war.html.

Kim, Yong Sik. "Eyewitness: A North Korean Remembers." http://www.kimsoft.com/korea/eyewit.htm.

"Korean War Aces": http://www.acepilots.com/korea_aces.html.

KoreanWar.com. History of the War: http://koreanwar.com/.

Korean War Commemoration: http://korea50.army.mil/.

Korean War Educator: http://www.koreanwar-educator.org/home.htm.

Korean-War.info, "Korean War": http://www.korean-war.info/.

The Korean War in Literature: http://www.illyria.com/korea_top.html.

The Korean War: 1950–1953, Information and Links: http://www.kimsoft.com/kr-war.htm.

Korean War Project: http://www.koreanwar.org/.

Korean War Veterans Association: http://www.kwva.org/.

MacroHistory: Prehistory to the 21st Century, "The Korean War": http://www.fsmitha.com/h2/ch24kor.html.

Military.com, "Korean War: The Forgotten War, 1950–1953—Overview": http://www.soldiertech.com/Content/MoreContent1?file=index.

National Museum of the United States Air Force: www.nationalmuseum.af.mil/factsheets/factsheet.asp?id=431.

National Security Agency, "NSA Korean War Commemoration": http://www.nsa.gov/korea/.

Navy Historical Center, "The Korean War: June 1950–July 1953—Introductory Overview and Special Image Selection": http://www.history.navy.mil/photos/events/kowar/kowar.htm.

Olive-drab, "Korean War History": http://www.olive-drab.com/od_history_korea.php3.

Out in the Cold, "Australia's Involvement in the Korean War": http://www.awm.gov.au/korea/intro_flash.htm.

The Presidential Papers of Dwight David Eisenhower: http://

www.eisenhowermemorial.org/presidential-papers/
index.htm.

Rutgers Oral History Archives, "World War II, Korea, Vietnam, Cold War": http://oralhistory.rutgers.edu.

2d Infantry Division, "Korean War Veteran Association:"
http://www.2id.org.

Spark Notes. "The Korean War (1950–1953)": http://
www.sparknotes.com/history/american/koreanwar/.

Spotlight Biography, "The Korean War": http://www.smith
sonianeducation.org/spotlight/start.html.

Truman Presidential Museum and Library, "Korea+50: No
Longer Forgotten": http://www.trumanlibrary.org/korea/.

United States Air Force Operations in the Korean Conflict: 25
June—1 November 1950: http://www.wpafb.af.mil/
museum/history/korea/no71.htm.

U.S. Army, "Reports of Nogun Ri Review": http://www.army.
mil/nogunri/.

U.S. Army Corps of Engineers, Baltimore District, "Korean
War Veterans Memorial": http://www.nab.usace.army.mil/
projects/WashingtonDC/korean.html.

U.S. Army in Action Series: John G. Westover, "Combat Support in Korea," Washington, DC: Center of Military History, U.S. Army, 1987, 1990: http://www.army.mil/cmh-
pg/books/korea/22_1_int.htm.

"A Vet Remembers . . . Jim's Korean War Page," Tech. Sgt.
James Barrett Kerins, Sr., USAF (Ret.): http://www.fru
goli.com/korea/.

Volkovskiy, N. L., ed. *Soviet View of the War in Korea*. "The
War in Korea, 1950–1953": http://www.korean-war.com/
Russia/RussianViewTranslation.html.

West, Bob. "Korean War Site": http://www.bob-west.com/.

BIBLIOGRAPHY

Chapter 1

This chapter is based on the sources cited in the following bibliography.

Chapter 2

Chinese Sources on the Korean War

CCP Central Archives. *Zhonggong Zhongyang Wenjian Xuanji* [Selected documents of the CCP Central Committee]. 14 vols. Beijing: CCP Central Academy Press, 1983–87 (restricted edition).

————. *Zhonggong Zhongyang Wenjian Xuanji* [Selected documents of the CCP Central Committee]. 18 vols. Beijing: CCP Central Archives and Manuscripts Press, 1989–92 (open edition).

Central Institute of CCP Historical Documents, ed. *Jianguo Yilai Zhongyao Wenxian Xuanbian, 1949–1950* [Selected important documents since the founding of the PRC]. Beijing: CCP Central Press of Historical Documents, 1991.

Chai Chengwen and Zhao Yongtian. *Banmendian Tanpan* [Panmunjom negotiations]. Beijing: PLA Press, 1989; rev. ed., 1992.

————. *Kangmei Yuanchao Jishi* [A chronicle of the war to resist America and support Korea]. Beijing: CCP Central Press of Historical Documents, 1987.

195

Chaoxian Wenti Wenjian Huibian [Selected documents of the Korean problem]. Beijing: People's Press, 1954.

Chen Yan, ed. *Kangmei Yuanchao Lunwenji* [Essays on the war to resist America]. Shenyang: Liaoning People's Press, 1988.

Chen Yun. *Chen Yun Wengao Xuanbian: 1949–1956* [Selected manuscripts of Chen Yun: 1949–1956]. Beijing: People's Press, 1984.

———. *Chen Yun Wenxuan: 1949–1956* [Selected works of Chen Yun: 1949–1956]. Jiangsu: People's Press, 1984.

CPVF Political Department. *Zhongguo Renmin Zhiyuanjun Kangmei Yuanchao Zhanzheng Zhengzhi Gongzuo Zongjie* [A summary of the CPVF political work in the war to resist America and aid Korea]. Beijing: PLA Press, 1989.

Da Ying. *Zhiyuanjun Zhanfu Jishi* [Stories about CPVF POWs]. Beijing: People's Liberation Army Press, 1986.

Deng Lifen. *Xin Zhongguo Junshi Huodong Jishi, 1948–1959* [A factual record of new China's military affairs, 1948–1959]. Beijing: CCP Central Press of the Historical Documents, 1989.

Division of Central Archives and Manuscripts, CCP Central Committee. *Documents and Commentaries on the Cease-fire and Armistice Negotiations in Korea.* 2 vols. Beijing: Foreign Language Press, 1953.

———. *Zhonggong Dangshi Fengyun Lu* [Records of the winds and clouds of the CCP history]. Beijing: People's Press, 1990.

Du Ping. *Zai Zhiyuanjun Zongbu: Du Peng Huiyilu* [At the CPVF Headquarters: Memoirs of Du Ping]. Beijing: PLA Press, 1989 and 1991.

He Ming. *Jianzheng: Chaoxian Zhanzheng Zhanfu Qianfan Jieshi Daibiao de Riji* [The memoirs of repatriated POWs of the Korean War]. Beijing: Chinese Literature Press, 2001.

Headquarters, Shenyang Military District. *Zhongguo Junzhi Baike Quanshu* [Encyclopedia of the Chinese military experience]. Shenyang: Shenyang Military District, 1990.

Hong Xuezhi. *Kangmei Yuancho Zhanzheng Huiyilu* [Recollections of the war to resist the United States]. Beijing: PLA Press, 1991.

Houmura Koonko. *Keaide Tongxue, Keaide Zhongguo: Yige Riben Shaonu Yanzhong de Chaoxian Zhanzheng* [Precious classmate,

Precious China: The Korean War in the eye of a Japanese girl].
Shenyang: Liaoning People's Press, 1995.

Hu Hua et al. *Zhonggong Dangshi Renwu Zhuan* [A collection of biographies of CCP historical figures]. 50 vols. Xian: Shanxi People's
Press, 1979–91.

Hu Qinghe. *Chaoxian Zhanzheng zhongde Nuren* [Women in the
Korean War]. Jinan: Yellow River Press, 1992 and 2000.

Huang Zhenxia. *Zhonggong Junren Shi* [Annals of the Chinese Communist soldiers]. Beijing: Institute of Contemporary History, 1968.

Jiang Siyi, ed. *Zhongguo Renmin Jiefangjun Zhengzhi Gongzuoshi* [His-
tory of the PLA's political work]. Beijing: PLA Political Institute
Press, 1984.

Lin Fu et al. *Kongjun Shi* [History of the PLA Air Force]. Beijing:
PLA Press, 1989.

Li Cheng, ed. *Jianguo Yilai Junshi Baizhuang Dashi* [A hundred major events in military history since the founding of the PRC].
Beijing: World Knowledge Press, 1992.

Li Weihan. *Huiyi yu Yanjiu* [Recollections and analyses]. 2 vols. Beijing:
CCP Central Press of Historical Documents, 1986.

Lin Yuansen. *Zhenhan Shijie Yiqian Tian: Zhiyuanjun Jiangshi
Chaoxian Zhanchang Shilu* [Brave 1,000 days: The records of
the Chinese army during the Korean War]. Beijing: Shehui University Press, 2003.

Liu Shaoqi. *Liu Shaoqi Xuanji* [Selected works of Liu Shaoqi]. 2 vols.
Beijing: People's Press, 1985.

Liu Wusheng et al. *Gongheguo Zouguo de Lu: Jianguo Yilai Zhongyao
Wenxian Zhuanti Xuanji* [The path the republic has walked
through: A selected collection of important historical documents
since the founding of the PRC]. 2 vols. Beijing: CCP Central
Press of Historical Documents, 1991.

Lu Liping. *Tongtian Zhilu* [The path to the sky]. Beijing: PLA Press,
1989.

Ma Jinhai and Hou Yunli, eds. *Zhonggong Hujiang yu Mingzhan*
[China's great generals and their famous battles]. Beijing: Social
Science Press, 1995.

Mao Zedong. *Jianguo Yilai Mao Zedong Wengao* [Mao Zedong's manuscripts since the founding of the PRC]. Vols. 1–4, *1949–1954.*

Beijing: CCP Central Archives and Manuscripts Press, 1987–90.

———. *Mao Zedong Junshi Wenji* [A collection of Mao Zedong's military papers]. Vols. 5–6. Beijing: Military Science Press and Central Press of Historical Documents, 1993.

———. *Mao Zedong Junshi Wenxuan—Neibuban* [Selected military works of Mao Zedong—internal edition]. Beijing: PLA Soldiers' Press, 1981.

———. *Mao Zedong Shuxin Xuanji* [Selected correspondences of Mao Zedong]. Beijing: People's Press, 1983.

———. *Mao Zedong Xuanji* [Selected works of Mao Zedong]. Beijing: People's Press, 1978.

The Military Library of the Chinese Academy of Military Science, ed. *Zhongguo Renmin Jiefangjun Zuzhi he Geji Lingdao Chengyuan Minglu* [A list of the historical evolution of organizations and leading members of the PLA]. 3 vols. Beijing: Military Science Press, 1987.

Mo Yang, Yao Jil, et al. *Zhongguo Renmin Jiefangjun Zhanshi* [The war history of the People's Liberation Army]. 3 vols. Beijing: Military Science Press, 1987.

Nie Rongzhen. *Nie Rongzhen Junshi Wenxuan* [Selected Military Works of Nie Rongzhen]. Beijing: PLA Press, 1992.

Pak Toufu. *Zhonggong Canjia Hanzhan Yuanyinzhi Yanjiu* [An examination of why the CCP decided to participate in the Korean War]. Taipei: Numin Cultural Service, 1975.

Pang Xianhi and Lie Jie. *Mao Zedong yu Kangmei Yuancho* [Mao Zedong and the war resisting America]. Beijing: Central Historical Material Press, 2000.

Peng Dehuai. *Peng Dehuai Junshi Wenxuan* [Selected Military Works of Peng Dehuai]. Beijing: The Central Press of Historical Documents, 1988.

Ruan Jiaxi. "The War to Resist America and Aid Korea and the Rise of the New China," *Junshi Shilin* [Studies of Military History] 6 (1993).

Shen Zhihua. *Chaoxian Zhanzheng Jimi* [Secrets of the Korean War]. Hong Kong: Cosmos Books, 1995.

———. *Mao Zedong, Sidalin, yu Hanzhan: Zhongsu Zuigao Jimi Dangan* [Mao Zedong, Stalin, and the Korean War: The Chinese-

Soviet top secret documents]. Hong Kong: Cosmos Books, 1998.

Shen Zonghong, Bi Jianzhong, et al. for the Academy of Military Sciences. *Zhongguo Renmin Jiefangjun Liushinian Dashiji: 1927–1987* [Records of important PLA events from 1927 to 1987]. Beijing: Military Science Press, 1988.

Shen Zonghong, Meng Zhoahui, et al. *Zhongguo Renmin Zhiyuanjun Kangmei Yuanchao Zhanshi* [The Chinese People's Volunteers Force in the war to resist America and aid Korea]. Beijing: Academy of Military Sciences, 1988 and 2000.

Su Kezhi. *Baqianlilu Yunheyue: Chaoxian Zhanzheng zhongde Disishierjun* [The moon and clouds in 8,000 li-long Way: The 42nd Army in the Korean War]. Beijing: Daily News Press, 1997.

University of National Defense. *Zhongguo Renmin Jiefangjun Zhengzhi Gongzuo Shi* [History of the PLA's political work]. Beijing: National Defense University Press, 1989.

Wang Debing. *Zhiyuanjun Zhanshi Chaoxian Zhanzheng Huiyilu* [Memories of the Chinese Volunteers Force in the Korean War]. Beijing: Wang Deping, 2003.

Wang Funian. "A Summary of the Negotiations on the Korean Cease-Fire," *Dangshi Yanjiu Ziliao* [Sources of the party history research] 6 (1983).

Wang Jiaxing. *Wang Jiaxiang Xuanji* [Selected works of Wang Jiaxiang]. Beijing: People's Press, 1989.

Wang Naiqing. *"Lianheguo": Junde Zhanfu Lishi: Yi Chaoxian Zhanzhengzhongde Bitong Zhanfuying* ["The UN Army": The story of the POW camp in Myedong during the Korean War]. Beijing: National Defense University Press, 2000.

Wang Suhong and Wang Yubin. *Kongzhan zai Chaoxian* [Air war in Korea]. Beijing: PLA Literature Press, 1992.

Wei Jie. *Wei Jie Hiuyilu* [Memoirs of Wei Jie]. Nanjing: Guangxi People's Press, 1989.

Wu Xinquan. *Chaoxian Zhanzheng Yiqian Tian: Sanshijiujun zai Chaoxian* [The 1,000 days of war in Korean War: The 39th Army in Korea]. Shenyang: Liaoning People's Press, 1996.

Xia Wei. *Shenbing: Zhongguo Fanghuabing zai Xingdong* [The operations of Chinese anti-chemical units]. Beijing: National Defense University Press, 2000.

Xie Lifu. *Chaoxian Zhangzheng Shilu* [Real records of the Korean War]. Beijing: World Knowledge Press, 1993.

Xu Xiangqian. *Lishide Huigu* [Remember history]. Beijing: PLA Press, 1987.

Yang Dezhi. *Weile Heping* [For the sake of peace]. Beijing: PLA Press, 1987.

———. *Yang Dezhi Huiyilu* [Memoirs of Yang Dezhi]. Beijing: PLA Press, 1992.

Zhang Wenyuan, ed. *Kangmei Yuancho Sanwen Xuanji* [The best of prose writings on the resist-America movement]. Beijing: People's Literature Press, 1990.

Zhang Zeshi. *Wode Chaoxian Zhanzheng: Yige Zhiyuanjun Zhanfude Zishu* [My war: The story of a Chinese POW]. Beijing: History and Literature Press, 2000.

Zhongmei Guanxi Ziliao Huibian [A collection of materials concerning Chinese-American relations]. Beijing: World Knowledge Press, 1957.

Zhou Enlai. *Zhou Enlai Shuxin Xuanji* [Selected telegrams and letters of Zhou Enlai]. Beijing: CCP Central Archives and Manuscripts Press, 1988.

———. *Zhou Enlai Xuanji* [Selected works of Zhou Enlai]. 2 vols. Beijing: CCP Central Archives and Manuscripts Press, 1984.

English-Language Sources

Bajanov, Evgeniy P., and Natalia Bajanova. "The Korean Conflict, 1950–1953: The Most Mysterious War of the 20th Century," 1998, manuscript history distributed by the authors.

Camilleri, Joseph. *Chinese Foreign Policy: The Maoist Era and Its Aftermath.* London: Martin Robertson, 1980.

Chang, Gordon. *Friends and Enemies: The United States, China, and the Soviet Union, 1948–1972.* Stanford, CA: Stanford University Press, 1990.

Chen Jian. *China's Road to the Korean War: The Making of the Sino-American Confrontation.* New York: Columbia University Press, 1994.

———. *Mao's China and the Cold War.* Chapel Hill: University of North Carolina Press, 2000.

Christensen, Thomas. *Useful Adversaries: Grand Strategy, Domestic Mobilization and Sino-American Conflict, 1947–1958*. Princeton, NJ: Princeton University Press, 1996.

Faculty of Futan University, trans. *Stories of the Chinese People's Volunteers*. Beijing: Foreign Language Press, 1960.

———. *A Volunteer Soldier's Day*. Beijing: PLA Press, 1961.

Gaddis, John Lewis. *The Cold War: A New History*. New York: Penguin Group, 2005.

George, Alexander L., et al. *The Chinese Communist Army in Action: The Korean War and Its Aftermath*. New York: Columbia University Press, 1967.

Goncharov, Sergei N., John W. Lewis, and Xue Litai. *Uncertain Partners: Stalin, Mao, and the Korean War*. Stanford, CA: Stanford University Press, 1993.

Gurtov, Melvin, and Hwang Byeong-mu. *China Under Threat: The Politics of Strategy and Diplomacy*. Baltimore, MD: Johns Hopkins University Press, 1980.

Harding, Harry, and Yuan Min, eds. *Sino-American Relations, 1945–1955*. Washington, DC: Scholarly Resources, 1989.

Headquarters, Korean People's Army. *The Heroic KPA: The Invincible Revolutionary Armed Forces*. Pyongyang: Korean People's Army Publishing House, 1990.

Heo Jeong-ho, Kang Sok-hui, and Pak Tae-ho. *The U.S. Imperialists Started the Korean War*. Pyongyang: Foreign Language Press, 1993.

Kim Ilpyong-jo, comp. *Historical Dictionary of North Korea*. Lanham, MD: Scarecrow Press, 2003.

Kim Kook-hun. "The North Korean People's Army: Its Rise and Fall, 1945–1950." PhD diss., King's College, University of London, 1989.

Khrushchev, Nikita. *Khrushchev Remembers*. Translated by Strobe Talbott. Boston: Little, Brown, 1970 and 1974.

Lankov, Andrei. *From Stalin to Kim Il-sung: The Formation of North Korea, 1945–1950*. New Brunswick, NJ: Rutgers University Press, 2002.

Mahoney, Kevin. *Formidable Enemies: The North Korean and Chinese Soldier in the Korean War*. San Rafael, CA: Presidio Press, 2001.

Mansourov, Alexandre. "Communist War Coalition Formation and the Origins of the Korean War." PhD diss., Columbia University, 1997.

———. "Korean War Studies in the United States." In *Fifty Years After the Korean War: From the Cold War Confrontation to Peaceful Coexistence,* edited by Dong-Sung Kim, Ki-Jung Kim, and Hahnkyu Park. Seoul: Korean Association of International Studies, 2000.

"Mao Informs Stalin of China's Decision to Enter the Korean War, 1950." In *Major Problems in American Foreign Relations.* Vol. 2, *Since 1914,* edited by Dennis Merrill and Thomas Paterson. Translated by Xiaobing Li and Chen Jian. New York: Houghton Mifflin, 2000.

"Mao's Dispatch of Chinese Troops to Korea: Forty-six Telegrams, July–October 1950." Edited and translated by Xiaobing Li, Wang Xi, and Chen Jian. *Chinese Historians* 5 (Spring 1992): 63–86.

"Mao's Forty-nine Telegrams During the Korean War, October–December 1950." Edited and translated by Xiabong Li and Glenn Tracy. *Chinese Historians* 5 (Fall 1992): 65–85.

Mao Zedong. *Military Writings of Mao Tse-tung.* Beijing: Foreign Language Press, 1967.

Roe, Patrick C. *The Dragon Strikes: China and the Korean War, June–December 1950.* San Rafael, CA: Presidio Press, 2000.

Schrader, Charles R. *Communist Logistics in the Korean War.* Westport, CT: Greenwood Press, 1995.

Shen Zhihua. *Mao Zedong, Stalin, and the Korean War.* Hong Kong: Tran Di, 1995.

———. "Sino-North Korean Conflict and Its Resolution During the Korean War." Translated by Dong Gil Kim and Jeffrey Becker. CWIHP *Bulletin* 14–15 (Winter 2003–Spring 2004): 9–24.

Simmons, Robert R. *The Strained Alliance: Peking, Pyongyang, Moscow, and the Politics of the Korean War.* New York: Columbia University Press, 1975.

Spurr, Russell. *Enter the Dragon: China's Undeclared War Against the U S. in Korea, 1950–1951.* New York: Henry Holt, 1988.

Tang Tsou. *America's Failure in China, 1941–1950.* Chicago: University of Chicago Press, 1963.

Torkunov, Anatoly. *The War in Korea, 1950–1953.* Tokyo: ICF Publishers, 2000.

The Victorious Fatherland Liberation War Museum. Pyongyang: Foreign Language Publishing House, 1997.

Westad, Odd Arne, ed. *Brothers in Arms: The Rise and Fall of Sino-Soviet Alliance, 1945–1963.* Stanford, CA: Woodrow Wilson Center and Stanford University Press, 1998.

———. *The Global Cold War: Third World Interventions and the Making of Our Times.* London and New York: Cambridge University Press, 2005.

Whiting, Allen. *China Crosses the Yalu: The Decision to Enter the Korean War.* New York: Macmillan, 1960.

Yu Bin. "What China Learned from Its 'Forgotten War' in Korea." *Strategic Review* 5 (Summer 1998): 4–16.

Zelman, Walter A. *Chinese Intervention in the Korean War.* Berkeley: University of California Press, 1967.

Zhang Shu Gang. *Mao's Military Romanticism: China and the Korean War, 1950–1953.* Lawrence: University Press of Kansas, 1995.

Zhang Zhu Gang and Chen Jian, eds. *Chinese Communist Foreign Policy and the Cold War in Asia: New Documentary Evidence, 1944–1950.* Chicago: Imprint Publications, 1996.

Zubok, Vladislaw, and Constantine Pleshkov. *Inside the Kremlin's Cold War: From Stalin to Khrushchev.* Cambridge, MA: Harvard University Press, 1996.

Russian Archives

Arkhiv Vnesheni Politiki Ministerstva Innostrannykh del Rossiyskoy Federatsii (AVP RF) (Foreign Policy Archive of the Ministry of Foreign Affairs of the Russian Federation)

Prezidentskiy Arkhiv Rossiyskoy Federatsii (PARF) (Presidential Archives of the Russian Federation, former Politburo Archive)

Rossiiskii Tsentr Khraneniia i Izucheniia dokumentov Noveishei Istorii (RTsKnIDNI) (former Central Party Archives, Russian Center for Storage and Treatment of Contemporary Documents, only documents after 1952)

Rossiiskii Tsentr Khraneniia i Obrabotki Sovremennoi Dokumentatsii (RTsKhOSD) (former Central Party Archives, Russian Center

for Storage and Treatment of Contemporary Documentation,
only documents prior to 1952)
Tsentral'nyi Voyenni Arkhiv (TsAMO) (Central Military Archive of
the Ministry of Defense of the Russian Federation)

Russian Sources on the Korean War

Abakumov, B. S. *V nebe Severnoi Korei* [In North Korea]. Kursk:
Raduya, 1997.

Gagin, V. V. *Vozdushnaia voina v Koree-2: glazami amerikantsev* [Aerial
war in Korea: Perspectives of an American]. Moscow: Penza, 1997.

———. *Vozdushnaia voina v Koree, 1950–1953 g.g.* [Aerial war in
Korea]. Voronezh: Poligraph, 1997.

Orlov, A. S., and Viktor A. Gavrilov. *Tainy koreiskoi voiny* [The secrets of the Korean War]. Moscow: Kuchkovo Polye, 2003.

Pepelaev, Evgenii. *"MiGi" protiv "Seibrov": vospominaniia letchika*
[MiG against Sabrejet: Lecture]. Moscow: Delta NPP, 2000.

Razuvaev, V. N., et al. *Nachal'niku General'nogo Shtaba SA Generalu
Armii Tovarishchu Shtemenko 5.M: Diestviia voisk KNA* [Reports
of the military mission to North Korea to the Fifth Directorate
of the Soviet Armed Forces General Staff (Gen. T. Shtemenko)].
3 vols. Moscow: FRS Army Press, 2002.

Savel'ev, R. V. *Koreiskii poluostrov: mify, ozhidaniia I real'nost': materialy
IV nauchnoi konferentsii, Moskva, 15–16.03.2000 g* [Korean Peninsula: Myths, expectations, and reality—proceedings of the 4th
academic conference, Moscow, 2000, March 15–16]. Moscow:
RTsKhIDNI, 2001.

Tikhomirov, V. D. *Koreiskaia problema I mezhdunarodnye faktory:
1945-nachalo 80-kh godov* [Korean problem and international
factors]. Moscow, 1998.

Torkunov, Anatolii Vasil'evich. *Zagadochnaia voina: koreiskii konflikt,
1950–1953 godov* [Mysterious war: Korean conflict, 1950–1953].
Moscow, 2000.

Torkunov, Anatolii Vasil'evich, and E. P. Ufimtsev. *Koreiskaia problema:
novyi vzgliad* [Korean problem: New perspectives]. Moscow,
1995.

Vanin, Urii Vasil'evich. *Voina v Koree, 1950–1953 gg.; vzgliad cherez
50 let: materialy mezhdunarodnoi naucho-teoreticheskoi konferentsii*

[The Korean War, 1950–1953; Perspectives after 50 years—materials from International Theoretical Science Conference]. Moscow, 2000.

Volkovskii, N. L. *Voina v Koree, 1950–1953* [The Korean War, 1950–1953]. St. Petersburg: Poligon, 2000.

Wada, Haruki, and G. A. Bordiugov. *Rossiia kak problema vsemirnoi istorii: izbrannye trudy* [Russia as the problem of world history: Selected works]. Moscow, 1999.

Yu Pyong-yong, E. P. Bajanov, and V. F. Li. *Vneshnepoliticheskaia strategiia Velikobritanii I koreiskii vopros v XX veke: politologicheskii analiz* [Britain's foreign policy and Korean issue in the 20th century: A political analysis]. Moscow, 1999.

Chapter 3

English-Language Sources

Acheson, Dean. *The Korean War*. New York: W. W. Norton, 1971.

———. *Present at the Creation*. New York: W. W. Norton, 1969.

Allen, Richard C. *Korea's Syngman Rhee: An Unauthorized Portrait*. Rutland, VT: Tuttle, 1960.

Allison, John M. *Ambassador from the Prairie*. Boston: Houghton Mifflin, 1973.

Armstrong, Charles K. *The North Korean Revolution, 1945–1950*. Ithaca, NY: Cornell University Press, 2003.

Baldwin, Frank, ed. *Without Parallel: The Korean-American Relationship Since 1945*. New York: Random House, 1973.

Cho Soong-sung. *Korea in World Politics, 1940–1950*. Berkeley: University of California Press, 1967.

Choi Duk-shin. *Panmunjom and After*. New York: Vantage Press, 1972.

Chung, Henry. *Korea and the United States Through War and Peace, 1943–1960*. Seoul: Yonsei University Press, 2000.

Clark, Donald N. *Living Dangerously in Korea: The Western Experience, 1900–1950*. Norwalk, CT: Eastbridge, 2003.

Cumings, Bruce, ed. *Child of Conflict: The Korean-American Relationship, 1943–1953*. Seattle: University of Washington Press, 1983.

———. *Korea's Place in the Sun: A Modern History,* rev. ed. New York: W. W. Norton, 2005.

————. *Origins of the Korean War*. Vol. 1, *Liberation and the Emergence of Separate Regimes*. Princeton, NJ: Princeton University Press, 1981.

————. *Origins of the Korean War*. Vol. 2, *The Roaring of the Cataract, 1947–1950*. Princeton, NJ: Princeton University Press, 1990.

Dobbs, Charles M. *The Unwanted Symbol: American Foreign Policy, the Cold War, and Korea, 1945–1950*. Kent, OH: Kent University Press, 1981.

Eckert, Carter J. *Offspring of the Empire: The Koch'ang Kims and the Origins of Korean Capitalism*. Seattle: University of Washington, 1991.

Eckert, Carter J., Lee Ki-baik, Young Ik Lew, Michael Robinson, and Edward W. Wagner. *Korea: Old and New*. Seoul: Iljogak for the Korea Institute, Harvard University, rev. ed., 1990.

Henderson, Gregory. *Korea: The Politics of the Vortex*. Cambridge, MA: Harvard University Press, 1968.

Kim Chum-kon. *The Korean War, 1950–1953*. Seoul: Kwangmyong Publishing, 1973.

Kim Gye-dong. *Foreign Intervention in Korea*. Dartmouth, NH: Dartmouth Publishing, 1993.

Kim Joung-won A. *Divided Korea: The Politics of Development, 1945–1972*. Cambridge, MA: Harvard University Press, 1975.

Kim Myung-ki. *The Korean War and International Law*. Claremont, CA: Paige Press, 1991.

Korean Institute of Military History. *The Korean War*. 3 vols. Seoul: Ministry of National Defense, 1998–2000, and Lincoln, NE: University of Nebraska Press, 2000–2001.

Kwak Tae-han, John Chang, Cho Soon-sang, and Shannon McCune, eds. *U.S.-Korean Relations, 1882–1982*. Seoul: Institute for Far Eastern Studies, Kyungnam University, 1982.

Lansdown, John R. P. *With the Carriers in Korea, 1950–1953: The Fleet Air Arm Story*. Wilmslow, Cheshire, UK: Crécy Publishing, 1997.

Macdonald, Donald Stone. *The Koreans*. Boulder, CO: Westview Press, 1988.

————. *U.S.-Korean Relations From Liberation to Self-Reliance*. Boulder, CO: Westview Press, 1992.

Matray, James I. *The Reluctant Crusade: American Foreign Policy in Korea, 1941–1950.* Honolulu: University of Hawaii Press, 1985.

McCune, George M., and Arthur L. Grey. *Korea Today.* Cambridge, MA: Harvard University Press, 1950.

Meade, E. Grant. *American Military Government in Korea.* New York: Columbia University Press, 1951.

Merrill, John. *Korea: The Peninsular Origins of the War.* Wilmington: University of Delaware Press, 1989.

Millett, Allan R. "Captain James H. Hausman and the Formation of the Korean Army, 1945–1950." *Armed Forces and Society* 23 (Summer 1997): 503–509.

———. *The War for Korea.* Vol. 1. *A House Burning, 1945–1950.* Lawrence: University Press of Kansas, 2005.

Nahm, Andrew C. *Korea, Tradition and Transformation: A History of the Korean People.* Elizabeth, NJ: Hollym International, 1988.

Nam Koon-woo. *The North Korean Communist Leadership, 1945–1965.* Tuscaloosa: University of Alabama Press, 1974.

Oh, Bonnie B. C., ed. *Korea Under the American Military Government, 1945–1948.* Westport, CT: Praeger, 2002.

Oliver, Robert T. *Syngman Rhee: The Man Behind the Myth.* New York: Dodd, Mead, 1955.

———. *Syngman Rhee and American Involvement in Korea, 1942–1960.* Seoul, ROK: Panmun Books, 1978.

Paik Sun Yup. *From Pusan to Panmunjom.* Washington, DC: Brassey's, Inc., 1992.

Pak Chi-young. *Political Opposition in Korea, 1945–1950.* Seoul: Seoul National University Press, 1980.

Pyun Yong-tae. *Korea: My Country.* Washington, DC: Korean Pacific Press, 1953.

Rose, Lisle. *Roots of Tragedy: The United States and the Struggle for Asia, 1945–1953.* Westport, CT: Greenwood Press, 1976.

Scalapino, Robert, and Lee Chon-sik. *Communism in Korea.* Berkeley: University of California Press, 1973.

Seiler, Sydney A. *Kim Il-sung: The Creation of a Legend, the Building of a Regime.* Landover, MD: University Press of America, 1994.

Song Hyo-soon. *The Fight for Freedom.* Seoul: Korean Library Association, 1980.

Stueck, William. *The Road to Confrontation: American Policy Toward China and Korea, 1947–1950.* Chapel Hill: University of North Carolina, 1981.

Suh Dae-sook. *Kim Il-sung: The North Korean Leader.* New York: Columbia University Press, 1988.

———. *The Korean Communist Movement, 1918–1949.* Princeton, NJ: Princeton University Press, 1967.

Underwood, Horace G. *Korea in War, Revolution, and Peace: The Recollections of Horace G. Underwood.* With Michael J. Devine. Seoul: Yonsei University Press, 2001.

Van Ree, Eric. *Socialism in One Zone: Stalin's Policy in Korea, 1945–1947.* New York: New York University Press, 1988.

Yim, Louise. *My Forty-Year Fight for Korea.* Reprint, Seoul: Chungang University, 1967.

North Korean Publications on the Korean War

Cha Chun-bong. *Nuga Choson Jeonjaeng Ireukyonneunga* [Who started the Korean War?] Pyongyang: Sahoe Kwahak Chulpansa, 1993.

Choson Inmin Daehan Migukjuui Jadeului Sikinjongjeok Manhaeng [Savage atrocities of the American imperialists against the Korean people]. Hyattsville, MD: Amerasian Data Research Services, 1952 and 1982.

Choson Inmineun Dosalja Mijewa Yi Sung-man Yeokdodeului Yasujok Manhaeng Boksuharira [The Korean people will seek vengeance against the brutal savagery of the butchers, America, and Syngman Rhee outlaws]. Hyattsville, MD: Amerasian Data Research Service, 1982.

Ho Chong-ho. *Mije Geukdong Chimnyak Jeongchaekgwa Choson Jeongjaeng* [The Far Eastern aggression policies of the U.S. and the Korean War]. Pyongyang: Sahoe Kwahak Chulpansa, 1993.

Jeonsi Gayo Yuraejip [The original collection of wartime songs]. Pyongyang: Munye Chulpansa, 1987.

Jogukui Tongil Dongrip Kwa Jayureul Wihayeo Jeonguiui Jeonjaenge Chon Gwolgi Haja [Let's stand up for the righteous war of the fatherland's unification, independence, and freedom]! Hyattsville, MD: Amerasian Data Research Services, 1950 and 1980.

Juneumhan Siryeneul Igyeonaen Hubang Chongneondeul [The youths in the rear who overcame the severe ordeal]. Pyongyang: Kumsong Chongnyon Chulpansa, 1977.

Kim Il-sung. *Eonjena Widaehan Suryeongnimgwa Hamkke* [We are always with the great leader]. Pyongyang: Kullo Tanche Chulpansa, 1977.

———. *Hyeon Gunsa Jeongsewa Dang Jeonggwon Gigwan Kwa Immingundaereul Ganghwahagi Wihan Myeotgaji Munje: Choson Rodongdang Jungang Wiwonhoe Je 5-cha Jeonwonhoeuiseo Han Gyeollon, 1952-nyon 12-wol 18-il* [Several problems in strengthening the present military and party, the political party apparatus, and the people's army: Conclusion of the 5th general meeting of the Korean Labor Party Central Committee, December 18, 1952]. Pyongyang: Choson Nodongdang Chulpansa, 1977.

———. *Singyang Wihan Tujaengeun Jogukeul Wihan Tujaengimyeo Chonson Seungrireul Bojanghagi Wihan Tujaengida: Pyongan Namdo Nongmindeulgwahan Damhwa, 1951-nyon 3-wol 15-il* [In the struggle for food there is the struggle for the fatherland and the struggle to guarantee frontline victory: A conversation with the peasants of South Pyongang province, March 15, 1951]. Pyongyang: Korean People's Press, 1977.

Kim Pyong-hyon and Kim Min-ju. *Cheju-do Inmindului Ui 4.3 Mijang Tujaengsa* [History of the Cheju Island people's 4.3 uprising]. Osaka: Munu-sa, 1963.

Kim Sun-yong. *Hanadoen Joguk Wihae* [For the sake of becoming one fatherland]. Pyongyang: Kumsong Chongnyon Chulpansa, 1991.

———. *Tto Dasi Jeokgueseo* [Again from the Communists]. Pyongyang: Kumsong Chongnyon Chulpansa, 1991.

Kwon Hyok-chang. *Hwason Cholli Choson Sugi* [Hwason: Frontline memoirs]. Pyongyang: Kumsong Chongnyon Chulpansa, 1984 and 1992.

Yeojeonsaui Bogo [An account of women soldiers]. Pyongyang: Gunro Danche Chulpansa, 1977.

Yeoksaga Bon Choson Jeonjaeng [History seen in the Korean War]. Pyongyang: Sahoe Kwahak Chulpansa, 1993.

Yi Mong-ho. *Choson Inminui Joguk Haebang Jeonjaeng Seungriui Gukjejeok Uiui* [The international significance of the Korean people's victory in liberating the fatherland]. Pyongyang: Choson Nodongdang Chulpansa, 1965.

Republic of Korea Sources

Cha Ilhyuk. *Palchisan Tobeoldaejang Cha Ilhyukui Sugi* [The memoir of Cha Ilhyuk: The commander of pacifying units]. Seoul: Kilinwon, 1990.

Chang Do-yeong. *Manghyang: Chunyukgun Chammo Chongchang Chang Do-yeong Huigorok* [Nostalgia: The Memories of ROK Army Former Chief of Staff Chang Do-yeong]. Seoul: Supsok, 2001.

Cho Pyong-ok. *Naui Hoegorok* [My recollections]. Seoul: Mingyosa, 1959.

Choi Myeng-san. *Hanguk Jeonjaengwa Gukje Gwangye* [The Korean War and international relationship]. Seoul: Gonggun Daehak, 1996.

Choi Sang-yong. *Migunjeonggwa Hanguk Minjokjuui* [American military government and Korean nationalism]. Seoul: Nanam, 1988.

Choi Young-hee. *Gyeokdongui Haebang Samnyeon* [The three violent years after national liberation]. Seoul: Hanlim University Press, 1996.

Chung Il-kwon. *Jeongjaeng gwa Hyujeon* [War and truce]. Seoul: Dongha Daily Press, 1986.

Gukbangbu Gunsa Pyeonchan Yeonguso [The Institute for Military History Compilation]. *Dae Bijeonggyu Jeonsa, 1945–1960* [The history of antiguerrilla war, 1945–1960]. Seoul: Gukbangbu Gunsa Pyeonchan Yeonguso, 1988.

———. *Hanguk Jeonjaeng* [The Korean War]. Seoul: Army Head-quarters Press, 1995.

———. *Hanguk Jeonjaenga Jiwonsa: Insa, Gunsu, Minganjiwon* [Supporting operations during the Korean War: Human resources, logistics, and civil affairs]. Seoul: Army Headquarters Press, 1997.

———. *Hanguk Jeonjaeng Pihae Tonggyejip* [Statistics of the damage during the Korean War]. Seoul: Army Headquarters Press, 1996.

———. *Hanguk Jeonjaeng Poro* [The Korean War and POWs]. Seoul: Army Headquarters Press, 1996.

———. *Hanguk Jeonjaengsaui Saeroun Yeongu: 6.25 Jeonjaeng* [A new study of the Korean War]. Seoul: Army Headquarters Press, 2002.

Hallim Daehakgyo Asia Munhwa Yeonguso [The Asian culture center at Hallim University]. *Palchisan Jaryojip* [The materials of Palchisan]. Chuncheon: Hallim University Press, 1996.

Han Tae-su. *Hanguk Jeongdangsa* [A history of Korean political parties]. Seoul: Sintaeyangsa, 1961.

Hangook Jeongsin Munhwa Yeonguwon. *Naega Gyeokeun Hanguk Jeonjaeggwa Park Jeong-hui Jeongbu* [The Korean War and Park Jeonghi Regime that I experienced]. Seoul: Seonin, 2004.

Hanguk Gunsa Hakhoe. *Hanguk Jeonjaengui Juyo Jaengjeom Jaejomyeong* [Reconsidering Controversial Arguments of the Korean War]. Seoul: Army Headquarters, 1998.

Hanguk Jeonjaengsa Hakhoe, ed. *Hanguk Jeonjaengwa Hyujeonchaeje* [The Korean War and the system of Truce]. Seoul: Jipmundang, 1998.

Hallim Daehakgyo Asia Munhwa Yeonguso. *Hanguk Jeonjaengui Ppira* [Leaflets in the Korean War]. Seoul: Hanlimdaehakgyo Chulpanbu, 2000.

History of the United Nations in Korea. 6 vols. Seoul: Ministry of National Defense, 1975.

Jeong Hae-ku. *Siwol Inmin Hangjaeng Yeongu* [A study of the October people's uprising]. Seoul: Yeoreumsa, 1988.

Jeong Jin-sang et al. *Hanguk Jeonjaenggwa Sahoe Gujoui Byeonhwa* [The Korean War and the change of social structure]. Seoul: Paeksanseodang, 1999.

Jeong Jinsang, et al. *Hanguk Jeonjaengwa Jabonjuui* [The Korean War and Capitalism]. Seoul: Hanwool, 2000.

Jeong Myong-hwan. *Bullanseo Jisikindeulgwa Hanguk Jeonjaeng* [French Intellectuals and the Korean War]. Seoul: Minumsa, 2004.

Jo Seong-hun. *Hanguk Jeonjaengui Yugyeok Jeonsa* [The commando operations during the Korean War]. Seoul: Gukbangbu Gunsa Pyeonchan Yeonguso, 2003.

Jung Il-hwa. *Daetongryongul Omkin Migun Daewi* [The U.S. Army captain who moved presidents]. Seoul: Hankuk Moonwon, 1995.

Kim Dongchun. *Jeonjaenggwa Sahoe (Uriege Hanguk Jeonjaengeun*

Mueot Ieotna) [War and Society: What is the meaning of the Korean War to us?]. Seoul: Dolbege, 2000.

Kim In-sik. *Imjingangeseo Naesorakkaji: Yukbon Jikhal Yugyeokdaeui Jeok Hubangjiyeokjakjeon 60il* [From the Imjin River to Mt. Sorak: The sixty-day operation of the commando unit under the direct command of the army headquarters in enemy rear area]. Seoul: Gukbangbu Gunsa Geonseol Yeonguso, 1991.

Kim Kye-dong. *Hanbandoui Bundangwa Jeonjaeng* [The division of the Korean Peninusla and the war].

Kim Kyu-sik. *Gwangbok Isimnyeon* [Twenty years of restoration]. Seoul: Kyemongsa, 1972.

Kim Yong-taek. *Hanguk Jeonjaenggsa Hampyeong Yangmin Haksal* [The Korean War and the massacre in Hampyeong]. Seoul: Sahoe Munhwawon, 2001.

Kim Young. *Palchisan Cheolchang Sucheop* [The memoir of a Palchisan in prison]. Seoul: Hangyeore, 1990.

Kim Young-ho. *Hanguk Jeonjaengui Giwongwa Jeongae Gwajeong: Stalingwa Migukui Rollback* [The origin and the development of the Korea War: The Rollback of Stalin and the U.S.]. Seoul: Dure, 1998.

Korean Institute for Military History Compilation (formerly Korean Institute for Military History). *History of the Korean War.* 3 vols. Seoul: Ministry of National Defense, 1998–2000.; and Lincoln: University of Nebraska Press, 2000–2002.

Korean War Studies Association. *Hanguk Jeonjaengwa Jungguk* [The Korean War and China]. Seoul: KWSA, 2004.

————. *Talnaengjeon Sidaeui Hanguk Jeonjaengui Jaejomyeong* [Illuminating the Korean War from the post–Cold War era]. Seoul: KWSA, 2002.

Lee Chi-op. *Call Me "Speedy" Lee: Memoirs of a Korean War Soldier.* Seoul: Won Min, 2001.

Lee Hijin and Oe Ihhwan. *Hanguk Jeonjaengui Susukkekki: Bundonui* [Mysteries of the Korean War: The division of the country and the beginning of the war!] Seoul: Garamgihoek, 2000.

Lee Hyong-kun. *Hoegorok: Gunbeon Ilbeonui Oegil Insaeng* [Memories: The lonely life of the man with service number one]. Seoul: Chungang Press, 1993.

Lee Janghee. *Hanguk Jeonjaeng 50nyeoni Namgin Gukje Indobeopjeok Munje* [The international humanitarian judicial problems that the Korean War left]. Seoul: Asia Sahoegwahak Yeonguso, 2000.

Lee Ki-bong. *Palchisanui Jinsil* [The truth of Palchisan]. Seoul: Dana, 1992.

Lee Mu-ho. *Eoneu Jolbyeongui Gyeokkeun Hanguk Jeonjaeng* [The Korean War of a private]. Seoul: Jisiksaneopsa, 2003.

Lee Wanbum. *Hanguk Jeonjaeng (Gukjejeonjeok Jomang)* [The Korean War (From the perspective of international war)]. Seoul: Baeksan Seodang, 1999.

Lee Won-bok. *Taigeo Changgun Sung Yo-Chan* [Tiger General Sung Yo-Chan]. Seoul: Army Publishing House, 1996.

Lee Yong-sik. *Gangdong Jeongchi Hakwon: Palchisan* [Gangdong Political Institute: Palchisan]. Seoul: Haenglim, 1998.

———. *Palchisan.* Seoul: Haenglim, 1988.

Paik Sun Yup. *Gun gwa Na* [The Army and I]. Seoul: Daeryak Yonkuson, 1989.

Park Du-bok, ed. *Hanguk Jeonjaenggwa Jungguk* [The Korean War and China]. Seoul: Baeksanseodang, 2001.

———. *San Jeungeoreul Tonghaebon Baekho Yugyeokbudaeui Binnaneon Jeontu: Hanguk Jeongjaengjung Jeokjineseo Junghoingmujin Hwalyakhan Bihwa* [The splendid combats of Baekho Unit based on real testimonies: The secret stories of dauntless operations in the enemy area during the Korean War]. Inchon: Hanguk Yugeokgun Baekhobudae Jeonwuhoi [The Veterans' Association of White Tigers—the Korean Commandos], 2004.

Park Keyju. *Jayugonghwaguk Choihuui Nal: Hanguk Jeonjaeng Baemyon Bisa* [The last day of the republic of freedom: The secret story of the Korean War]. Seoul: Jeongupsa, 1995.

Park Myenglim. *Hanguk Jeonjaengui Balbalgwa Giwon* [The origin and beginning of the Korean War]. Seoul: Nanam, 1996.

Park Myenglim and Kim Gyedong. *Hanguk Jeonjaenggwa Gukje Galdeung* [The Korean War and International Conflicts]. Seoul: Tongilbu, 1998.

Park Nam-ki. *Uimubyeongui Hanguk Jeonjaeng Cheheom Sugi* [The memoir of a paramedic in the Korea War]. Seoul: Muneumsa, 2004.

Sin Young-duk. *Hanguk Jeonjaenggwa Chonggun Kija* [The Korean War and war correspondents]. Seoul: Gukhakjaryowon, 2002.

So Jinchol. *Gukje Gongsanjuuiui Eummo* [The plot of international Communism]. Seoul: Wongwang Daehakgyo Chulpanbu, 1996.

Son Sae-il. *Yi Seungman gwa Kim Ku* [Syngman Rhee and Kim Ku]. Seoul: Iljogak, 1970.

Song Nam-hon. *Haebang Samnyeonsa, 1945–1948* [A three-year history of liberation, 1945–1948]. Seoul: Kkachi, 1985.

War History Compilation Committee. *Hankuk Jeonjaengsa* [History of the Korean War]. 9 vols. Seoul: Ministry of National Defense, 1967–70.

Yang Young-jo. *Hanguk Jeonjaeng Ijeonui 38 doseon Chungdol* [The conflicts over the 38th Parallel before the Korean War]. Seoul: Gukbangbu Gunsa Pyeonchan Yeonguso, 1999.

Yi Chong-sik. *Kim Kyu-sik Saengae* [The life of Kim Kyu-sik]. Seoul: Singu Munhwasa, 1974.

Yi Pom-sok. *Minjokgwa Chongnyeon* [Nation and youth]. Seoul: Paeksu-sa, 1947.

Yo Un-hyong. *Mongyang Yo Un-hyong* [The life of Yo Un-hyong]. Seoul: Chongha-gak, 1967.

Yu Jae-hung. *Hoegorok: Gyeokdongui Sewol* [Memoirs: Violent times]. Seoul: Yeulyou Numhwasa, 1994.

Yukgunbanbu [Army headquarters]. *Chunggun Jeonsa* [History of the army before 1948]. Seoul: ROK Army Press, 1980.

Yukgunbanbu Jeongboguk [G-2 of the Army Headquarters]. *Gongbi Yeonhyeok* [The history of guerrillas]. Seoul: Yukgun Gunsa Pyeonchan Yeonguso, 1956.

———. *Yukgun Baljeonsa, 1945–1953* [History of the formation of the national army, 1945–1953]. Seoul: ROK Army Press, 1961.

Yukgunbanbu Jeonsagamsil [Military History Center of the Army Headquarters]. *Gongbi Tobeolsa* [The history of antiguerrilla war operations]. Seoul: Yukgun Gunsa Pyeonchan Yeonguso, 1954.

Yukgunsangsa Pyeonchan Wiwonhoe. *Hanguk Jeonjaeng Yeongung Yeon Je-gun Yukgun Sangsa: Pohang Hyungsangang Jeontueseo* [The Korean War hero: Army Sergeant Yeon Je-gun: At the Hyunsangang Battle in Pohang]. Seoul: Yukgunsangsa Pyeonchan Wiwonhoe, 2001.

Yun Jangho. *Hoguk Gyeongchal Jeonsa* [The history of police antiguerrilla war operations to protect the fatherland]. Seoul: Jeil, 1995.

Chapter 4

English-Language and Other Western Sources

Alexander, Bevin. *Korea: The First War We Lost.* New York: Hippocrene,
1986.

Bailey, Sydney D. *The Korean Armistice.* New York: St. Martin's
Press, 1992.

Barclay, C. N. *The First Commonwealth Division: The Story of British
Commonwealth Land Forces in Korea, 1950–1953.* London: Gale
and Polden, 1954.

Bercuson, David J. *Blood on the Hills: The Canadian Army in the Korean War.* Toronto: University of Toronto Press, 1999.

Blair, Clay. *The Forgotten War: America in Korea, 1950–1953.* New
York: Times Books, 1987.

Bohlen, Charles E. *Witness to History, 1929–1969.* New York: W. W.
Norton, 1973.

Bowie, Robert R., and Richard H. Immerman. *Waging Peace.* New
York: Oxford University Press, 1998.

Bradley, Omar N., and Clay Blair. *A General's Life.* New York: Simon
& Schuster, 1983.

Braim, Paul. *The Will to Win: The Life of General James Van Fleet.*
Annapolis, MD: Naval Institute Press, 2001.

Briggs, Ellis. *Farewell to Foggy Bottom.* New York: McKay, 1964.

Caridi, Robert. *The Korean War and American Politics.* Philadelphia:
University of Pennsylvania Press, 1968.

Clark, Mark W. *From the Danube to the Yalu.* New York: Harpers,
1954.

Cohen, Warren I., and Akira Iriye, eds. *The Great Powers in East Asia,
1953–1960.* New York: Columbia University Press, 1990.

Collins, J. Lawton. *War in Peacetime.* Boston: Houghton Mifflin, 1969.

Condit, Doris. *History of the Office of the Secretary of Defense.* Vol. 2,
The Test of War, 1950–1953. Washington, DC: Office of the Secretary of Defense, 1988.

Cotton, James, and Ian Neary, eds. *The Korean War as History.* Atlantic Highlands, NJ: Humanities Press, 1989.

Cowdrey, Alfred E. *The Medic's War*. Washington, DC: Center for Military History, 1987.

Crahay, B. E. M. *Les Opérations du Premier Contingent Belge en Corée*. Brussels: Institute Géographique Militaire RDN No. 74, 1954.

Donovan, Robert. *Tumultuous Years: The Presidency of Harry S. Truman*. New York: W. W. Norton, 1982.

Edwards, Paul, ed. *To Acknowledge a War: The Korean War in American Memory*. Westport, CT: Greenwood Press, 2000.

Farrar-Hockley, Anthony. *The British Part in the Korean War*. Vol. 1, *A Distant Obligation*. London: Her Majesty's Stationery Office, 1990.

———. *The British Part in the Korean War*. Vol. 2, *An Honourable Discharge*. London: Her Majesty's Stationery Office, 1995.

Fehrenbach, T. R. *This Kind of War: A Study of Unpreparedness*. New York: Macmillan, 1963.

Ferrell, Robert H. *Harry S. Truman and the Modern American Presidency*. Boston: Little, Brown, 1983.

Flint, Roy K. "The Tragic Flaw: MacArthur, The Joint Chiefs and the Korean War." PhD diss., Duke University, 1975.

Foot, Rosemary. *The Practice of Power: U.S. Relations with China Since 1949*. New York: Oxford University Press, 1995.

———. *A Substitute for Victory: The Politics of Peacemaking at the Korean Armistice Talks*. Ithaca, NY: Cornell University Press, 1990.

———. *The Wrong War: American Policy and the Dimensions of the Korean Conflict*. Ithaca, NY: Cornell University Press, 1985.

Foreign Office, Great Britain. *Documents Relating to the Discussion of Korea . . . at the Geneva Conference*. London: HMSO, Cmd 9186, 1954.

Futrell, Robert F. *The United States Air Force in Korea, 1950–1953*, rev. ed., Washington, DC: Office of Air Force History, 1983.

Gahide, J. P. *Belgium and the Korean War*. Brussels: Belgian Center of Military History, 1991.

Goodman, Allen E., ed. *Negotiating While Fighting: The Diary of Admiral C. Turner Joy at the Korean Armistice Conference*. Stanford, CA: Hoover Institution Press, 1978.

Gordenker, Leon. *The United Nations and the Peaceful Unification of Korea: The Politics of Field Operations, 1947–1950*. The Hague: Nijhoff, 1959.

Gough, Terrence J. *U.S. Army Mobilization and Logistics in the Korean War.* Washington, DC: Center of Military History, 1987.

Goulden, Joseph. *Korea: The Untold Story.* New York: Times Books, 1982.

Gradjdanzev, Andrew J. *Modern Korea.* New York: Institute of Pacific Relations, 1944.

Grey, Jeffrey. *The Commonwealth Armies and the Korean War.* Manchester, UK: University of Manchester Press, 1988.

Hagiwara, Ryo. *The Korean War: The Conspiracies by Kim Il-sung and MacArthur.* Tokyo: Bungli Shanja Press, 1993.

Halliday, Jon, and Bruce Cumings. *The Unknown War: Korea.* New York: Panther Books, 1988.

Hamby, Alonzo L. *Man of the People: The Life of Harry S. Truman.* New York: Oxford University Press, 1995.

Haruki, Wada. *Chosen Senso* [The Korean War]. Tokyo: Iwanami Shoten, 1995.

Hastings, Max. *The Korean War.* New York: Simon & Schuster, 1987.

Haynes, Richard F. *The Awesome Power: Harry S. Truman as Commander in Chief.* Baton Rouge: Louisiana State University Press, 1973.

Heefner, Wilson A. *Patton's Bulldog: The Life and Service of General Walton H. Walker.* Shippensburg, PA: White Mane Books, 2001.

Heller, Francis H., ed. *The Korean War: A 25-Year Perspective.* Lawrence: Regents Press of Kansas for the Harry S. Truman Library, 1977.

Hickey, Michael. *The Korean War: The West Confronts Communism, 1950–1953.* London: John Murray, 1999.

Higgins, Rosalyn, ed. *United Nations Peacekeeping, 1945–1967: Documents and Commentary.* 4 vols. London: Oxford University Press, 1970.

Higgins, Trumbull. *Korea and the Fall of MacArthur.* New York: Oxford University Press, 1960.

Historical Section, General Staff, Canadian Army. *Canada's Army in Korea.* Ottawa: Queen's Printer, 1956.

History Division, General Staff. *The Battles of the Turkish Armed Forces in the Korean War, 1950–1953.* Istanbul: Turkish General Staff, 1975.

History Section, Department of the Army. *The Greek Expeditionary Force in Korea (1950–1955).* Athens: Ministry of Defense, 1977.

Hogan, Michael J. *Cross of Iron: Harry S. Truman and the Origins of the National Security State, 1945–1954.* New York: Cambridge University Press, 1998.

Huston, James A. *Guns and Butter, Powder and Rice: U.S. Army Logistics in the Korean War.* Susquehana, PA: Susquehana University Press, 1989.

———. *Outposts and Allies: U.S. Army Logistics in the Cold War, 1945–1953.* Susquehana, PA: Susquehana University Press, 1989.

James, D. Clayton. *The Years of MacArthur.* Vol. 3, *Triumph and Disaster, 1945–1964.* Boston: Houghton Mifflin, 1985.

James, D. Clayton, and Anne Sharp Wells. *Refighting the Last War: Command and Crisis of Korea, 1950–1953.* New York: Free Press, 1993.

Jarman, Robert, ed. *Korea: Political and Economic Reports, 1982–1970.* 14 vols. Chippenham, UK: Anthony Rove, Ltd. for Archives Edition, 2005.

Johnson, U. Alexis, and J. Olivarious McAllistor. *The Right Hand of Power.* New York: Prentice-Hall, 1984.

Joy, C. Turner. *How Communists Negotiate.* New York: Macmillan, 1955.

Kaufman, Burton I., ed. *The Korean Conflict.* Westport, CT: Greenwood Press, 1996.

———. *The Korean War: Challenges in Crisis, Credibility, and Command.* Philadelphia: Temple University Press, 1986.

Kennan, George. *Memoirs.* Vol. 1, *1925–1950.* Boston: Little, Brown, 1967.

———. *Memoirs.* Vol. 2, *1950–1963.* Boston: Little, Brown, 1972.

Kim, Stephen Jin-woo. *Master of Manipulation: Syngman Rhee and the Seoul-Washington Alliance, 1953–1960.* Seoul: Yonsei University Press, 2001.

Kohn, Richard H., ed. "Military Situation in the Far East, May–June 1951," in *American Military Experience.* New York: Arno Press, 1979.

Korean War Research Committee. *The Historical Reillumination of the Korean War.* Seoul: War Memorial Service, 1990.

Kort, Michael. *The Columbia Guide to the Cold War.* New York: Columbia University Press, 1998.

Lee Chai-jin, ed. *The Korean War: 40-Year Perspective*. Claremont, CA: Keck Center for International and Strategic Studies, 1991.

Leffler, Melvyn P. *A Preponderance of Power: National Security, The Truman Administration, and the Cold War*. Stanford, CA: Stanford University Press, 1992.

Levine, Steven I., and Jackie Hiltz, eds. *America's Wars in Asia: A Cultural Approach to History and Memory*. London: M. E. Sharpe, 1998.

Lie, Trygve. *In the Cause of Peace*. New York: Macmillan, 1954.

———. *Containing the Cold War in Asia: British Policies Towards China, Japan and Korea, 1948–1953*. New York: St. Martin's Press, 1997.

———. *The Korean War*. New York: St. Martin's Press, 2000.

Lowe, Peter. *The Origins of the Korean War*. London: Longman, 1986.

Lyons, Gene M. *Military Policy and Economic Aid: The Korean Case, 1950–1953*. Columbus: Ohio State University, 1961.

MacArthur, Douglas. *Reminiscences*. New York: McGraw-Hill, 1964.

MacDonald, Callum A. *Korea: The War Before Vietnam*. New York: Free Press, 1986.

Matray, James I., and Kim Chull-baum, eds. *Korea and the Cold War*. Claremont, CA: Regina Books, 1993.

McCormack, Gavan. *Cold War, Hot War: An Australian Perspective on the Korean War*. Sydney, Australia: Hale and Iremonger, 1983.

McCoy, Donald. *The Presidency of Harry S. Truman*. Lawrence: University of Kansas Press, 1984.

McCullough, David. *Truman*. New York: Simon & Schuster, 1992.

McGibbon, Ian. *New Zealand and the Korean War*. 2 vols. Wellington, NZ: Oxford University Press, 1992 and 1996.

McGlothlen, Ronald L. *Controlling the Waves: Dean Acheson and U.S. Foreign Policy in Asia*. New York: W. W. Norton, 1993.

Meador, Daniel J., ed. *The Korean War in Retrospect: Lessons for the Future*. Lanham, MD: University Press of America, 1998.

Mount, Graeme S. *The Diplomacy of War: The Case of Korea*. With André Laferriere. Montreal: Black Rose Books, 2004.

Murphy, Robert. *Diplomat Among Warriors*. New York: Doubleday, 1964.

Nitze, Paul H. *From Hiroshima to Glasnost: At the Center of Decision—a Memoir*. With Ann M. Smith and Steven L. Rearden. New York: Weidenfeld and Nicholson, 1989.

Noble, Harold J. *Embassy at War.* Seattle: University of Washington Press, 1975.

Office of the Surgeon General, Department of the Army. *Battle Casualties and Medical Statistics: U.S. Army Experience in the Korean War.* Washington, DC: The Surgeon General, U.S. Army, 1973.

Offner, Arnold A. *Another Such Victory: President Truman and the Cold War, 1945–1953.* Stanford, CA: Stanford University Press, 2002.

Okonogi Masao. *Chosen Senso: Beikoku no kaingu katei* [The Korean War: The process of U.S. intervention]. Tokyo: Chou Koronsha, 1986.

O'Neill, Mark A. "The Other Side of the Yalu: Soviet Pilots in the Korean War—Phase One, 1 November 1950–12 April 1951." PhD diss., Florida State University, 1996.

O'Neill, Robert. *Australia in the Korean War.* 2 vols. Canberra: Australian War Memorial, 1981 and 1985.

Paige, Glenn D. *The Korean Decision: June 24–30.* New York: Free Press, 1968.

Pierpaoli, Paul G., Jr. *Truman and Korea: The Political Culture of the Early Cold War.* Columbia: University of Missouri, 1999.

Pogue, Forrest C. *George C. Marshall.* Vol 4, *Statesman, 1945–1959.* New York: Viking, 1987.

Polo, Lily Ann. *A Cold War Alliance: Philippine–South Korean Relations, 1948–1971.* Manila: Asian Center, University of the Philippines, 1984.

Prasad, S. N. *History of the Custodian Force (India) in Korea, 1953–1954.* Delhi: Government of India Press for the Ministry of Defense, 1976.

Rees, David. *Korea: The Limited War.* New York: Macmillan, 1964.

Ridgway, Matthew B. *The Korean War.* New York: Doubleday, 1967.

Rose, Lisle. *The Cold War Comes to Main Street: America in 1950.* Lawrence: University Press of Kansas, 1999.

Ruiz Novoa, Alberto. *El Batallion Colombia en Korea.* Bogota: Imprenta Nacional, 1956.

Rusk, Dean. *As I Saw It.* With Richard Rusk and Daniel S. Papp. New York: W. W. Norton, 1990.

Satyasnguan, Snit, et. al. *The Thai Battalion in Korea, 2495–2496.* Bangkok: Toppan, 1956.

Schaafsma, M. D. *The Dutch Detatchment of the United Nations in Korea, 1950–1954.* The Hague: History of War Section, Royal Netherlands Army General Staff, 1960.

Schaller, Michael. *Douglas MacArthur: The Far Eastern General.* New York: Oxford University Press, 1989.

Schmitt, Michael, and Leslie C. Green, eds. *Levie on the Law of War.* Vol. 70, *International Law Studies.* Newport, RI: Naval War College, 1988.

Schnabel, James F. *United States Army in the Korean War: Policy and Direction—the First Year.* Washington, DC: Office of the Chief of Military History, 1972.

Schnabel, James F., and Robert J. Watson. *The Joint Chiefs of Staff and National Policy.* Vol. 3, *The Korean War.* Washington, DC: JCS Joint History Office, 1998.

Skordiles, Kimon. *Kagnew: The Story of the Ethiopian Fighters in Korea.* Tokyo: Radio Press, 1954.

Smith, Gaddis. *Dean Acheson.* New York: Cooper Square, 1971.

Spanier, John W. *The Truman-MacArthur Controversy and the Korean War.* Cambridge, MA: Harvard University Press, 1959.

Stairs, Dennis. *The Diplomacy of Constraint: Canada, the Korean War, and the United States.* Toronto: University of Toronto Press, 1974.

Stone, I. F. *The Hidden History of the Korean War, 1950–1951.* Boston: Little Brown, 1952.

Stueck, William. *The Korean War: An International History.* Princeton, NJ: Princeton University Press, 1995.

———, ed. *The Korean War in World History.* Lexington: University Press of Kentucky, 2004.

———. *Rethinking the Korean War: A New Diplomatic and Strategic History.* Princeton, NJ: Princeton University Press, 2002.

Thimayya, K. S. Gen. (Indian Army). *Experiment in Neutrality.* New Delhi: Vision Books, 1981.

Thorgrimsson, Thor, and E. C. Russel. *Canadian Naval Operations in Korean Waters, 1950–1955.* Ottawa: Naval Historical Section, Canadian Forces, 1965.

Thorton, Richard C. *Odd Man Out: Truman, Stalin, Mao, and the*

Origins of the Korean War. Washington, DC: Brassey's, Inc., 2000.

Truman, Harry S. *Memoirs.* 2 vols. Garden City, NY: Doubleday, 1955 and 1956.

U.S. Congress, Committee on Armed Services and Committee on Foreign Relations, 82nd Congress, 1st sess. "Military Situation in the Far East, May–June 1951." 5 vols. Washington, DC: Government Printing Office, 1951.

U.S. Department of State. *Korean Problem at the Geneva Conference, April 26–June 15, 1954.* Publication 5609. Washington, DC: Government Printing Office, 1954.

U.S. Department of State, Office of Historian, Bureau of Public Affairs. *Foreign Relations of the United States.* Vol. 3, *The Far East, 1946* (1971); Vol. 6, *The Far East, 1947* (1972); Vol. 6, *The Far East and Australia, 1948* (1974); Vol. 7, *The Far East and Australia, 1949* (1974); Vol. 6, *Korea, 1950* (1976); Vol. 7, *Korea and China, 1951,* 2 parts (1983); Vol. 15, *Korea, 1952–54,* 2 parts (1984). Washington, DC: Government Printing Office.

Vatcher, William H., Jr. *Panmunjom: The Story of the Korean Military Armistice Negotiations.* New York: Praeger, 1958.

Wainstock, Dennis D. *Truman, MacArthur and the Korean War.* Westport, CT: Greenwood Press, 1999.

Weintraub, Stanley. *MacArthur's War: Korea and the Undoing of an American Hero.* New York: Free Press, 2000.

Westover, John G. *Combat Support in Korea.* Washington, DC: Office of the Chief of Military History, 1955.

Whitney, Courtney. *MacArthur: His Rendezvous with History.* New York: Knopf, 1956.

Wilhelm, Alfred D., Jr. *The Chinese at the Negotiating Table.* Washington, DC: National Defense University Press, 1996.

Williams, William J., ed. *A Revolutionary War: Korea and the Transformation of the Postwar World.* Chicago: Imprint Publications, 1993.

Wood, Herbert Fairlie. *Strange Battleground: The Official History of the Canadian Army in Korea.* Ottawa: Queen's Printer, 1956.

Yonosuke, Nagai, and Akira Iriye, eds. *The Origins of the Cold War in Asia.* New York: Columbia University Press, 1977.

Yoo Tae-ho. *The Korean War and the United Nations: A Legal and Diplomatic History.* Louvain, Belgium: Librairie Deobarax, 1965.

Zhang Xiaoming. *Red Wings Over the Yalu: China, the Soviet Union, and the Air War in Korea*. College Station: Texas A&M University Press, 2002.

German-Language Source

Steininger, Rolf. *Der Vergessene Krieg: Korea, 1950–1953*. Munich: Olzog, 2006.

Chapter 5

English-Language Sources

Aerospace Studies Institute. *Guerrilla Warfare and Air Power in Korea, 1950–1953*. Maxwell AFB, AL: Aerospace Studies Institute, Air University, 1964.

Aid, Matthew M. "HUMINT and COMINT in the Korea War." In *The Clandestine Cold War in Asia*, by Richard Aldrich, Gary Rawnsley, and Ming-yeh Rawnsley. London: Frank Cass, 2000.

Alexander, James E. *Inchon to Wonsan: From the Deck of a Destroyer in the Korean War*. Annapolis, MD: Naval Institute Press, 1996.

Alexander, Joseph H. *Battle of the Barricades: U.S. Marines in the Recapture of Seoul*. Washington, DC: History and Museums Division, HQMC, 2000.

———. *Fleet Operations in a Mobile War, September 1950–June 1951*. Washington, DC: Naval Historical Center, 2001.

Anderson, Ellery. *Banner Over Pusan*. London: Evans Brothers, 1980.

Apel, Otto F., and Pat Apel. *MASH: An Army Surgeon in Korea*. Lexington: University of Kentucky, 1998.

Appleman, Roy E. *Disaster in Korea: The Chinese Confront MacArthur*. College Station: Texas A&M University Press, 1989.

———. *East of Chosin: Entrapment and Breakout in Korea*. College Station: Texas A&M University Press, 1987.

———. *Escaping the Trap: The U.S. Army in Northeast Korea, 1950*. College Station: Texas A&M University Press, 1987.

———. *Ridgway Duels for Korea*. College Station: Texas A&M University Press, 1990.

———. *South to the Naktong, North to the Yalu*. Vol. 1 of *The United*

States Army in the Korean War. Washington, DC: Office of the Chief of Military History, 1961.

Baker, Roger G. *A USMC Tanker's War.* Oakland, OR: Elderberry Press, 2001.

Baldovi, Louis, ed. *Foxhole View: Personal Accounts of Hawaii's Korean War Veterans.* Honolulu: University of Hawai'i Press, 2002.

Ballenger, Lee. *The Final Crucible: U.S. Marines in Korea, 1953.* Washington, DC: Brassey's, Inc., 2001.

———. *The Outpost War: The U.S. Marines in Korea, 1952.* Washington, DC: Brassey's, Inc., 2000.

Barker, A. J. *Fortune Favors the Brave: The Battle of the Hook, Korea, 1953.* London: Leo Cooper, 1974.

Barth, G. Bittman. "Tropic Lightning and Taro Leaf in Korea." Unpublished Memoir, 1952–1953, library, U.S. Army Military History Institute.

Bateman, Robert L. *No Gun Ri: A Military History of the Korean War Incident.* Mechanicsburg, PA: Stackpole Books, 2002.

Berebitsky, William. *A Very Long Weekend: The Army National Guard in Korea, 1950–1953.* Shippensburg, PA: White Mane Publishing, 1996.

Berry, Henry. *Hey, Mac, Where Ya Been? Living Memories of the Korean War.* New York: St. Martin's Press, 1988.

Biderman, Albert D. *March to Calumny: The Story of American POWs in the Korean War.* New York: Macmillian, 1963.

Birtle, Andrew J. *The U.S. Army Counterinsurgency and Contingency Operations Doctrine, 1941–1975.* Washington, DC: Center of Military History, 2006.

Black, Robert. *A Ranger Born: A Memoir of Combat and Valor From Korea to Vietnam.* New York: Ballantine, 2002.

Blair, Clay. *Beyond Courage: Escape Tales of Airmen in the Korean War.* New York: Ballantine Books, 1956.

Bowers, William T., William M. Hammond, and George L. MacGarrigle. *Black Soldier, White Army: The 24th Infantry Regiment in Korea.* Washington, DC: Center of Military History, 1996.

Brady, James. *The Coldest War: A Memoir of Korea.* New York: St. Martin's Press, 2000.

Brainard, Morgan. *Men in Low Cut Shoes.* Great Neck, NY: Todd and Honeywell, 1985.

Breuer, William. *Shadow Warriors: The Covert Wars in Korea*. New York: John Wiley, 1996.

Bruning, John R. *Crimson Sky: The Air Battle for Korea*. Washington, DC: Brassey's, Inc., 1999.

Burchett, Wilfred, and Alan Winnington. *Koje Unscreened*. London: Britain-China Friendship Association, 1953.

Bussey, Charles M., Lt. Col., USA (Ret.). *Firefight at Yechon: Courage and Racism in the Korean War*. Washington, DC: Brassey's, Inc., 1991.

Butler, D. M., A. Argent, and J. J. Shelton. *The Fight Leaders: Australian Battlefield Leadership: Green, Hassett and Ferguson, 3rd RAR-Korea*. Canberra: Australian Army History Unit, 2002.

Cagle, Malcolm W., and Frank A. Manson. *The Sea War in Korea*. Annapolis, MD: Naval Institute Press, 1957.

Chappell, Richard G., and Gerald E. Chappell. *Corpsmen: Letters From Korea*. Kent, OH: Kent State University Press, 2000.

Chauncey, Jennie Ethell, and William R. Forstchen. *Hot Shots: An Oral History of the Air Force Combat Pilots of the Korean War*. New York: Morrow, 2000.

Chinese People's Committee for World Peace. *United Nations POWs in Korea*. Beijing: CPCWP, 1953.

Chinnery, Philip. *Korean Atrocity! Forgotten War Crimes, 1950–1953*. Annapolis, MD: Naval Institute Press, 2000.

Choi Duk-shin. *Panmunjom and After*. New York: Vantage Press, 1972.

Chung, Donald. *The Three-Day Promise*. Tallahassee, FL: Loiry Publishing, 1988.

Clark, Eugene F. *The Secrets of Inchon: The Untold Story of the Most Daring Cover Mission of the Korean War*. New York: Penguin Putnam, 2002.

Cleaver, Frederick W., et al. *UN Partisan Warfare in Korea, 1951–1954*. Chevy Chase, MD: Operations Research Office, the Johns Hopkins University, 1956.

Cleveland, William M. *Mosquitos in Korea*. Portsmouth, NH: Peter E. Randall Publishers, 1991.

Cole, Charles F. *Korea Remembered: Enough of a War: The USS Ozborurn's First Korean Tour, 1950–1951*. Las Cruces, NM: Yucca Tree Press, 1995.

Coleman, J. D. *Wonju*. Washington, DC: Brassey's, Inc., 2000.

Condon, John P., Maj. Gen., USMC (Ret.). *Corsairs to Panthers: U.S. Marine Aviation in Korea*. Washington, DC: History and Museums Division, HQMC, 2002.

Cooling, Benjamin Franklin, III, ed. *Close Air Support*. Washington, DC: Office of Air Force History, 1999.

Cooper, Paul L. *Weekend Warriors (VF-871)*. Manhattan, KS: Sunflower Press, 1996.

Courtney, Vincent R. *Hold the Hook: With the Princess Patricia's Canadian Light Infantry in Korea*. Leamington, Ontario: North American Heritage, 1996.

Cowart, Glenn C. *Miracle in Korea: The Evacuation of X Corps From the Hungnam Beachhead*. Columbia: University of South Carolina Press, 1992.

Crane, Conrad. *A Rather Bizarre War: American Airpower Strategy in Korea, 1950–1953*. Lawrence: University Press of Kansas, 2000.

Crawford, C. S. *The Four Deuces: A Korean War Story*. New York: Simon & Schuster, 1989.

Cunningham, Cyril. *No Mercy, No Leniency: Communist Mistreatment of British Prisoners of War in Korea*. London: Leo Cooper, 2000.

Cunningham-Boothe, Ashley, and Peter N. Farrar. *British Forces in the Korean War*. Leamington Spa, UK: British Korean Veterans Association, 1989.

Danisman, Basri. *Situation Negative*. The Hague, the Netherlands: Interdoc, 1973.

Dannenmaier, William D. *We Were Innocents: An Infantryman in Korea*. Urbana and Chicago: University of Illinois Press, 1999.

Davis, Larry. *The 4th Fighter Wing in the Korean War*. Atglen, PA: Schiffer Military History, 2001.

Day, William W. II. *The Running Wounded: A Personal Memory of the Korean War*. Riverton, WY: Big Bend, 1990.

Endicott, Stephen, and Edward Hagerman. *The United States and Biological Warfare*. Bloomington: Indiana University Press, 1998.

Ent, Uzal W., Brig. Gen., ANG (Ret.). *Fighting on the Brink: Defense of the Pusan Perimeter*. Paducah, KY: Turner Publishing, 1996.

Evanhoe, Ed. *Dark Moon: Eighth Army Special Operations in the Korean War*. Annapolis, MD: Naval Institute Press, 1995.

Evans, Douglas K. *Sabre Jets Over Korea: A First Hand Account.* Blue Ridge Summit, PA: Tab Books, 1984.

Field, James A., Jr. *History of United States Naval Operations Korea.* Washington, DC: Director of Naval History, 1962.

Galloway, Jack. *The Last Call of the Bugle: The Long Road to Kapyong.* Queensland, Australia: University of Queensland, 1994.

Geer, Andrew. *The New Breed: The Story of the U.S. Marines in Korea.* New York: Harper's, 1952.

Gibby, Bryan R. "Fighting in a Korean War: The American Advisory Missions From 1946–1953." PhD diss., The Ohio State University, 2004.

Gilbert, Bill. *Ship of Miracles: 14,000 Lives and One Miraculous Voyage.* Chicago: Triumph Books, 2000.

Gugeler, Russell A. *Combat Actions in Korea.* Washington, DC: Office of the Chief of Military History, 1970.

Haas, Michael E. *Apollo's Warriors: United States Air Force Special Operations During the Korean War.* Honolulu: University Press of Hawai'i, 2002.

———. *In the Devil's Shadow: UN Special Operations During the Korean War.* Annapolis, MD: Naval Institute Press, 2002.

Hall, R. Cargill, ed. *Strategic Bombardment.* Washington, DC: Office of Air Force History, 1998.

Hallion, Richard P. *The Naval Air War in Korea.* Baltimore, MD: Nautical and Aviation Publishing, 1986.

Hamburger, Kenneth E. *Leadership in the Crucible: The Korean War Battles of Twin Tunnels and Chipyong-ni.* College Station: Texas A&M University Press, 2003.

Hammel, Eric M. *Chosin: Heroic Ordeal of the Korean War.* New York: Vanguard Press, 1981.

Hanley, Charles J., Sang-hun Chol, and Martha Mendoza. *The Bridge at No Gun Ri.* New York: Henry Holt and Company, 2001.

Hansen, Kenneth. *Heroes Behind Barbed Wire.* Princeton, NJ: Van Nostrand, 1957.

Hansrath, Alfred H. *The KMAG Advisor: Roles and Problems of the Military Advisor in Developing an Indigenous Army for Combat Operations in Korea.* Chevy Chase, MD: Operations Research Office, Johns Hopkins University, 1957.

————. *Problems of the Development of a Local Army (ROKA)*. Chevy Chase, MD: Operations Research Office, Johns Hopkins University, 1956.

Heinl, Robert D. *Victory at High Tide: The Inchon-Seoul Campaign*. Philadelphia: Lippincott, 1968.

Hermes, Walter, Jr. *Truce Tent and Fighting Front*. Vol. 3 of *The United States Army in the Korean War*. Washington, DC: Office of the Chief of Military History, 1966.

Hess, Dean E. *Battle Hymn*. New York: McGraw-Hill, 1956.

Hinshaw, A. L. *Heartbreak Ridge: Korea, 1951*. New York: Praeger, 1989.

Hone, Thomas C. "Korea," in *Case Studies in the Achievement of Air Superiority*, edited by Benjamin Franklin Cooling. Washington, DC: Office of Air Force History, 1994.

————. "Strategic Bombing Constrained: Korea and Vietnam," in *Case Studies in Strategic Bombardment*, edited by R. Cargill Hall. Washington, DC: Office of Air Force History, 1998.

Hopkins, William B. *One Bugle, No Drums: The Marines at Chosin Reservoir*. Chapel Hill, NC: Algonquin Books, 1986.

Jordan, Kelly C. "Three Armies in Korea: The Combat Power in the U.S. 8th Army in Korea, 1950–1952." PhD diss., The Ohio State University, 1999.

Kim Chull-Baum, ed. *The Truth About the Korean War*. Seoul, ROK: Eulyoo Publishing, 1991.

Kinkead, Eugene. *In Every War but One*. New York: Norton, 1959.

Knight, Peter G. "MacArthur's Eyes: Reassessing Military Intelligence Operations in the Forgotten War, June 1950–April 1951." PhD diss., The Ohio State University, 2006.

Knott, Richard C. *Attack From the Sky: Naval Air Operations in the Korean War*. Washington, DC: Naval Historical Center, 2004.

Knox, Donald. *The Korean War: An Oral History*. New York: Harcourt Brace Jovanovich, 1985.

————. *The Korean War: Uncertain Victory*. New York: Harcourt Brace Jovanovich, 1988.

Leckie, Robert. *March to Glory*. New York: Simon & Schuster, 1960.

Linklater, Eric. *Our Men in Korea*. London: HMSO, 1954.

Lott, Arnold S. *Most Dangerous Sea: A History of Mine Warfare and an*

Account of U.S. Navy Mine Warfare Operations in World War II and Korea. Annapolis, MD: Naval Institute Press, 1959.

Maher, William L. *A Shepherd in Combat Boots: Chaplain Emil Kapaun of the 1st Cavalry Division.* Shippensburg, PA: Burd Street Press, 1977.

Maihafer, Harry J., Col., USA (Ret). *From the Hudson to the Yalu: West Point '49 in the Korean War.* College Station: Texas A&M University Press, 1993.

Malcom, Ben S., and Ron Martz. *White Tiger: My Secret War in North Korea.* Washington, DC: Brassey's, 1996.

Manhurin, Walker M. *Honest John: The Autobiography of Walker M. Manhurin.* New York: Putnam's Sons, 1962.

Mark, Eduard. *Aerial Interdiction in Three Wars.* Washington, DC: Office of Air Force History, 1994.

Marshall, S. L. A. *Infantry Operations and Weapons Usage in Korea.* Report GRO-R-13. Baltimore, MD: Operations Research Office, Johns Hopkins University, 1951.

———. *Notes on Infantry Tactics in Korea.* Report GRO-T-7 (EUSAK). Baltimore, MD: Operations Research Office, Johns Hopkins University, February 28, 1951.

———. *Pork Chop Hill.* New York: William Morrow, 1956.

McLaren, David R. *Mustangs Over Korea: The North American F-51 at War, 1950–1953.* Atglen, PA: Schiffer Military History, 1999.

McWilliams, Bill. *On Hallowed Ground: The Last Battle for Pork Chop Hill.* Annapolis, MD: Naval Institute Press, 2004.

Meyers, Edward C. *Thunder in the Morning Calm: The Royal Canadian Navy in Korea, 1950–1953.* St. Catherines, ON: Vanwell Publishing, 1991.

Meyers, Samuel M., and William C. Bradbury. "The Political Behavior of Korean and Chinese Prisoners of War in the Korean Conflict: A Historical Analysis," in *Mass Behavior in Battle and Captivity: The Communist Soldiers in the Korean War,* edited by Samuel M. Meyers and Albert D. Biderman. Chicago: University of Chicago Press, 1968.

Millett, Allan R. "Korea, 1950–1953" in *Case Studies in the Development of Close Air Support,* edited by Benjamin Franklin Cooling. Washington, DC: Office of Air Force History, 1990.

———. *Their War for Korea: American, Asian, and European Combatants and Civilians, 1945–1953*. Washington, DC: Brassey's, 2002.

Mills, Randy K., and Roxanne Mills. *Unexpected Journey: A Marine Corps Reserve Company in the Korean War*. Annapolis, MD: Naval Institute Press, 2000.

Montross, Lynn. *Cavalry of the Sky: The Story of U.S. Marine Combat Helicopters*. New York: Harper and Brothers, 1954.

Montross, Lynn, et. al. *U.S. Marine Operations in Korea*. 5 vols. Washington, DC: Historical Branch, G-3, Headquarters Marine Corps, 1954–1972.

Moore, Dermont, and Peter Bagshawe. *South Africa's Flying Cheetahs in Korea*. Johannesburg: Ashanti Publishing, 1991.

Mossman, Billy. *The United States Army in the Korean War*. Vol. 2, *Ebb and Flow*. Washington, DC: Office of the Chief of Military History, 1990.

Muir, Malcolm, Jr. *Sea Power on Call: Fleet Operations, June 1951– July 1953*. Washington, DC: Naval Historical Center, 2005.

Murphy, Edward F. *Korean War Heroes*. Novato, CA: Presidio Press, 1993.

Nalty, Bernard C. *Long Passage to Korea: Black Sailors and the Integration of the U.S. Navy*. Washington, DC: Naval Historical Center, 2003.

No Kum-sok [Kenneth H. Rowe]. *A MiG-15 to Freedom*. Jefferson, NC: MacFarland, 1996.

O'Dowd, Ben. *In Valiant Company: Diggers in Battle, Korea, 1950– 1951*. Queensland, Australia: University of Queensland, 2000.

Office of the Provost Marshal General, Department of the Army. *Prisoners of War*. 3 vols. Washington, DC: Department of the Army, 1968.

O'Rourke, G. G. *Night Fighters and Korea*. With E. T. Woolridge. Annapolis, MD: Naval Institute Press, 1998.

Owen, Joseph R. *Colder than Hell: A Marine Rifle Company at Chosin Reservoir*. Annapolis, MD: Naval Institute Press, 1996.

Paschall, Rod. *Witness to War: Korea*. New York: Perigee Books, 1995.

Pate, Lloyd. *Reactionary!* New York: Harpers, 1956.

Peters, Richard, and Li Xiaobing, eds. *Voices From the Korean War:*

Personal Stories of American, Korean, and Chinese Soldiers. Lexington: University Press of Kentucky, 2004.

Polk, David, comp. *Ex-Prisoners of War.* Paducah, KY: Turner Publishing for the Association of Ex-POWs from the Korean War, Inc., 1993.

Price, Scott T. *The Forgotten Service in the Forgotten War: The U.S. Coast Guard's Role in the Korean Conflict.* Annapolis, MD: Naval Institute Press, 2000.

Raschen, Dan. *Send Port and Pajamas!* London: Buckland Publications, 1987.

Rishell, Lyle. *With a Black Platoon in Combat.* College Station: Texas A&M University Press, 1993.

Russ, Martin. *The Last Parallel.* New York: Rinehart, 1957.

Sams, Crawford. *Medic!* Armonk, NY: M. E. Sharpe, 1998.

Sauter, Jack. *Sailors in the Sky: Memoir of a Navy Aircrewman in the Korean War.* Jefferson, NC: McFarland, 1995.

Sawyer, Robert K. *Military Advisors in Korea: KMAG in War and Peace.* Washington, DC: Center of Military History, 1962.

Sheldon, Walt. *Hell or High Water: MacArthur's Landing at Inchon.* New York: Macmillan, 1968.

Shinn, Bill. *The Forgotten War Remembered, Korea 1950–1953.* Elizabeth, NJ: Hallym, 1996.

Simmons, Edwin H., Brig. Gen., USMC (Ret.). *Frozen Chosin: U.S. Marines at the Changjin Reservoir.* Washington, DC: History and Museums Division, 2002.

———. *Over the Seawall: U.S. Marines at Inchon.* Washington, DC: History and Museums Division, HQMC, 2000.

Slater, Michael P. *Hills of Sacrifice: The 5th RCT in Korea.* Paducah, KY: Turner Publishing, 2000.

Smith, Neil C., ed. *Home by Christmas: With the Australian Army in Korea, 1950–1956.* Melbourne, Victoria, Australia: Mostly Unsung, 1990.

Smurthwaite, David. *Project Korea: The British Soldier in Korea, 1950–1953.* London: National Army Museum, 1988.

Snyder, Don J. *A Soldier's Disgrace* [Maj. Ronald Alley]. Dublin, NH: Yankee, 1987.

Spiller, Harry, ed. *American POWs in Korea: Sixteen Personal Accounts.* Jefferson, NC: McFarland, 1998.

Stanton, Shelby L. *America's Tenth Legion: X Corps in Korea, 1950.* Novato, CA: Presidio, 1989.

Stewart, Richard W. *Staff Operations: The X Corps in Korea, December 1950.* Ft. Leavenworth, KS: USA Command and General Staff College, 1991.

Sullivan, John A. *Toy Soldiers: A Memoir of a Combat Platoon Leader in Korea.* Jefferson, NC: McFarland, 1991.

Taplett, Robert. *Dark Horse Six.* Williamstown, NJ: Phillips, 2002.

Terry, Addison. *The Battle of Pusan: A Korean War Memoir.* Novato, CA: Presidio Press, 2000.

Thompson, Wayne, and Bernard C. Nalty. *Within Limits: The U.S. Air Force and the Korean War.* Washington, DC: Air Force History and Museums Programs, 1996.

Thorton, John W. *Believed to Be Alive.* Annapolis, MD: Naval Institute Press, 1981.

Toland, John. *In Mortal Combat: Korea, 1950–1953.* New York: John Morrow, 1991.

Tomedi, Rudy. *No Bugle, No Drums: An Oral History of the Korean War.* New York: John Wiley, 1993.

Utz, Curtis A. *Assault From the Sea: The Amphibious Landing at Inchon.* Washington, DC: Naval Historical Center, 2000.

Vetter, Harold. *Mutiny on Koje Island.* Rutland, VT: Charles E. Tuttle, 1965.

Voelkel, Harold. *Behind Barbed Wire in Korea.* Grand Rapids, MI: Zondervan Publishing, 1953.

Walker, Adrian. *A Barren Place: National Servicemen in Korea, 1950–1954.* London: Leo Cooper, 1994.

Watts, John Cadman. *Surgeon at War.* London: Allen & Unwin, 1955.

Weintraub, Stanley. *War in the Wards.* Garden City, NY: Doubleday, 1964.

Werrell, Kenneth P. *Sabres Over MiG Alley: The F-86 and the Battle for Air Superiority in Korea.* Annapolis, MD: Naval Institute Press, 2005.

White, William L. *The Captives of Korea: An Unofficial White Paper on the Treatment of War Prisoners.* New York: Scribner's, 1957.

Willis, Morris R., and J. Robert Moskin. *Turncoat: An American's 12 Years in Communist China.* Eaglewood Cliffs, NJ: Prentice-Hall, 1966.

Wilson, David. *Lion Over Korea: 77 Fighter Squadron RAAF, 1950–1953*. Canberra: Banner Books, 1994.

Winnington, Alan, and Wilfred Burchett. *Plain Perfidy: The Plot to Wreck Korean Peace*. London: Britain-China Friendship Association, 1962.

Y'Blood, William T. *MiG Alley: The Fight for Air Superiority*. Washington, DC: Office of Air Force History, 2000.

Chapter 6

Anderson, Christopher J. *The War in Korea: The U.S. Army in Korea, 1950–1953*. St. Paul, MN: Greenhill Books, 2001.

Boose, Donald W., Jr. *U.S. Army Forces in the Korean War, 1950–1953*. Botley, Oxfordshire, UK: Osprey Books, 2005.

Brune, Lester, ed. *The Korean War: Handbook of the Literature and Research*. Westport, CT: Greenwood Press, 1996.

Collier, Rebecca L., comp. *The Korean War*. Washington, DC: RIP 103, National Archives and Administration Records, 2003.

Ecker, Richard E. *Korean Battle Chronology: Unit-by-Unit United States Casualty Figures and Medal of Honor Citations*. Jefferson, NC: MacFarland, 2005.

Edwards, Paul, ed. *The Korean War: A Historical Dictionary*. Lanham, MD: Scarecrow Press, 2003.

Epley, William W., ed. *International Cold War Military Records and History*. Washington, DC: Office of the Secretary of Defense, 1996.

Hoare, James, and Susan Pares, eds. *Conflict in Korea: An Encyclopedia*. Santa Barbara, CA: ABC/CLIO, 2000.

Jager, Sheila Miyoshi. *Narratives of Nation Building in Korea*. Armonk, NJ: M. E. Sharpe, 2003.

Koo, John H., and Andrew C. Nahm. *An Introduction to Korean Culture*. Elizabeth, NJ: Hollym, 1997.

Korean Overseas Information Service. *A Handbook of Korea*. Elizabeth, NJ: Hollym, 1990.

Lautensach, Hermann. *Korea: A Geography Based on the Author's Travels and Literature*. Reprint, Berlin: Springer-Verlag, 1988.

Lee, Steven Hugh. *The Korean War.* London: Longman, 2001.

Lentz, Robert J. *Korean War Filmography.* Jefferson, NC: MacFarland, 2003.

Malkasian, Carter. *The Korean War, 1950–1953.* Botley, Oxfordshire, UK: Osprey Books, 2001.

Matray, James I., ed. *Historical Dictionary of the Korean War.* Westport, CT: Greenwood Press, 1991.

McFarland, Keith D., ed. *The Korean War: An Annotated Bibliography.* New York: Garland, 1986.

Milliken, Jennifer. *The Social Construction of the Korean War: Conflict and Its Possibilities.* Manchester, UK: Manchester University Press, 2001.

Pratt, Keith, and Richard Rutt. *Korea: A Historical and Cultural Dictionary.* London: Curzon, 1999.

Rottman, Gordon L., ed. *Korean War Order of Battle.* New York: Praeger, 2000.

Sandler, Stanley. *The Korean War: An Encyclopedia.* New York: Garland, 1995.

Summers, Harry G., ed. *Korean War Almanac.* New York: Facts on File, 1990.

Thomas, Nigel, Peter Abbott, and Mike Chappell. *The Korean War, 1950–1953.* Botley, Oxfordshire, UK: Osprey Books, 1986.

Tucker, Spencer, ed. *Encyclopedia of the Korean War.* 3 vols. Santa Barbara, CA: ABC/CLIO, 2000.

Varhola, Michael J. *Fire and Ice: The Korean War, 1950–1953.* El Dorado Hills, CA: Savas Publishing Company, 2000.

ABOUT THE AUTHOR

Allan R. Millett is the director of the University of New Orleans Eisenhower Center for American Studies and the Ambrose professor of American history. A retired colonel of the Marine Corps Reserve, Millett specializes in the history of the American armed forces, military policy, military innovation, and America's twentieth-century wars. His previous books include *Their War for Korea: American, Asian, and European Combatants and Civilians, 1945–1953* (Potomac Books, 2004); *The War for Korea, 1945–1950: A House Burning*; and the bestsellers *A War to Be Won: Fighting the Second World War* (with Williamson Murray), *For the Common Defense: A Military History of the United States* (with Peter Maslowski), and *Semper Fidelis: The History of the United States Marine Corps*. He lives in New Orleans.